EPISODES

1/7/14
BOB,
MY IRISH BROTHER
+ SCOTTISH FRIEND,
A TRUE MASTER
STORY TELLER. THANKS
SO MUCH FOR INSPIRING
ME. BEST ALWAYS,

1

IMPORTANT NOTICES

Front Cover: Designed by the author, composited by Spud Grammar. Some photos used by arrangement with Dreamstime.

Back Cover: Designed by Spud Grammar. Terraces photo, Author Arash Heshemi. See 11.0 Permissions.

*   *   *

"This is a work of non-fiction. These situations were real. Words, feelings, behaviors and thoughts were/are real. All experiences and dialogue are to the best of my recollection. The narrative is my own. If this period of my life sounds embellished (which it isn't), then it's not embellished enough." -- R.R.

DISCLAIMER

I'm just one person and not a spokesman for anyone other than myself.

Episodes

A poetic memoir

from

Rodney Richards

A Blessed Life in America® Book

ABLiA Media Co

Trenton New Jersey

Forthcoming

A Blessed Life in America® Books:

summary memoirs

wild youth

NJ State contracting

Baha'i Movement

observations

states of being

autobiography

CONTENTS

Contents, continued

TO

Janet — my love in all the worlds of God, my supporter, defender and protector. Also to my family and friends, but especially **Janet, Jesse** and **Kate** who live with my antics daily.

How grateful I am that our love is mutual.

Mom and her faith and love in me, always. To my father, **Rodney Senior**, a temporary caretaker; and to my Dad, **Ralph Daloisio**, who was there for me for over fifty years.

All led me to universal values and ethics.

All let me live free.

Now two of those bodies are resting in peace and all three souls are progressing in heaven.

'Abdu'l-Baha who said and wrote:

"Truthfulness is the foundation of all human virtues." [1]

ACKNOWLEDGEMENTS

To Janet, my indefatigable and unflappable soul mate of over 46 years, who told me in 2009 after I retired,
    "You're not doing anything, why don't you write your memoir or something?"

Jesse and Kate, who have been supportive, and surprised, thruout this 16-month writing process, when they could have ripped *Episodes* or me to shreds.

Thank you's to Dr. Kathleen Pike and Dr. Susan Fuchs for their kind words.

Special thanks to my first writing coach, Maria Okros, since passed, and to Rita Breedlove-Wolf, editor, mentor, and accomplished author of *Lured to Death* and past editor of Microsoft's Encarta.

And to my beloved Writing Groups in Lawrence, Philly, Hamilton, Princeton, Warminster/ Hatboro and Doylestown.

Not only have these **Ideal Readers** taught me what craft I may have, they also corrected grammar and content; and suggested major improvements. My family helped correct memories as well.[2]

Every word was informed and invaluable.

REVIEWS FROM EARLY DRAFTS

"We have many accounts of mental illness by psychologists, psychiatrists and other mental health professionals. We also need to hear directly from those who experience mental illness first-hand. Rodney Richards' book is a passionate, personal account of one man's journey living with bipolar disorder. It is raw, honest and powerful.

Mr. Richards' story of wrestling and coming to terms with bipolar disorder doesn't sugarcoat the difficulties, but it also proves that these individuals [with bipolar disorder] can live full and rewarding lives."

Kathleen M. Pike, PhD
Clinical Professor of Psychology
Columbia University
The doctor also has presented two TED Talks
on mental illness and bipolar.

"Rodney's book about his struggle with bipolar disorder is a revealing account which is blatantly and refreshingly honest. It describes the havoc and chaos caused by mental illness not just on its innocent and unsuspecting victims, but also on their families and the people who love them. Above all this is an inspirational tale of Rodney's drive and determination to overcome the ravages of the illness, and is a testimony to the love and support of family and friends who were there with him along the journey."

Dr. Susan Fuchs M.D., practicing in Hamilton NJ

My psychiatrist and friend

PREFACE

1. There's many references to the Movement called the **Baha'i Faith,** founded by the Persian nobleman **Baha'u'llah**, in mid-18th century Persia (Iran). **The Faith** is a recognized independent worldwide religion with over 5 million adherents in almost every country and principality on the globe. It's watchword is simple, but not simplistic: **"The world is but one country, and mankind its citizens."** [3]

Pronunciations: Buh-high and Ba-ha-ol-lah.

1. For the full effect *Episodes*, start with the **Forward** on page 13. To skip to my exciting first person manic Self, start at Chapter **1.10 Conversing with an Infinite** (p. 63).

2. During My five manic episodes, I don't think or hear pronouns and conjunctions, or use correct grammar, like "a's," "ands," "or," "the's," except when I speak. They don't exist in My manic Mind racing away with Me. These words are only added, if added at all, for your benefit. Evelyn Wood has written that the brain is capable of producing as many as 50,000 words per minute. [4]

3. Story narration may be indented or not, extra spaces added or not. My spoken words and thoughts are usually **not** indented. **Words of others are <u>always</u> indented.** In his book *On Writing,* Stephen King also refers to dialogue attribution often, and symbolism is okay. [2]

4. I grew up in **Trenton New Jersey** in the '50s and '60s with its vernaculars, so I may say ""hafta" (have to), "cuz" or "'cause" (because), "gotta" (got to), etcetera. Also used are informals like "info" for information or "nite."

5. I hate long forms of "though," "although," "throughout," "through," and "until." For 40 years all my written notes use the short versions. Therefore the following mean the same but may be shown as "tho," "altho, "thruout," "thru," and "til."

6. Ellipses (. . .) are used often to indicate either time, meditations or thoughts passing, or intervening. Asterisks (* * *), indicate a break in the story; again, time passing, or circumstances changing. A $^?$ means I'm not sure of the exactitude.

*   *   *

Personal note

"I don't apologize for my views and perceptions, but am willing to change based on rational truthful arguments and the greater good. I'm a cheerleader for decent jobs for all, morals, The Great State of New Jersey, world peace, universal education, good government, WHYY-FM and others . . . ." -- R.R.

Epigraphs

Truly, there's **absolutely nothing in this universe**

including ourselves,

that isn't perfectly timed.

- Dr. Wayne W. Dyer, *Inspiration Your Ultimate Calling*

The 8th Habit

To **find our voice** and inspire others to find theirs

is an idea whose time has come.

- Stephen R. Covey

There are eight million stories

in the Naked City.

This is one of them.

- *Naked City,* 1958-1962 ABC TV show

Emphasis added

FORWARD by AUTHOR

I have a manageable disease. Thank God and my doctors for finding the right medications early so I can live a normal life. The disease I have was unnamed until the work by Frenchman Jules Falret in 1854 (may be disputed). The **American** medical establishment didn't utilize **Lithium**, the first treatment medicine, until the early '70's. Today, an estimated 10 million Americans are infected with it. Correct diagnosis is difficult, and not definitive thru blood or laboratory tests. Average length of time from onset of symptoms to diagnosis is 10 years. It is a chronic and lifelong disorder. There is no cure. Treatment is often haphazard, and may take years to be effective. Even those lucky enough to be on medication, can be their own worst enemies. Approximately thirty percent of those who go untreated commit suicide. [5]

"Starting in 2009, more people died of suicide than car accidents," wrote National Alliance on Mental Illness.

These are five episodes so far of one such afflicted, including a few close calls, and how he coped.

How I coped.

How I became copasetic.

How I compensated

*   *   *

Please turn the page so episodes can begin . . .

1.0 FIRST EPISODE

1.1 Beginning a 17-year Expedition — A Telling.

Demanding obligations were festering.
Decisions had to be made.

*   *   *

I had been preoccupied upon waking.

Alone in my cubicle at work, uncontrolled feelings of loss and fear after Dad's death had been building since having left **California** two weeks earlier, in late September. Flying out there alone, I'd made final arrangements and taken care of things like a dutiful son.

It had been draining and stressful. Too stressful.

A week after returning My emotions had reached their breaking point. At work at my desk, I'd shut My eyes tightly, lain My head on my arms . . . and had an epiphany. Staring into My black closed eyelids, a thought came unbidden, *What's happened to my soul? Is this what happens after death?* All I see is **Blackness . . .** *Swirling shapes. . .*

I'm empty; empty, nothingness. Why can't I hope? I can at least hope? But no, Soul's irrelevant. Another thought, *I'm going to die -- soon.* I had scribbled on My yellow pad . . . **"Meditation # 1: Noon Day Prayer: What exists? Nothing exists. Who exists? God exists."** Rapidly writing seven more. . ..

I had cried, sobbed, nothing to live for anymore. . . . Taking effort . . . slow . . . easy . . . . calm Yourself.

I'd been concentrating on the well-known **Baha'i** quotation: **"He should forgive the sinful, and never despise his low**

14

estate, for none knoweth what his own end shall be. How often hath a sinner attained, at the hour of death, to the essence of faith, and, quaffing the immortal draught, hath taken his flight unto the Concourse on high!" I had thought, *Dad had drunk it. When would I drink 'the immortal draught?"*

Then I remembered the rest of it: **"And how often hath a devout believer, at the hour of his soul's ascension, been so changed as to fall into the nethermost fire!"** [6]

Asking, What would be My end? I had shivered right then.

The rest of that day I'd been in a trance; going through motions, not able to focus. **Fearful.**

Pretended everything was normal when I got home after work, for wife Janet's and two-year old son Jesse's benefits. However, beginning with My racing thoughts, something hadn't been right. By then feelings of omniscience and righteousness, turbulence and doubt consuming Me. Being uncommunicative, I hadn't shared my feelings with Janet. Not telling her . . . *feeling strange.*

Going to bed at 10, having closed My eyes, and staying motionless; no sleep came. Wide open. See thru glow of moon. Thoughts without pause wouldn't let Me slumber. Clock shines 2 a.m. Compelled to get out of bed, quietly rising, not waking Janet. Softly pick up jeans, T-shirt, loafers, no socks. Tiptoeing out our room to Jesse's. Pausing . . . a moment. *I have to leave him. I gotta go, I gotta go,* driving Me, no destination in mind -- not yet.

Dressing in kitchen with lights off.

The Toyota Corolla had started right up, and I'd begun driving thru Yardville and Allentown, onto Rt. 539, two miles from our home, toward the shore. Voices on the radio telling Me what to do and how I should feel. I heard, "You'll love the Sparkomatic! Our new digital AM/FM Cassette car radio, with exceptional reception. Comes in 8-track version as well." I had shouted, "You can't tell me what to buy!" I'd been mad   as hell at the announcer, but hadn't turned off the radio. Seemed to know the next words proceeding from his lying mouth.

During the news report I'd screamed, "Let the priests marry for Christ' sake!" when they mentioned Pope John Paul II's visit on the newsbreak.

Other times, I'd loudly sung all the words to every song, no matter what kind of station. Switched stations often, and each time had been caught in the moment and the flow, melody and lyrics, upbeat or down.
        Not once had I thought of smoking since I'd left, un-usual, even though I was addicted. Then, "I need to stop smoking" — and tossed cigarettes and matches thru the open window, tho freezing out.

Mind . . . in hyper-drive, senses on high alert. I'd counted the telephone poles as they had whizzed past. As I had flown by cars on the road, I'd queried, "I wonder where that person's going?" or "Why is that driver going left?"

"Ugh. that billboard's ugly!" I had shouted, as I passed it going 75 in a 50 MPH zone. Traffic had flowed lightly with big gaps at that time in the morning, and I had sailed in and out smoothly. My eyes and ears missed nothing;   Senses — **hypersensitive.** The mileposts flashed past. Everything connected. I'd been oblivious of time passing, but everything else has meaning.

Continually racing. Thoughts, images, rapidly replacing one after the other, easily distracted. Declaring, "No more nuclear tests," remembering Russia's recent one. I had jumped from solving world problems, to how many miles I'd driven since leaving home.

Only solvable problems existed except one, and all the world's problems easily solved. I'd felt entirely confident and full of energy, power. Fingers drumming the steering wheel incessantly. I hadn't thought of eating or going to the bathroom. However, the thought came, *Must go to bathroom.*

I'd rounded the corner and *"Perfect. A gas station, just what I need." Just in time* I had stopped and gone.

No need for a **Wawa** coffee although hot coffee was another addiction. Already high, wired. "I'm all-powerful," *as if I had all the answers.*

"Received" overwhelming feeling *I'll never see Janet or Jesse again!* When I had begun driving again, crying, I'd screamed, "Bob and Barb will look after you both! It'll be Okay. The Baha'is will help!"

Compelled to continue. I'd travelled a few more miles and pulled into **Crestwood Village** on route 530 near Toms River. Stopping the car at the only development house with lights on, had walked purposefully to the door and knocked. Doing so boldly, no compunctions. An aged, white-haired couple had answered, fully dressed. "Hi, I'm Rodney, and I'm lost. Can you tell me the best way to the shore?"

*I must go to **Haifa.*** The sudden compulsion wouldn't leave. He gave directions and I zoomed away without leaving thanks for their offers of hot tea. I'd been suddenly obsessed with *My goal.* A few miles down the road, I'd swerved right, down a dirt road, had reached a clearing in the pines, and ground to a halt. Bursting from the car, screaming and ranting, tearing my clothes off "I'm coming!" "Nothing can stop Me. It's time the world was saved and mankind must listen."

Have a great debate -- about tossing my gold wedding ring, but because it was engraved with **Allah'u'abha**, kept it on. [7] The only thing I had on, cuz I had also tossed my glasses.

Searching for the ocean. At no time had any roadblocks entered My mind like the water would be too cold, or I wouldn't have the stamina to swim 5,000 miles.
Continually stomping eastward in beam of my headlights.
Nothing's going to stop Me . . . **not Me!**
          Continued to scream and rant.

A revelation! like lightning. **"I'm the lion of indomitable strength, I am the next manifestation of God!"** [8] I'd shouted, **"Mankind must listen. It's time!"** Had to bring peace and cooperation to the world, following Baha'u'llah's teachings.

Great calm had washed over Me.

Listened intently. Mumbling . . . **"Yes Lord!"** and "**O Lord! Increase my astonishment at Thee!"** [9] Immediately endowed with the knowledge and power of the Lord, the All-Mighty. *Words appeared before my eyes . . . .*

> **"O King! I was but a man like others . . . asleep upon My couch, when lo, the breezes of the All-Glorious were wafted over Me . . . and taught Me the knowledge of all that hath been. This thing is not from Me . . . but from One Who is Almighty and All-Knowing . . ."** [10]

conversing with . . . the **One** *. . . .Earth, passing away . . .*

embracing My new World.

1.2 The Departures [Three weeks earlier]

[Monday September 24, 1979]

Janet wakes immediately, curly short red hair in clumps, cute freckles coming alive. "Who can this be before 7?" as she grabs the phone by her side of our bed. Listening intently for 3 full minutes and sitting upright. Slowly turning toward me, watching me with her "quizzical" look. Half-surprise, half-worry. Dressing for work, looking at her, pausing.

"Rod, it's your mom. You need to speak with her." Handing me the phone.

"Rodney, I have some bad news." As soon as I hear those words, I perk up — and plop on the bed with just my shirt and tie on. *Someone in the family has died.* I know the drill; I just don't know who. We have a big family; it could be someone close, or someone I met only once — or never.

"Donny called me half an hour ago." Mom says.

"Dad?" *He's the only one I sorta care about* in California, where Donny is. Dad and cousin Donny are best friends. They live near each other. They're close.

"Um, Yes, I'm sorry. Donny told me your father died in his sleep just past midnight. Donny found him shortly after."

"But he's so young!" Blurting out as I gaze up at Janet standing near me. Knowing little about Dad because I haven't seen or heard from him in twelve years except for a few notecards and **Polaroids.**

Knowing he's ex-Marine, divorced twice, lived alone in Irvine, and is, was, a school custodian. Oh, and a smooth-talking womanizer, as well as a weekend alcoholic. Wondering *How will my 27 year-old brother Stephen take the news. Stephen's never met him.*

19

"The coroner told Donny it was a massive heart attack, a silent myo, ah, my-o-card-i-al infarction." Listen intently as she fills me in. Still surprised but calm, looking up gain and seeing she understands what this means to us.

Rodney Carroll Richards Senior was gone just like that. Within a month his death would have unforeseen consequences for me and my family. Me twenty-nine, with college educated wife Janet a year older, and our son Jesse, two. All young and healthy, at the low end of middle-class. Our '57 two-bedroom rancher, which Janet and I had bought only five months earlier, needed work. I'd barely begun clearing the half-acre property full of wild firethorn bushes and trimming a ring of 12-foot tall purple lilacs. The 60-foot Norway maples canopied, and made it hard for grass to receive sunlight. Challenges. Interior cleaning and painting as well, tidying up, buying supplies, cutting grass on the Murray sit-down that Bill and Kathy Cross had left for us. Busy. **Preoccupied.** *Not a good time.*

Can't hesitate, or even consult my diminutive sweetheart, telling Mom "I'll go today and take care of things. You call Stephen." Thinking, *Dad and I had never been close, but someone has to go.*

I'm the only logical person who can: Mom has a new family with a husband and three teenagers of their own, *Stephen can't afford it,* and Janet can't because of her severe flying sickness — besides needing to stay home with Jesse. *Except for Mom, they don't need to come; they've never met Dad either.* The rest of the relatives aren't going to fly 3,000 miles from Jersey, especially Dad's 80-year-old mother, whom we're close to.

I wonder how she's taking it. I can't imagine her pain, but know she's tough Irish Catholic, like Mom.

Another obligation. Janet and I paying for this; no one else has money. Of course, we don't either, but as the eldest son, feel responsible. *Janet must understand.*

After hanging up, my wise redhead of 8 years plus simply says, "I'm so sorry Rod. Do whatever you have to. Can I help?"

"Yeah, thanks Hon," hugging her small frame for comfort, more because it's the expected response, rather than real emotion. "I'll go today and make his final arrangements. Can you get me a plane ticket? I hafta call Chris at work too."

"Let me check on Jesse first."

Sitting ruminating about what's coming as she checks. *I haven't been to Orange County California in a long time.*

Waiting for my boss to get in at 8, her usual time. Sifting thru past funerals in the family. Don't know much. I have accrued sick and vacation time, which will be paid leave for at least three days for a death in the family. Calling her desk number with the news.

"Do whatever you need to Rod, just go and the State will wait," Chris says. Surprisingly understanding; a change from her usual demanding self. Chris, a go-getter, always looking for work and piling on responsibilities. Intelligent, driven and capable. *No beatin' 'roun' the bush.* Also calling my assistant Alice with the news and bringing her up-to-date on current projects and consulting on what can wait.

Knowing I have 3 State personal days available for the trip.

Getting off the phone, *quickly looking up myocardial infarction in our medical dictionary to be* sure I know what's happened. A part of Dad's heart had died within minutes. Mom had said after work, Donny had gone over to

21

visit him as he often did. They were buddies. Altho Donny was 12 years younger than he, they went carousing together. When I had lived out there, Donny had sorta taken me under his very open wing to dance clubs in LA looking for women.

A quick death. A blessing. *I hope my fate is similar. Only, why so young?* Remembering the old joke: "Yup, my Dad died peacefully in his sleep, and I hope to go that way too. At least, not kicking and screaming like his passengers." Wondering, *How did he really die, had he been with a woman? Too strenuous maybe?*

Brought back to present. Janet, who had worked as a bookkeeper at Mercury Travel in Trenton for years,, quickly orders one plane ticket on United with a phone call and 206 on our credit card. We agree that paying for all this will come later. Having no idea how much money it'll take, or how much time I'll be away, *but feeling obligated to do whatever's necessary to get the job done.* We have credit cards. We both know Dad didn't have assets like us, *and doubted he had savings..*

It's raining. Entering the garage and lighting a **Kool.** *First long   puffs always tasting great. Feel nicotine coursing . . . thru my blood stream . . . Going back to California . . . will it be   different?*

*   *   *

Thinking, *Ahh Dad . . . .* while speeding from Newark Airport, to LAX in Los Angeles.

His death   not   hitting   me   yet.

Will it hit?

Sitting in my comfortable seat looking out the United DC-10's window, thinking, *I don't really love him, do I? But*

I certainly don't hate him. I've no reason to hate him; after all, he took me under his wing when I'd needed it most. I was a juvenile delinquent —   he'd actually done a lot to straighten me out, in his own low-key way. Remembered novelties of living with him: how meeting girls, and having new experiences, changed me; the almost unlimited freedom because he had treated my   15 year-old self as an adult; and how, without being aware of his training me, I've acquired a degree of discipline.

Regardless of emotions now, or lack of them, cementing my desire to do best by him.

Lost in two years

of teenage memories;

three-hour flight

passing swiftly.

Donny met me at Baggage Claim just after 8. *Our greeting subdued.* Speedily inhaling cigarette on the way to the car, Donny begins driving to Irvine on the 12 lane Santa Ana freeway. *I had learned to drive on this freeway when I had been 16.* The sprawling city we were heading to was only 37 miles south of LA, close to where Dad and I had lived, '65 and '66, and again in '68.

My older cousin by 15 years had never married, and had kept his clean-shaven dark Italian good looks. His thick black hair just like Dads. Donny sharing with me he's still working in janitorial services, now as a regional manager. We had been kinda friends, cuz he had given me a job back then nights. *And the clubs:* pounding music, young and middle-aged people dressed alike, and me on the dance floor near Donny, him doing a spread eagle kinda movement with arms and legs akimbo, me, stepping casually right and left, moving arms briefly up and down, with half-fists. I'd been surprised when I went in their john and saw a colorful metal wall dispenser selling Trojans for 50 cents.

Buying one to say I had. Just in case?

Wake-up riding south. "So what've you been doing all these years Junior? Where do you live? Rodney told me you had a son." I had always been Junior to my relatives out here, even Dad. Never had minded it. They were the only ones who called me that. No one back home even knowing *I'm a Junior.* Only Janet, Mom and Ralph.

Explained my computer-purchasing job with the **State** in **Resource Development,** then the house Jan and I had bought earlier in a small rural development outside Trenton, New Jersey, and the new joy of our lives, 2 year-old son Jesse.

Donny not commenting much, nor asking further questions. Time passing in silence as I stare out the window, immersed in traffic and garish billboards, and the good days I'd had in the past. The free times.

Entering Irvine, can't help noticing major difference as the highway narrows from 6 to 3 lanes.

"Donny, what happened to the orange groves?"

"Yeah, construction's boomed since you left, Junior. Wait until you see."

When I had lived in Orange County, Irvine consisted of two words: "**El Toro.**" The Marine Air Station was a sprawling, 4,600 acre, military base built in the '40s. Dad had hung out at its non-commissioned officers club maybe once every month. The base had been surrounded by orange and grapefruit groves for dozens of miles, wide swaths of fruit trees thruout the county.

24

Now groves gone too. I didn't know what to miss more: familiar settings, my carefree youth spent some nights and all weekends at Newport Beach, *or Dad.*

1.3 The Apartment

Entering Irvine, *Donny hadn't been kidding.* The area, a sprawling megalopolis composed of new roads, strip malls, and walled housing complexes, only looks somewhat familiar, the familiar that only California can bring. No buildings over three or four stories, and, no orchards. Donny exiting the freeway 10 minutes later onto Culver Avenue, pulling into a one-row parking lot on Pinestone.

"See that midnight blue **Chevy** parked there? That's your dad's, and you should use it while you're here. I guess you'll have to sell it." The '75 **Impala** looks in perfect condition and I have a vision of driving it home cross-country on Route 66 — by myself this time.

The 2-story adobe motel has a dozen units. Trudging up wide outside steps to the 2nd floor walkway.

"Number twenty-three."

He lived alone, but was never alone on weekends I'll bet — not if he could help it.

Door creaking ominously as Donny unlocks and opens it. Handing me a Budweiser key ring. "The car key's on it too."

"Flip," light turns on and my eyes visualize our 1966 apartment in Tustin, where we had lived next door to my high school in a garden apartment. This living room is also dark beige with only two paintings on the walls, the most prominent being the white stallion on black velvet bordered with its golden frame. I had been with Dad when he had bought it in Tijuana for four bucks. *Still eye-catching,* altho dull and dusty now. His **RCA** stereo system sitting on a small metal table under the stallion, with stacks of LPs standing upright. *He'd played those tunes constantly:* Sinatra, Al Martino, Tony Bennett, Dean Martin; Alpert, Williams, Mathis. A small black TV with rabbit ears sitting nearby on tiny table along wall. Square coffee table, wooden end tables with green lamps and faded lampshade, book endings for a spartan tan couch, no pillows. Small black rocking chair completes the furnishings.

Have a surge of **deva vu.**

"So Dad, you listen to this great music all the time. What's your favorite song?"

"Ah, *Spanish Eyes* by Al Martino. He's the greatest."

I attest to that, *cuz Dad plays the album of the same title frequently. Moon River* by Andy Williams another of his favorites, and of course anything by Dino.

Even as a young hippie, I had come to appreciate the classics. Remembering this past praise, recalling well refrains I had heard so often. "You and your Spanish eyes will wait for me," Al Martino crooned. *The perfect description for Dad's love 'em, leave 'em style of romance.*

Spying the light blue **Princess Phone** on the end table, jerking my mind out of that vision into another. All those years before, how it had been a black rotary. That phone, and that spot on the couch next to it, a mainstay in the apartment. *A mainstay of Dad's weekends*

26

Never had sat in that corner seat or next to it, not if I could help it.

Small kitchen with yellow dinette set, bathroom and good-sized bedroom, completing the scene. Looking into bedroom, Dad has an old wooden dresser, pressed white shirts and colorful sports shirts, a few blazers, and two dark suits hanging in the single closet. Not many clothes really, *for a bachelor.*

Three pairs of highly polished black wingtips *Do I still have mine?* lined neatly in a row on the closet floor. His Kiwi shoeshine box lies near them. High school friends had called him "Sharpie;" everything always cleaned and pressed.

The Marine in him meant he always dressed up, except for his sweatpants, leatherneck blue sweatshirt and white flip-flops whenever alone in the apartment. He was *a neatnik* in all other ways, nothing out of place.

Tossing my bag on the stripped bed, a recent stain on its left side, Donny saying, "We had to call somebody, so your Uncle John called **Donegan-Beckenbauer Mortuary** in Orange early this morning to handle the arrangements. I'll leave you their number. Ask for Richard, the owner. John and Charlotte set the viewing for Wednesday afternoon, not sure what else to do. Besides that, I don't know what to tell you **Junior**, except to say again that they and I are all broken up about Rodney."

"Thanks Donny, and thanks for your help. You were a good friend to Dad and me years ago. We had some good times, didn't we?" Recalled sleeping on his couch during the two months we had stayed with him and his strapping blonde-haired roommate Virgil, who stayed in his room every evening til late with his yellow-blonde German girlfriend..

"Yeah Junior, except for you runnin' up my phone bills." *He'll never let me live that down.* That had been later in August '68. I had returned from Jersey to live with Dad while I attended Fullerton Junior College for *nuthin' but fun and* the cost of a few books. Sad Janet had been back home, studying at Trenton State College; missing me, *our romance is separated by 10 states.* The AT&T long distance charges had been $4.00 for 10-minutes. I had called my sweetheart twice a week back then, oftener if I could — *in secrecy. On Donny's phone. Dad wouldn't permit it.*

"Hi hon, I've missed you. .... Yeah, school's going well, but I didn't have a lot to choose from at registration. So I'm in a literature class and shockingly -- modern dance.. . . "Yeahh." "And guess what? . . . Donny gave me a nite job to earn some money." . . .

'Yeah, definitely pumped!"

Breaking out of reverie, "About Donegan, I'm sure they'll be fine. Thanks to you all for calling someone. By the way, do Uncle John and Aunt Charlotte still live in Orange?"

"Yep, same place. I'll give you their number, too," which he does, writing it on a yellow legal pad on the kitchen table. "Junior, I gotta get going. I'll be at work until after midnight, but you can call me at noon if you need to, okay?"

"Yeah, thanks again for all your help Donny. I gotta lot to do. I'll call tomorrow."

"All right, bye kid." Putting the chain on the door behind him, lounging on open couch, striking match and lighting up, "What'll I do next?"

Also remembering working for Donny as a janitor on 2nd shift, cleaning offices nites. **Motor Trend Magazine,** in Anaheim. *The shiny sports cars.* Large color photos of silver Ferraris and red Lamborghinis hung in glass and silver matching frames along private hallways. I'd dust them, desktops, and windowsills, photos in the halls, then empty the small trashcans and vacuum the carpets, walled office by walled office. My only spending money, for pot and Kools, and cafeteria lunches, first at Estancia High, then at Tustin.

Dad said, **"Work for it."**

Donny was still a confirmed bachelor; and he was Dad's only other friend besides Uncle John, as far as I could tell.

I on the other hand am ***now confirmed husband.*** Five years longer than my father's failed marriages. Mine would later save me.

1.4 No Ghostly Dreams

At the apartment, sitting at the kitchen table with its yellow Formica® top, pulling out the list Jan and I made before I'd left:

Must call Janet

Make funeral arrangements. Order flowers from us and from Grandmom. I add: "Thru Donegan's?"

Check Dad's papers for bills, checkbook, and a will

Call Uncle John and Aunt Charlotte

Check at school for pension or life insurance

Adding: Sell car or drive home?

Past midnight Jersey time, calling home. She's been waiting for me . . . and is relieved to hear I'd made it okay.

Then she says, "I'll call your mom in the morning; she's worried about you. What're you going to do for the funeral?"

"The family here already called a funeral parlor, so I'll visit it tomorrow. It's called Donegan-something. I'll call the Richard's patriarch first and see what else they've arranged."

"Okay, but try to get some sleep. Call me tomorrow when you know what's going on." Hearing concern in her voice, placating her, reassuring her, "It'll go okay. I'll be home as soon as possible."

Saying, "Love you," **in that casual way,** and sending hugs and kisses to Jesse, hang up looking around closely. Walk to bedroom dresser, opening drawers. Socks and skivvies neatly arranged. One drawer quarter-full of loose papers. Pulling it out and carrying it to the Formica® kitchen. Separating papers of all sizes into smaller piles of a few bills, photos of him and women, letters from some of them, and personal papers. *Not a lot here.* Dad hadn't kept many invoices or records. *At least I found his check book. He's got some funds at least.* Few souvenirs or mementoes. *He wasn't sentimental except for good music. Not cold --* **direct.**

One thing *touching me* however, an envelope addressed to Dad with our return address on it. Inside, a picture of Jesse sitting on our bed, arms wide, in his print pajamas and blue-striped robe. Huge happy grin . . . *I ponder his fate --how and when I will lose him, or if I will die first as I'm supposed to . . . .*

Tiny paper heaps seeming so little for a man's whole life. Too young. Glancing thru his brown address book, wondering, *Should I call any of these numbers tomorrow?* However, deciding against it. *No one I call will have an idea of who I am other than perhaps hearing of my junior status. Too much time has passed.*

I'd first come to live with Dad in late August '65, together with his 2nd wife Marilyn and her two teenage boys, Freddie, 15 like me, and Warren, 13. Both from her past marriage. Upon my arrival, and for the first 6 months, I attended the brand new high school, Estancia. *No classroom doors or windows, built under one roof, and had a huge rotunda with a* **Taco Bell** *in its interior food court.* I ate more beef tacos than I had classes, like biology and dissecting dogfish sharks. While there thinking, *Wow, this is classy, and tasty.* Much more wonder-filled *than when pinning a boiled frog at Ewing High.*

My sojourn in the Eureka State had been during my juvenile delinquent phase. Sometimes I'd tow the line, others not coming home after school or evenings, just like Jersey. When the last bell had rung for the day, I'd hitched rides in friend Ray Hamburghey's open Jeep to girl's we had met at Newport. Drinkin' beer and takin' parent's whiskeys we'd smoke grass between gulps and shots. I wouldn't call home. Hitchin' a ride back from these *pleasure* sites was just as easy; never a long wait as long as I had stayed ahead in line before other hitchers, *no easy task if at the wrong end of the line.*

Together with close friend Mike, Ray'd drive us to Anaheim and Disneyland often, *a favorite haunt.* Grass passed easily between us. *Practically free,* it was sooo cheap. Only a fin for a coupla' heavy ounces, sometimes with rolling papers. Those early mornings I had stumbled back to the condo and Dad rattled off the riot act in his loud Marine voice.

"Junior! Whaddya want me to do, tell your mom you won't straighten up? Should I send you back to Jersey?"

Head down, no response.

"Look up at me when I'm talkin' to you!" Look up.

31

"Straighten up." Dad's favorite phrase with me, especially since he had always exclaimed, "I'm straight as an arrow." no matter how drunk he'd been. I'd play nice for a week, then right back to my cat-nipping ways.

I'd get pissed at Dad. I'd thought *sure, I'll travel back to Jersey* after Mike and I decided to hitch to Tijuana, doing our first leg on route 101. We had gotten far before jumpin' a fence onto our second leg, Interstate 5 — *big mistake.* Highway Patrol pulled us over just as Mike had stuck his thumb out, and he'd driven us to San Diego jail. Later that night our dads had come and paid fines to get us out. But Dad had just muttered, "Hitch on the roads, not on the highways shithead. Entrances are okay."
    I shudda known that.

By February the following year, Marilyn and Dad had separated. *Was it my erratic behavior that had anything to do with their break-up?* Dad then rented us a two-bedroom apartment in a large complex next to Tustin High School, where he was a janitor. I transferred in as a sophomore.   Dad was a bachelor again.

        His preferred mode. **Free spirit,** *un-tie-a-ble.*

Settling into our new place, we'd fallen into basic routines. I cleaned every week *under Dad's strict supervision.* He trained me specifically to wipe trash cans, toss the house and kitchen garbage into green dumpster outside; scrub the "commode" (toilet) his way and clean the rest; then vacuum, every Saturday morning. But I didn't mind, or groan, *especially not near Dad.* He'd always done our laundry and his ironing. Only wearing T-shirts and jeans, I hadn't minded, and he paid all the bills. I was used to cleaning and emptying trash back home — *my way,* which wasn't nearly as regular or neat.

For Dad's part, every Friday nite at 5:30 he'd eat a **Swanson** frozen dinner, take a shower and dress to the nines: clean dark pants, wingtips over black stretchy socks, colored pressed shirt open at the collar, often a tie, and dark blazer; ready to go out or welcome a "guest." Sitting on the corner of the couch next to the black rotary phone, *he'd thumb thru his* ***little black book . . .***

"Hello Jennifer[?]. It's Rodney, how've you been? . . . Really, yeah, it's been awhile . . . How 'bout meeting me at the NCO Club like old times?" A favorite ploy of his, *usually working.* Once, I was there picking him up after-hours, and the place seemed deserted.

I have full run of the joint. I searched thru the club's industrial silver refrigerators and found slabs of cheese and bread for a sandwich. I'd sung along with **Creedence Clearwater Revival** crooning *Suzie Q* blaring on the sound system. Past 2 a.m. I had shouldered him to "our" '57 Chevy Bel Air, no posts, after his date slunk out, seated him in front, rolled down windows, and drove to our pad.

Dad had always assumed I could, and would, take him and/or pick him up from these rendezvous; and I had, Never put out he "told" me to. *At least he knows he's too drunk to drive.*

In between calls made from his couch, he'd smoke a **Marlboro**, pour **Smirnoff** into a shot glass, hoist it up to his lips and down it, without a wince. The bottle and glass sat next to each other on the end table. *I can easily picture them standing under the light yellow glow thru the green shade.* Alternatively, Dad had hit nearby, or far, bars, and invited women back to the apartment, *or they'd invite him to their place.* Some nights I'd driven him miles to those meetings. *Most of his "date's" usually drove.* When commanded, it'd been between 2 or 25.

Rarely picked him up, unless at bars.

They hadn't been chores Cuz having had a semi-car of my own, cruisin' in Dad's immense salmon Chevy, no posts, *had thrilled me.* Dad had taught me what I already knew, so I'd gotten my license May 14th, at age 16, altho hoppin' 2 curbs.

I'd especially enjoyed cruisin' thru the local **A&W** car hop nites when alone or with date, with all the rods parked facing out, and the girls on roller skates in short, very short, pants — skimpiest I'd had ever seen. I'd become good friends with Dave, age 30, who had a cherry 2-tone '55 Chevy, with souped up 265 hp V8 and its slightly raised body. *Vroom,* **vroom, C h h I r r p p p . . .**Magnificent vehicles squealed out of the place *all evening.*

However, early every Monday morning Dad had always — *always,* been sober as a judge, and never missed a day of work. *I had ta give him credit for that.* Maybe the V8 juice he downed had helped?

He'd taught me how important it was to be reliable for work, *and both neat and organized.* In addition, we had never had money problems *that I knew of.*

He'd also taught how to give someone a firm handshake.

"A little lighter for the ladies, but use a full grip."

For men or women, one shake meant meeting for first time, two if we knew each other, possibly three if I were meeting someone important.

"It builds more trust."

Never three. Moreover, never grasp their hand with both of yours unless they're exceptional. *But always firm,* not a dead fish. I had only grasped JFK's hand lightly in '61[?] at **Mercer County Airport** near our Ewing Twp. home when he had visited the area.

*   *   *

Here I am, turning a page in his "new" brown address book., *Hey, there's Donna's and Leslie's names! 20-something's Dad and I had double-dated.* Dad, 15 years older than Donna, wooed his slippery blonde bombshell like the pro he was. I'd courted Leslie, petite longhaired blonde *with plain but pleasing looks.* She'd always driven the 2 of us in her dilapidated green **Plymouth**, and we'd neck at drive-ins or when parked on the beach, *or sometimes, in my top bunk when Dad was married to Marilyn for a while.* My only step-mom and *only for 6 months.*

Leslie's ex had come back and had warned me off. *It had been effective.* He had a buzz-cut, was tall and wide with huge biceps and anchor tattoos. ***I buzzed off.***

Whether Dad had nailed his own Marilyn Monroe or not, she had discarded him abruptly over drinks and an argument at her place, a month before Leslie's Tom had entered the picture again *and she discarded me.*

Coming out of these lovely memories, *it struck me, Why am I here?* Lighting up cuz I was stressing from thinking of Dad's sudden, inglorious end. Turning on TV to ease my low-key jitters. Spooky being here alone. Nevertheless, not superstitious. Enjoying Hart to Hart with Robert Wagner and Stephanie Powers. By the end, tired, going to bed, but carrying in my smokes and ash tray.

First turning the mattress over so the stain would be on the other side. Next, putting clean sheets on, no other covers, undressing, and climbing in, *I'm too tired to brush.*

Don't feel sad — only **dutiful.** *The natural cycle.
But, tomorrow'll be stressful at the mortuary,* tossing the
thought away after a last *Ahh,* For the nicotine. Turning off
the lamp and getting cozy on my right side, *how I always
snore.*

He died in this bed 24 hours ago. *That doesn't faze me.*

I always sleep soundly . . .

Becoming impossible in the coming weeks.

1.5 The Mortuary

[Tuesday, September 25, 1979]

Early next morning, after showering briskly, hopping into **Levi**
bell-bottoms and burgundy **Polo** shirt, brown loafers, then
calling Uncle John. While their phone rang, *taking inventory
and. feeling blue.* However, not one to dwell on unpleasant
things, sighing a Baha'i Prayer for Dad, **"O God! Refresh and
gladden his spirit . . . ,"** *helping me at the same time.*[11]
Making funeral arrangements not morbid, *just necessary.*
Handling this like everything else: *do the best I can
whatever comes.* No expectations anything'd be easy.
Never asking "Why me?" when smacked with difficulties.

I rang the Richards.

"I'm so sorry for you Rodney, you're dad was special to us." *She should know he wasn't that close to me.* I knew what a close relationship Dad had with them tho, particularly his Uncle John, carousing together. Aunt Charlotte acknowledging they'd used Donegan before and how good they had been. *She seems in a hurry to get to work.*

"Is it okay we set the viewing for tomorrow?"

"Sure, no problem, I'm calling Richard next. I'll let you know the outcome. Don't worry, get to work. Bye." Hangin' up.

Never had liked small talk. This'll all be over in a coulpa' days and I'll probably never see or hear from them again. Now that our mutual connection — Rodney Senior — was gone, *no reason to communicate existed.*

Calling Donegan's and speaking to Richard who has a pleasant manner, and seems kind, accommodating. He suggests we meet at 11. Gives directions to the funeral home, on Chapman Avenue, the main drag in Orange. At 10:30, hopping into Dad's Chevy, which starts right up and drives well, it strikes me, *I like this car, maybe I will drive back for the heckuv' it. Hell with the gas cost.*

Leery thinking about how expensive funerals can be, *try to keep an open mind.*

20 minutes later, finding the place, on my right, and parking. As I approach, in the front door of a large converted red brick home, appears Richard, who seems middle-aged but with a full head of blonde hair. *Shaking hands once,* he holds the door open and we enter. Leading me toward his office, I ask, "Can I take a look around first?"

"Of course."

Showing me main viewing room. Like a small chapel, *with muted gold lame wallpaper and heavy red velvet curtains.* Four dull salon chairs in front. *Not much natural light. I like light.* 40 folding chairs lined behind, quite nice actually. *Okay, this'll do fine, wonder what the cost will be?* Even Janet has never arranged a funeral, so she hadn't been able to give me helpful tips, *unlike her usual abilities.*

Janet and I are moderate people, *so we aren't planning on extras;* I know paying for the basics will be tough enough. Totally clueless, *yet I trust things will work out.*

Oh well, **Inshallah.** God's Will be done.

Soulfully yearning,

psyche changin' voice

. . . in only weeks.

1.6 Arrangements

After looking thru large entrance lounge with salon couches and chairs, more muted greys, Richard and I walk into his office. He offers me a seat in one of two plush high-backed, black, cushioned leather chairs. *Comfortable.* Made to relax, I *wasn't relaxed.*

Richard looks at the paperwork in front of him and opens, "Do you like the facilities?"

The interior's plain - except for the red velvet curtains.

"Yeah, everything's fine. Very nice in fact." And true it is.

"Very good. I'm, I'm, sorry for your loss. Understand it was unexpected?" *How many times has he said that to previous family members?*

"Yeah, I still can't believe he was only fifty.**" *Only fifty. Why so young?* In shock for fifth time.

"Don told me you'd be calling. Would you like us to call you Rodney or Mr. Richards?"

"Rodney will be fine; my Dad was Mr. Richards." *I only ever called him Dad.* However, when I was with him and around his women or other adults, he had asked me to call him Rodney, *whereas **I was always Junior.***

"You're a Junior, right?" *Oh no, he just called me Junior.*

"Right, I guess Dad became a Senior when I was born in '50." *You just add Sr period to your last name, and it makes it legit?*

"Should we start with what I know about Rodney Senior?"

"Yep, go ahead." Richard rattles off Dad's full name, address, and so forth, which he must have gotten from Donny. Richard confirms that Dad had been head custodian at San Joachin Middle School in Irvine.

"I knew he was a custodian, but wasn't sure of the school." *I guess that's it if Donny said so.*

Richard asks if Dad had been in the military.

"As a matter of fact, I just discovered he was a master gunnery sergeant last nite, honorably discharged in '53. He was a Marine." Becoming numb and anxious at the same time, *want a smoke.*

All of a sudden *This is stressing me.* I know nothing else about his military service. I realize *I don't know much about Dad at all. I need that smoke.*

"Because he was a veteran, one option we can offer is a burial plot in a military cemetery, including a standard service and grave marker."

"Really? How much does that cost?" *Hey, that could be cool and a real cost saver.*

"Actually, nothing. He's entitled as a Vet. All we do is transport the body to there and they take care of everything else. By any chance do you have his discharge papers?"

Nothing? Hope rises. "I do, I found 'em last night. That's how I knew he was a sergeant." *Thank goodness, I had the papers!*

"Well, please call me with his service number and we'll make the arrangements."

"Great. And what cemetery is it?"

"**Riverside National Cemetery,** over the San Bernadino mountains, about 40 miles away. A beautiful location. It just opened about three years ago from part of **March Air Force Base.**"

"Wow, he would've loved that, so let's do it, okay?"

"Sure, we'll arrange it, we've worked with them multiple times," says Richard.

Okay, this could be a big problem solved!

Already his easy manner and promise part of this will be free, encouraging calm; less anxious. *Maybe this won't be so bad after all.* As Grandmom had requested, ordering spray of red roses for the hardwood casket. Aunt Joan, Dad's sister, had asked that I place one red rose next to him inside it. Also ordering flowers from Janet, Jesse and I. Choosing the contents for 25 prayer cards and equal number of **In Memorial** programs.

Nothing reminding me to consult with Janet about arrangements, costs, *even tho it's her money as much as mine.*

She'll be happy about the cemetery. So will Grandmom.

Richard suggests a black limo to take us, which I agree to, and fills me in on other details like death certificate copies and the obit. I know there's no turning back. Still, a lot of 25 hundred, although it could've been double. We are now committed to pay for all this. Either my pride or status as the eldest son, instills the strong feeling it's my sole duty to pay — *and no one else's. And -- we don't have the money.*

"I'll call you back with a number for the limo, probably me, Donny, Uncle John and Aunt Charlotte and their daughter Janie. Doubtful their son Muffie will come."

We set the final service, at Riverside, Thursday at 11, in 2 days. He also confirms tomorrow's viewing at 3 pm for the family and the public, and his friends.

Boy they move quickly here *with arrangements.*

Richard had briefly explained the processes for what follows, and I'm certainly familiar. *But not foretelling what will actually happen at the viewing and the cemetery.* He passes over the document.

Reading line items, some costs in pencil to be filled in later. *Don't question.* Sign, not getting copy. No legal or contracting experience.   Preoccupied.

Leaving Donegan's, gratefully smoking outside, takin' the freeway thru Costa Mesa to Newport Beach. Park a block from the pier I had spent most days and nites on. Also in its bars and clubs, surf shops, and, *it hadn't changed a bit* — but now quiet except for the white and grey gulls squawking, scrambling, for scraps.

Ambling out on the mainly deserted pier, overlooking blue frothing waves. 4 casters tending their lines. Slap, slap sounds of waves lapping the tall pylons bringing back memories of carefree, warm sunny days and very gorgeous tanned girls. Watching the black-suited surfers on their light-colored boards and picking up their girls *had been my favorite pastimes.* Walking out past the surf, riding the cresting waves, just like Jersey. Never tried surfing, but envied those who did *with such ease and sure-footed grace.*

Remembering longhaired, long-legged, pretty brunette. At 5'11," a meek Las Vegas showgirl whom I'd met on this beach one lazy afternoon in '66. She and her mom had been sunning topless. I had walked over barefoot and in trunks and chatted them up.

She called that same evening at 6.

"Ah, Hi, Rod? It's Michelle, from the beach."

Michelle! It's great you called. Can you go out tonite?"

"Well, remember you insisted you'd show me the sights?" *Bitchin'. Not too meek.* I had told her we'd hit some bars and go dancing. Disco and Watusi were in.

She was only visiting until the next day, when mom was driving her back. She gave me her mom's number and I promised, "I'll call you right back with details; I'll need directions to your house."

I phoned Donny full of anticipation for a great nite out. "No Junior, not tonight, Willy's out." Willy was my cleaning buddy. Donny, and then Dad, insisted Donny drive me to work as scheduled. I begged to work some other nite, even a weekend, any time . . . but to no avail. *Goddamn it.!* I felt shitty calling Michelle back; she was disappointed but gracious. *Mature for 23, sweet, amazingly not jaded, with a bright personality.*

On the way home from the pier, stopping at an old haunt, Jack in the Box, and gorgin' on two beef tacos. Beef is the only kind they have and their hard shells are greasy and orange, *tasting great.* Weather's beautiful, naturally — sunny and high 70's, *never humid like Jersey,* 'specially in hot summers. Sitting outside at wood picnic table chewing, *meditating. None around us back home.* I had forgotten them as soon as I had returned to the **Garden State.**

Finish eating and having my mandatory cigarette *as I do after every meal.*

Back at the apartment, finding the discharge papers and calling Richard with Dad's service number. Dialing Janet who's holdin' down the fort, telling her about the funeral costs. She's happy about Riverside; *not the cost of other stuff.*

"When you get back we'll set up an account for everything. I'll help you with it. It'll work out, I'm sure."

Not as optimistic as she, but knowing with her background doing Mercury Travel's books, it'll be much easier. She knows accounting, and along with another volunteer, had annually audited my Baha'i Treasurer's Assembly records every year. She also handled our personal banking and bill paying; all I had to do was know how to use my **ATM** and credit cards, which I did frequently. Rarely writing checks *and maintaining 30- bucks in my pocket on average.*

When calling Mom, finding she's detached about the whole process. Hasn't seen Dad since '54 when they had divorced, so she has some distance. Mom hadn't had an easy time raising me and Stephen on her own, *but she had never held it against Dad.* Mom had never bad-mouthed him *altho he'd broken her heart.* Luckily, others had seen her good heart and had helped her when she needed it.

It's a short call, but reassuring -- things are proceeding well.

Talking with Grandmom Richards however, *is tougher.* Janet and I had visited every coupla' months, and she loved seeing little Jesse. I could always picture her sitting in her black Princeton rocking chair and thin grey frock, brown eyes and saggy face. Some kind of short brownish stockings covering her ankles.

"Hi Grandmom, it's Rodney."

"How are you taking it?"

"Me? Fine, it's been almost 12-years since I saw him last. He really did right by me. But I'm more concerned about you, how're you?" *I'm sorry Grandmom.*

"I'm doing well Rodney; it happens to all of us.   I will miss his weekly phone calls though . . . ." I didn't know what to say, so I fill her in on the arrangements, telling her how great the Donegan people are, how nice their place is. Telling her about the spray of red roses I've ordered in her name for the casket. Telling her about Riverside and a veteran's burial, and then she becomes more than pleased. "He would like that," said emotionally. I can hear her invisible tears, *Or are they real?* **But she's tough Irish.**

"I thought so too, Grandmom, I thought so too. I'll say a nice prayer at his funeral, okay?"

"Please do, Rodney. I trust you'll handle everything."

"I will," hanging up. A heavy load, but . . . *I can do this*. She's made no other demands of me. *I'm on my own.* No different from makin' project deadline pressure at work —
I can handle this.

Walking outside smoking and thinking about her. Chinese proverb pops into my head, "Grandfather dies, father dies, son dies." *Children aren't supposed to die before their parents, regardless of age. Dad had never met his only other son since knowing him at age two.*

Dad had never met his only grandchild either. But we had sent pictures.

Back in the apartment, remembering to look for my Ewing High yearbook, Clepsydra. Hoping against hope it'll turn up. All my friends had signed it. That book and my 12th grade wallet photos are my only mementoes. I had brought it with me after graduating in '68, when I'd come back to live with Dad.

Fullerton Junior College had been a failure, and I withdrew after 4 months, but, *I'd had fun.* Only, *I missed Janet.* Taking the Greyhound bus home in December '68, I had only one suitcase and two boxes packed with clothes and – the yearbook. I arrived at the **Trenton Bus Station** and the boxes had disappeared. *Son-of-a-bitch!*

Now, over 10 years later, I'm sorely disappointed Dad doesn't have my yearbook by some miracle. The thought crosses my mind, *I'm more attached to that yearbook than I am to Dad.* **Is that the case?**

Then I get to work. Calling Donny and Uncle John first, sharing the arrangements, and seeing if they want anything of Dad's.

Uncle John saying, "I'd like his LPs Junior, if that's alright with you."

"Fine, I may take a couple tho." He also says his daughter Janie's boyfriend will buy the Chevy for $500. *That'll help. Oh well. No adventurous trip home.* Donny saying he can use most of the furniture for a friend — *girl I presume*, and that's a BIG help.

Call electric and gas companies and Ma Bell, close the accounts for September 30. Go downstairs to see the super and arranging for the apartment inspection and security deposit to be returned. *Luckily, Dad isn't liable for lease payments since he died mid-term.* The super promises to send a few hundred bucks. *Nice enough guy, but he hadn't really known Dad.*

Conflicted about disposing of Dad's things, thinking, *Were they mine to keep as the oldest? Should I share with my brother Stephen? Would Stephen, picky as he was, even want anything?* Finding nothing I think he'd want. Spending an hour bagging up Dad's clothes, dishes, sheets and towels, except what I need, for the Salvation Army. The rest of his things, like his old Marine blues, a few medals, miniature photo album and similar items, boxed up. Wanting them for Grandmom more than anything else. Throwing out kitchen stuff *except my beloved **Pepsi's.***

Hopping in the Chevy touring the area looking for old landmarks in Santa Ana, as well *as the **Trailways** Bus Station*. Finding the station first and shipping both boxes of Dad's things home — well, shipping them as far as the Trenton Bus Station. Dropping off clothes at **Salvation Army** and receiving contributed receipt for 20 bucks. *I think the Chevy and I'll do mere explorin'.*

     Circling blocks to get back to main drags.

The old **Tustin Car Wash** where I'd worked in high school is on the same street and is bigger, fancier. Get the Chevy washed.

Remembering sweaty days brushing the rears of cars and vans, outside wiping interior and exterior windows with damp blue cotton-plied cloths. Next the pool hall *where I'd hustled a few bucks,* and had been hustled, was closed; replaced by a Chinese restaurant. Driving back past my old high school, apartments next door where we had lived. Past Marlene's place, *my girlfriend livin' in the same complex, who's faded green apple '55 Chevy I'd secretly stolen and trashed.* I'd known she left the key under the passenger-side car mat.

Only for a short time, seeing I'm not missing anything but the tacos, *noticing proliferation of strip malls and **7/11's.*** Heading back to Dad's.

At the apartment, lighting up and reflecting. *Well, I've done the best I can. Even tho Janet and I don't have the money, **I'm gonna pay it.** The least I can do.* Luckily having no problem making decisions, and haven't called Janet to consult today. She and I had never considered getting big, clunky, expensive, cellphones.

By then trusting Richard implicitly, and really appreciating Donegan's. *They've made it easy for me.* Only one problem remaining: *how to pay for it.*

Belt tightening probable;

But lack of wealth,

least of it.

Sleep needed.

1.7 The Viewing

[Wednesday, September 26, 1979]

Waking up early again, lighting up and thinking, ***Gotta get to the viewing by 2 p.m.*** Watching TV to kill time. Now 10:30, *in middle of Bob Barker's The Price is Right.*

Oh no! I hafta go to the courthouse. Second most important thing I gotta do! Richard had filled me in on the probate process, and had said, "You'll have to go to the Santa Anna Courthouse and file. Just fill out their form and give them a certified copy of your Dad's death certificate. I took the liberty, here's five." *I hafta go in person as next of kin.*

Rushing to their county admin building and parking. Inside waiting in line for forms, filling them out.   15 minutes later handing them over with death cert. Paying the examiner's fee. *Done! **Easy.*** Dad had so few assets, I was out in half-an-hour. All perfunctory — *Oh, it makes me feel so . . . callous.* Enjoying my 3rd smoke outside, driving to Bank of America.

Have checkbook, handing over another death cert, my ID, and copy of the county certificate to a forgettable, perfunctory **Bank of America** associate, closing Dad's checking account. She comes back with two hundred or so in cash.

Feeling numb again, going thru all the right motions, adrenalin pumping harder.

It'll shoot sky high by the time I'm in Janet's welcoming embrace . . . .

Meeting the family at the funeral home at 2:30, Uncle John, daughter Janie, and Donny, Aunt Charlotte at her nursing job, which she couldn't get out of. Sitting at the front of the room sits the open oak casket with Grandmom's spray of **roses** on top, hanging down. Smelling the attar, refreshing. Taking one long stemmed rose from above, placing it on Dad's shoulder for Aunt Joan. A floral arrangement of glads From Janet, Jesse and I, on the right.   Family's on the left.   Another from his sister Joan, husband Pete, and daughter Suzanne.

None others.

Relatives outside shootin' the bull. Minutes later, walkin' up to me, alone, a brunette Barbie slightly taller than me, so many in southern Cal. My age and long legged — wearing sexy, short burgundy cocktail dress showing her well-defined, well-tanned shape.

"Hi, I'm Rod Junior. Are you here for my Dad?"

I'd seen her enter and take his prayer card, a picture of the Pieta on green background, the beginning words on the other side, "Lord, make me an instrument of thy peace . . . " by Mary Lee Hall.

"Yes, I saw the notice in the paper. I'm sorry. Is that the casket?"

"Yes," as she strides up to it purposefully, standing near Dad, gazing down, slight nod, and leaving by the side door. *Checki — didn't sign guestbook. No card left. The only visitor besides our foursome.*

Altho Dad, **Catholic** in name (like me), hadn't been religious, no one had called a priest. I had found membership cards for **VFW, B.P.O.E.** (Elks), and others, but hadn't seen phone numbers. *Hadn't thought to call.*

Looking well heeled in his best dark blue suit, white starched shirt with gold cufflinks and capital letter "R," red paisley tie and gold tiepin, polished black featherweights on. Dressed to kill. *Squeezing his ice-cold hand.* Ashen, mouth mercifully closed, peaceful while asleep, whisper of rouge on cheeks. Even at fifty, jet black hair. *So young.* By 3 pm — alone.

Thinking, What a shame no one else showed up, but while shrugging, sit on the tan brocade love seat facing the casket.

Spending a few minutes looking at Dad's body, alone with 40 padded folding chairs. Having my first moment of silence with him, and *mentally saying the prayer for the departed.* Not touching his cold flesh again.

How am I feeling? Don't feel too much. Is something wrong with me? He was my Dad! Why can't I find my feelings right now? Fond isn't quite right, 'cause of being called shithead often, and our past verbal arguments. After one bad one, I had stayed for two weeks with my friend, Willie, and his "aunt," in their one room/kitchenette weekly rental, *and hadn't called Dad.* He just let me cool off.

Admiration totally out of place; even tho he was a reliable worker, his lifestyle as a swinger, and his alcoholism, aren't for me, especially now. Is respect the closest? He had always treated me that way. Understanding maybe? **How can you ever really understand someone** *you don't watch 7/24?*

Especially wishing *how did he first met Mom,* altho I can easily guess, 'cause in '49 she'd been beautiful, kind and smart. I had seen her high school graduation picture, and wedding pictures from both marriages. *She's kept her good looks, is the kindest person I know, as well as a good haggler. She had to negotiate alone for many years with Stephen and I.*

Also wanting to know what he had done in the service, how had he made sergeant? *Where did he and mom live during their times together? What had it had been like?*

They knew each other from Princeton, their hometown, and ended up in Washington D.C. where I'd been born on May Day of '50, just after their marriage. *How'd all that happen? And were they there 'cause they'd lived close to Quantico Marine Base where Dad had been stationed?*

He can't answer all the questions I have now. When we meet in the Abha Kingdom — the next world —I'll hug him, our first real hug, and ask. Can't wait. More than mere curiosity now. *Burning to know. Wanting to know the real story.*

Out of my thoughts, Donny and Uncle John coming in, asking if I knew the woman in the pretty dress, since neither does. "She's Miss Anonymous."

Mrs.? Shudda looked for a ring.

Dad had always taught,

"Junior, treat women well."

He loved them all;

briefly.

1.8 No Others

[Thursday, September 27, 1979]

Donnie, Uncle John, Aunt Charlotte, and I, riding in a black limo 40+ miles to Riverside National Cemetery following the hearse. *No conversations* — I'm looking out the window, comfortable with the air on. Weaving and speeding thru mountainous countryside, brown desolate earth, forested in some areas, mostly dirty chaparral dotting the hills.

No flower car; the spray of roses not accompanying us — can't be used. None of the flowers can be. Janie not with us. Home babysitting Muffie, her 15 year-old retarded brother, my sweet and powerful cousin who bellows with rocks in his mouth. [12]

No other cars with headlights on.

At the cemetery, driving under stone and black iron gate, following major path, stopping not far from tall, wide, white concrete canopy. A man in khaki's and open shirt collar silently greets us. I'm lifting the coffin from the grey hearse with darkened windows onto a wheeled metal cart with help from Donegan's pallbearers, Uncle John and Donny, rolling it to the designated position under that dark canopy, with Silent Man guiding us. Cemetery man draping the it with a large wrinkled flag. Family sitting down on a wooden bench 8 feet in front of casket. *Silent Man* switching on the loudspeaker which plays *Taps* from a recording. *Sounding* **rushed.**

    Three of us face forward in silence.

When the music's over, me standing up, walking behind the casket, turning, facing the others. Begin reciting short ***Baha'i Prayer for the Departed*** from memory. **"O, Ah, O my God! O Thou forgiver of sins, bestower of gifts, dispeller of afflictions."** Intoning in my loud clear voice. Three-quarters thru, can't help myself . . . *choking up.* Tears welling in eyes, but continuing to the end: **". . . and, and, grant them. . . to . . . to behold Thy splendors, on the loftiest mount."** [13]

At that moment, my quavering stops and I realize in my heart, I love him but I've lost him, not really knowing who he truly was, only his outward appearances. Breath catching, *"uh,"* dying with him right on that spot, a bright, airy, blue sky day, air fragrant and fresh, 1,000 miles from home. Plunging into melancholy *staring at the light brown coffin six inches from me with its brushed aluminum handles.*

No one else saying anything or moving. Looking down. I change, look forward,   ahead, across the fields of low white crosses.   *No one getting up to console me.*

*Alone. It's **oveerr**. Moving   to bench,   sitting back down . . . but not for long.*

My head lowered, but hearing wheels rattling over the dark fieldstones as Silent Man pushes the cart/casket behind a low wall. Same guy coming back, *to me*, handing me a **pre-folded flag,** *not wrinkled.*

I don't remember him saying "On behalf of the **President of the United States** from a grateful nation," but I'm sure he has. He's been rushin' cuz another funeral's pulling up.

Wow, is that all Dad gets? Not just thinking now of the service. Thought hitting me, *We'd been hoping for enough money to pay this, and my expenses.* We're concerned about the costs, including those for plane tickets, especially because Janet hasn't been working at a salaried job since Jesse's birth, *having sacrificed and pausing teaching from the **Hamilton School Board.***

*Service   is   .   .   .   **so   final** — everything   over.* We're not even asked if we want to visit actual burial site.

Silent Man politely motioning us to leave. *Someday I hope to return and find his plot, and say the **Congregational Prayer for the Dead,** even tho he isn't Baha'i.*

Silence again in the limo on way back to Donegan's. After goodbyes, driving to the apartment, changing into jeans and T-shirt, lighting up. I looked and looked and still haven't found a will or notes. No clear idea of Dad's last wishes. *Not a mistake Janet and I'll make.*

Had our wills drawn up after Jesse's birth, for 2 reasons: to comply with Baha'u'llah's exhortation to have a will, and to name Guardians. With their permission, best friends Bob and Barb accepted. At that moment, *I wish they and Janet had been here with me.*

I hope Dad's spirit is adjusting to the next world, and he's on a better path. The Baha'i Writings state, **"As to the question whether the souls will recognize each other in the spiritual world: This fact is certain; for the Kingdom is the world of vision where all the concealed realities will become disclosed. How much more the well-known souls will become manifest."** [14]

I'm going to see him again. I know I'm going to see Dad again — and converse with him, on the next plane.

Calling Janet all I can say is, "It's done. I'll call Mom and Grandmom later." She wants details but can't recount them just then, *too burnt out.*

How could I describe this sinking feeling to anyone?

Telling her I'll be on a plane home the next day, if she can book a flight. Then closing call and laying down for a rare nap. I've barely dozed off when the phone rings unexpectedly.

"Rodney? It's Richard from the funeral home." *Uh-oh, what's wrong?*

"Yeah, Richard, did we forget something?"

"Well actually, I'm not sure. Your dad worked for the **Irvine Unified School District**, right?"

"Yeah, for about 20-years I think."

"That means he should've had a pension. Have you inquired into that?"

54

"Oh wow, no, I forgot."

Notorious for forgetting things, Janet constantly reminding me where we were going, what we were doing, my appointments and times. *Even for those I'd set up for myself.*

Janet never forgets, or would show up late for a meeting or appointment, not once. Nor allow me to either. *Neither would have my father. I missed them both.*

[Friday September 28, 1979]

Early next morning Richard picks me up and we drive to the schools administration building. Located in central Orange County. The district is huge, but seems to run efficiently as we cover details with the staff. Accepting their condolences.

"He was such a nice guy."

"A hard worker, and you're his son?"

"Yes, thank you for knowing him."

Confirming me as the beneficiary on Dad's pension. *Really?* Taken aback but pleased, very pleased. *Really?* I had always guessed, *Dad's only close to Uncle John and Donny. Why me?* Sliding my driver's license and a death cert and copy of the county doc across the counter, slight pause then signing their form, so they can send a check for 14-thousand. **Thousand?!** *Besides paying these bills, those funds will help with our home improvements and cars. It's almost my annual salary. Janet will be extremely pleased.*

Next, *Next?* handing me another shock, telling me he had 15k in life insurance and had also named me. *O my God! Thank you Dad! Did you ever imagine how this could change our lives? Wow.* In shock. *We could practically pay off our new mortgage if we wanted to. What are we going to do with all this money?* Thinking about my beat up, used yellow Chevette at home, and the circular saw blade I had used to prop up the left shock absorber. I'd wondered why it'd been so cheap when we'd bought it.   *Almost 30-grand?*

Richard dropping me back at the apartment, and I thanked him profusely, over and again. *I'll have to send a tip.* Not smart enough to realize that Richard, probably only looking after Donegan's — is more interested in being paid ASAP. *He's gone above and beyond standard funeral practice, in a slew of ways.*

After the big news pointing this out to Janet when I call. She states, "Perfectly normal that he'd want to get paid sooner." Of course, *that would occur to Janet's practical mind.* Nevertheless, **I'm touched** *by Richard's considerations.*

Surprised and extremely happy about the money! Especially being able to pay my expenses, Jan's also relieved. After filling me in on her doings, Jesse, family and Baha'i stuff, she calls to confirm the plane ticket and departure time.

Calling Donny for a ride to the airport the next day, *without telling him about the money.* Afterwards hanging up, opening a Pepsi, and striking a match for my cigarette. *A long, satisfying smoke.* Relaxing for the first time, thinking, *Awesome, all done. And we don't hafta worry about money! About anything anymore.*

Not remembering flight back to Jersey. New, racing thoughts also flying — *in and out of my head, sideways.*

Three brief weeks then soaring heavenward.
*Not done **at all.** Just starting.* **Just.**

1.9 Unbalancing

Hungry greetings at Newark Airport, Janet, Mom, and stepdad Ralph are solicitous. *Do they know what I've been thru? Jan's lucky, both parents still alive. Dad's parents gone. Better not to tell 'em all of it. Keep it positive.*
Janet's Mom Doris is babysitting, which drowns her in magic. *So happy and grateful to be* **home!**
Hugs around, handshake with my Italian Dad. Seeing Janet smiling makes me comfortable and relaxed. However, she's puzzled also. Janet recognizing My altered mental state immediately. Years later, she told me she knew I was "wacko" (her word) as soon as we met in the terminal and she saw my wild eyes, *bloodshot from lack of sleep.* She also said I was acting strange in little ways, running at the mouth, forgetting things, being easily distracted.

"Are you alright?"

"Ah, yeah, fine." ***Standard response.***

Overjoyed at seeing my son and holding him in my arms again. "Hi little man!" Big grasping smile. I give Doris a big hug also. *But not all normal;* rambling on about California orange groves and bigger freeways. *Unrelated?* thoughts trickling up constantly *and having to express them verbally,* forced to get them out of me.

Forced to recount story in car, Janet listening *closely. Thinking elsewhere now. Be slow.* Soon home, asking, "Jan, I think we should take a vacation to **Disneyland™**. We've never been."

"Rod, Jesse won't remember it, so what's the point?"

"Oh," *disappointing, but continue planning for some day.* Janet's always able to bring me down to earth, *but not down.*

During the week **obsessing** over Dad's bills, especially Donegan's. Spending hours decoding them. We open a checking account in my name for the estate, with cash I'd already received. The school district won't send check without my father's divorce decree, so we enlist our lawyer, Mr. Robinson, to straighten it out. He had previously helped us with our wills. Kind, *wise and considerate,* speaking from his experience and his heart to our best interests.

Paying past due bills such as Donegan's, 14 hundred, dentist 30, annual Time magazine 14.97, Chiropractor 43, and others, adding up to over 2 thou. Later discovering Dad had only owned the Impala a year, yet owed 4 thousand on it. Luckily, finding insurance on it that pays it off upon his premature death, which is important. *Uncle John has already paid me 500 for it.* Using that to pay smaller bills. We're shocked to receive one for 37 dollars in back taxes on Dad's **1977 California Income Tax return.** Other bills have to wait *til we receive pension or life insurance monies.* "UUNG" More surprising, some stranger filed bankruptcy papers against Dad the day after he died. *A scam?* Another job for Mr. Robinson.   The surprises won't quit.

Without knowing it, My brain is chemically imbalanced from the stress that started the day I left California.

Janet later told me I'd been obsessed with paying all Dad's debts. **Adamant.** Even tho one credit card bill stated outright "charges are forgiven in the event of death," I insisted on paying it, **developing distorted sense of obligation and purpose.**

Telling Janet, "Look, this is the noble thing to do."

Next morning outta nowhere throwing away my half-pack of Kools, announcing, "I'm done with these."

Janet not saying anything.

Before our **Baha'i council** meeting a nite later, Janet asks, "Why don't you stay in the bedroom tonight? Watch TV and relax." *The Assembly meeting always takes place in our living room, on a two-week cycle.* Not really thinking, or caring, "Okay," and go in our bedroom and watch a movie on HBO, eating fudge swirl ice cream, another favorite.

Rarely missed a meeting, but not important. Other thoughts goin' on.

Our Assembly took care of all Baha'i affairs in Hamilton, and Janet and I were heavily involved with Baha'i activities. Our 9-member council practiced the principles of consultation and met with individuals or couples who had personal issues, career questions, financial problems, marriages to be officiated, and even divorces granted. Best was processing new declarations.

We also were the only assembly for a wide area, so people came to us with their questions, difficulties and joys, from central and most of south Jersey,

Since '74 and April officer elections, *Barb had always been elected* **Chair,** and was again, as was Janet to **Secretary.** It was the hardest position by far. Our correspondence writer and spokesperson conveying assembly decisions thru verbal and written communications, as well as: preparing the Agenda, setting up meetings with guests and adjudicating and approaching and treating callers with respect.

I had been elected Treasurer again, with an annual community budget of over 11 thousand. Issuing receipts, making deposits, writing checks and keeping the cash journal had become second nature. In '77 when the Assembly had incorporated, I'd spent 4 months going back and forth with the **NJ Division of Taxation,** to get our non-profit legal designation. *Ungh! The same questions and documents, over and again.* Finally succeeded in obtaining tax-exempt status for all our purchases. Now we could use an ST-5 with vendors. I'd also developed a guidebook for other assemblies and groups, and we announced it in *'Amru'llah,* our monthly community newsletter, put together by Janet.[15]

Getting the exemption had taken longer *because Taxation hadn't been familiar with the Baha'i Faith — at all. And who could blame them?* Many thought of us as an obscure middle-eastern sect of Islam, even tho the Persian nobleman Baha'u'llah, our founder, and His **Precursor,** the **Blessed Bab,** had both declared religious independence. Repeatedly.

Around   Me   lives   passing   normally.
*Thought   Mine   was   too -- *but sure wasn't.

During this phase, *conjuring up an idea for a unique* **Corporation.** *I'm committed. It's gonna happen.* Positive this company would quickly become a major player in the world of international commerce *by creating popular products. Greeting cards, books, knickknacks, and doodads, with a spiritual twist, will sell like hotcakes, and I have ideas for dozens. We'll use quotations from all the great figures and religious* **Teachers.**

On   Corp   plans   write   ***Inshallah***   nine   times,
for future growth and success.

Also jotting down 13-pages of notes *in my usual block printing,* in the space of an hour. Outlining precepts and structures: directors, departments such as art, publishing, games and media. These departments utilizing talents of all our local Baha'is, my friends, like Linda for art, Spud for media and marketing, and Bob for photography. Barb, his attractive young wife, would be spokesperson, since, having years of experience as our assembly chairperson, *she approached people easily and was quick on her feet with either deflecting repetition, or drawing out hidden motives, as could Janet.*

My decisions while writing were quick also. Convinced *the Corporation will be a* **worldwide success** *instantly.* Everyone shared in the profits, a Baha'i principle.

This without the slightest notion of what starting a business required, *let alone running one.*

After excitedly telling Janet these ideas, she calmly says, "Rod, why don't we share this with the Assembly, and you can meet with them and get their advice? It can't hurt and it might help. It would make me feel better if you did."

"I'll share your plans with them. Please?"
"I'm worried about you. You're erratic.
You're not acting like yourself."

Thinking a minute. *Can it hurt? They might say "No." Then what?* Hearing **Proceed**

Not acting Myself? This is a great idea. Saying, "Yes," knowing I'm going ahead with it.

Jan giving them My plans with my high hopes, convictions.

*   *   *

Entering our living room a week later, the other 8 members standing, ringed around Me, smiling and welcoming, friends and co-members.
Barb beckons as chair, "Welcome Rod, please take a seat." She's our best friend, but now she's something else. I cannot fear My own assembly.   No trepidation.
This   assembly   loves   Me.
After Barb's warm greeting and sharing the confidential relationship *I was so familiar with*, asking sweetly, "So Rodney, why don't you tell us why you're here?" Without thanking the institution for seeing Me, I open up a rambling description of the purpose of the Corporation and its divisions for 20-minutes.

Just getting started.

Pausing in My enthusiasm, Barb interjects kindly, "Rod, we know this is important to you, but what would you like us to do to help?"

"I need to meet with the **Universal House of Justice** about this. And not just a representative. Can you call and tell them I'll be coming?" This supreme governing council of the Baha'is is located at its world headquarters in Haifa, Israel.

Instead of shocked faces, everyone's deadpan and Barb calmly says, "Rod, you know how the Assembly works. We read your printed papers. Let us consult on this and get back to you with a response in a few days. Would that be alright?"

"Of course," *then rambling on.* With humble patience, they listen 10 more minutes *until repeating Myself for the 3rd time.*

Barb politely puts up her palm.   I pause.

"Rodney, thank you so much for sharing this with us. I'd like to ask, does anyone have a question?" My friends have none.

Jan rises to help me leave.

Barb closes, "Rod, you know there's a power just by coming to an assembly, and we promise to review what you've given us and what you've asked. Evelyn will contact you shortly, okay?"

That's enough then. They'll take care of it. Standing up, turning and heading to our bedroom, *before the members can even stand and show respect.*

Knowing how it all works.

*   *   *

Janet was hoping consulting with the Assembly would appease me. The institution sent me two letters of advice, the first dated October 9th, a week after returning home. The second October 18th. Neither suggested I visit the Universal House of Justice now, but rather wait until settling down. *Settling   down.   Taking   a   break.*

One letter says, "Although your desire to quit smoking now is commendable, it would not be a good idea at this time." *I consider it a temporary pass. One thing's sure, as a past Catholic, my flesh can still be obedient, sometimes.* [A1]

Buying a pack of Kool's after those 2 weeks, lighting the match, sucking on it, I didn't know that smoking would become so important to me in the mental hospitals I was heading toward.

It's My "moderate" **manic phase.** Janet and all my friends had tolerated my erratic words and behavior because they were clueless as to the real problem.

It would take everyone, including me, just a few more weeks to find out.

1.10 Conversing with an Infinite

Preoccupied from the moment the new Me awakes, around 6. *Pretend to sleep* til 7. Usual level disposition is missing in action. Dressing, leaving, driving to work. Alone in my cubicle, uncontrolled *feelings of loss for Dad and fear of my own mortality are building, building.* Since leaving California weeks earlier, flying out and making arrangements, alone, taking care of the his estate, ever more draining, *upsetting and bringin' more tension.*
Feelings reach breaking point. Shutting eyes tightly, lying head down on arms, staring inside eyelids, purple shapes, nothing, experiencing . . .

epiphany,   then hurt,   *loss*

*What's happening to Me? Is this what happens . . .
    after death?*

Blackness   *emptiness, nothingness.   Losing all hope,
but deep,   deep down,   knowing soul lives   eternally.
    I'm going to die — soon.*

    Scribbling   on   yellow   work   pad,   *"**Meditation:
1.   Noon Day Prayer: What exists?   Nothing exists.
    Who   exists?   God   exists.**"*
    Rapidly writing seven more.

Crying.   Sobbing.   Self-control vanquished.
    Taking   great . . . effort . . . not   stopping . . .

    Dying inwardly, *not the first time.* Fear of loss *enters
Me many times.* Fears of *losing Janet, Jesse or Mom. No
way to help.* Knowing me, always impulsive; interrupting
others while they're speaking, blurting out opinions as if
gospel. *Self-righteous from Catholic guilts? Imperfect . . .*
    Mourning quotation interjects: " **. . . none knoweth
what his own end shall be. How often hath a sinner attained,
at the hour of death, to the essence of faith, and, quaffing
the immortal draught, hath taken his flight unto the
Concourse on high!**" *What had Dad drunk? Would I drink
"**the immortal draught?**"*
        Recalling scarifying   rest: **"And how often
hath a devout believer, at the hour of his soul's
ascension, been so changed as to fall into the
nethermost fire!"** [6]

    *Shivering . . . Me?   **Only when extremely cold.***

Rest of day, workplace, in a trance; painfully stepping thru
motions, *acting   normal,* unable   to   concentrate.
    Fearful.

    Arriving home and pretending everything normal for
Janet's benefit. But beginning with random thoughts, *usually*

connected, knowing something's . . . not right. Feelings of *omniscience and righteousness,* turbulence and confidence. Being my usual uncommunicative self, *not sharing My turmoil with Janet.*

Not telling . . .feeling stranger. **Stronger.**

Grope thru the evening. Undercover by 10, yellow, warm stifling. Lights out, but full moon. Closing eyes again, lying motionless; *not sleeping.* Can't dispel . . . flashing, speeding thoughts without pauses or periods. *Don't disturb Janet! Faster thoughts . . .* Her on her side, facing away. My eyes land on lighted green dial. 2 a.m. *Compelled.* In slow motion, *Can't wake Jan!* rising from bed, hands pushing down on mattress, easing up, pick bell bottoms off chair, pulling out white T-shirt from hamper. No socks, picking up brown loafers. Tiptoeing, silently opening, closing, bedroom door behind Me. Padding 'cross hall to Jesse's door, *pause a split-second.*

I gotta leave him. **Gotta go**, gotta go. No destination yet.

Toyota Corolla starting right up, I'm driving thru Yardville, nearby Allentown, onto Route 539 toward the shore. Scrolling thru stations. **Voices** . . . on . . . radio . . . telling me what to do and how to feel. "You'll love the Sparkomatic! A new digital AM/FM cassette car radio, with exceptional reception. Comes in 8-track version as well!"

Shout, "You can't tell me what to buy!" Mad as hell at them, but don't turn off radio. Intuiting next words proceeding from announcer's lying mouth.

During news report, screaming, "Let the priests marry for Christ' sake!" after he mentions Pope John Paul II's visit. Other times singing words to every song, no matter station. Switching channels after a few verses. Caught up . . . *in the moment* . . . **the flow,** melodies, lyrics, upbeat or down. Down not affecting My Up.

65

Not once thinking of smoking. Not once had I thought of smoking, *even though I was addicted.*

Striking Me, "I need to stop smoking" -- throw Kools and matches out open window. Freezin' air blast *invigorating.*

       Both windows wide open, Mind in hyper-drive, *senses on high alert.* "11...12...13...14...," as telephone poles whizz past at 75, *whizzing thru traffic,* asking "Wonder where that person's going?" or "Why is that driver up ahead going left?" Concocting fanciful tales "Okay, he's got a tie on. He looks like he's on his way to work. I wonder where he works? Is it the newspaper because it's so early in the morning?" *Wonder if it's the* **Times** *or the* **Trentonian**? Prattling on whenever noticing something new. Barely looking . . . *but seeing all.*

Shooting thru intersection quickly.
Quicker   Faster   blinking   sign   posts

Speed

limit

50

Soon making note of **R.C. Maxwell** logos, immediately *composing missive to send them* re: improving their signs. *Searching,* finding, same name on other flashy boards. Traffic gliding lightly, big gaps early in the morning, *sailing in and out smoothly.* Eyes and ears miss nothing; *senses, inner sight registrin' everything   now* — note, note, note.
      File, file, file.   ***Unlimited capabilities***

Milepost 25 "whooshing" past, and noted. *Every flash connected.* Oblivious of time passing, sandy 2-lane county

road thru pine barrens holds infinite meanings.
Thoughts   continually   racing . . .

racing,   can't fathom, focus, rapidly replacing one on top of another . . . at once clear, complete,   then mislaid. Remembering **Russia's** recent test, declaring, "No more nuclear bombs, what are you, stupid!" jumping from solving world problems   to how many miles have been added to   My trip meter in past 5 minutes.

Only solvable problems exist; the 8 major barriers to peace identified by the House of Justice -- *overcome. FFFEEELIN'* entirely confident,   full   of   energy;   euphoria   *the world is right again.*

Completely confident, boundless energy. Fingers drumming steering wheel incessant *tap, tap, tap*. Not thinking of eating, or going to the bathroom.

I hafta go.

Rounding blind corner, "Perfect. **Sunoco**, just what I need." *Prescient*. Stopping to go. Feeling powerful, *having all the answers.*   Not needing coffee.

Sailing   again   .   .   .   crying   uncontrollably. Over-whelming-ness-washing-thru-Me.
I'll never see Janet or Jesse again.

Screaming, "Bob and Barb will look after you both! It'll be okay. The Baha'is will help." Knowing *they'll take good care of my family.* Can't take the intensity . . . feelings . . . *unable to separate thoughts . . .* whisperered **End it all,** floating, then still . . . *moving again . . . thru my head . . .* life pointless.   *Where'm I heading?*

Compelled to continue, life . . . leading straight for telephone pole number 325x471 . . . last moment, street lamp shines, poster, **Megan's Bar** [(?)] getting close,   pole looms, swerving away   swaying   skidding   my   bullet.

Don't hit brakes.

Prior   moment,   life   pointless. *Oh how next world beckons . . . Must go faster.*

One   (whisper)   wants to see **You**

That **Voice**. Living   exciting   Me   again. Careening on, pulling hard left into Crestwood Village on route 530 near Toms River.   One Cape cod with lights on, tilting into driveway at last minute, jolting car to a stop, rushing to the windowed door rapping three times.   Boldly.

Man moves curtain, looks out. Moving. Opens door wide. I open screen door. Couple facing Me, he fully dressed, she in robe matching thinned white hair.

"Hi, I'm Rodney, and I'm lost. Can you tell me the best way to the shore?" *I'm not a serial killer.*   Both smiling. He invites me in, wrinkled face and neck.   She also.

Chatting. Citing the chill outside, she offers me hot tea, "Oh, no thank you, but it's a dear thought." More chatting, but rubbing fingers in haste. Asking how they like the neighbor-hood, then rudely asking directions.

        "Okay son, turn around, make a right, and then left at the stop sign onto Route 530. You'll be there in no time," the nice man says. "Thank you both so, so much!" Leaving just as suddenly as I 'd arrived.

Continuing driving east   towards . . . water.

Hear secret Voice interrupt . . .   *H A I F A*

Now obsessed, " Must . . . go . . . to . . . Haifa."

Gotta get to Haifa to Haifa can't stop must stop where can I stop do I stop. Approaching large "Sand Co." sign with clearing behind it. Squealing rear tires on asphalt, veering right sharply, down 2-lane dirt road. 30 more yards, reaching large space, ringed by scruffy pines. Grinding to a halt, already unbuckled, bursting out screaming and ranting, pacing, kicking off shoes, tearing off shirt, unzipped pants dropping. Throwing them all as mightily as possible, not caring where they fall to earth.   Wallet   too . . . .

"I'm coming!"

"Nothing can stop Me!"

Great debate. *Toss gold ring. Keep it. Toss it.* Keeping it only because it's engraved with *Allah'u'abha*. And ignore wedding date 6/12/71.   *Searching   for   beach.*

No roadblocks entering Mind: the water won't be too cold, don't need a boat, I'll have stamina to swim the ocean. Only focusing on next second. Continually stomping eastward in path of headlights,   underwear off, bunching them up and tossing as hard and as far as I can.

Nothing . . . is going to stop Me.

Continuing, screaming, at top of lungs . . . raving at . . .

the world.   *My poor disintegrating world.*

Raising head . . . arms,   to full height,
         yellow moon   waiting . . . knowing . . .

Sudden breeze hits face and torso . . . . blowing hard . . .

Pushed back,   **Lightingstruck!**   A, a Revelation . . .

striking faster than a rattler, without warning I'm the lion of indomitable strength. [8] The next manifestation of God! Shouting **"Mankind must listen! It's time**!" Wanting to bring peace and cooperation to the world's peoples more than anything, never before feeling . . .
such burning desire . . . connection

Great calm washing thru Me. Listening intently. Mumbling . . . **"Yes Lord!"** and "**O Lord! Increase my astonishment at Thee!"** [9] Breathing in the knowledge and power of the Lord, the Omniscient, the All-Mighty. **Bold script appearing before my eyes . . . .**

Baha'u'llah's well-known words materializing inside seeing Eyes, Mind; feeling Heart; streaming thru hearkening Ears:

> **"I was asleep on My couch, when lo, the Breeze of God wafting over Me roused Me from My slumber. His quickening Spirit revived Me, and my tongue was unloosed to voice His Call."** [10]

Sensing . . . welcoming . . . fathoming . . .

Suns bursting . . . Explosioning . . . engulfing Us

Immersed . . .

earth's   existence . . . floating away . . .

imbued . . . permeating

exbued . . . entering

. . . other world . . .

What's left dies to this world.

Mind and heart, beating . . . rapidly . . . expanding . . .

inner eyes beholding new script . . .
slowly   fashioning . . .

hearing . . . forming . . .

one, two, three, four . . . WORDS.

Fusing.

*

Waves of warmth love hope embracing:
Seeing   feeling   hearing   tasting   smelling   touching

contentedness . . . respond **"Yes Lord. . . . "**

Filled with the knowledge   and the power
of the   spiritual world —

All-Merciful, All-Knowing, All-Good, All-Loving.

blackness engulfs

1.11 Jail Time

The black and white, *no flashing light*s, drags up slowly, stopping ten yards away. Two officers slide out, approaching cautiously. *Name badge reads DiPetro* in silver. Short husky guy, dark hair, asking, "Why don't you get in the car?"

"We will."

Not embarrassed. Not resisting.   Moving peacefully.

Searching briefly, they can't find clothes, shoes, wallet. Not cuffing me, placing me in back seat. One of them, retrieves blanket from trunk to cover nakedness. Barely noticing, laying it on lap. Sweating, glistening . . . *warm.*

Another says, "It's 4 a.m., we'll get you home. Have to make a stop."

Not paying attention.

Driving in blackness, *no siren, no strobe light*s, to brick two-story building. Braking, door opened, step out, blanket falling to ground. Entering, down hall, in back now, barred gate unlocked, swung open on thick hinges, officer handing me *drab* one-piece olive-green jumpsuit, which a climb into with no self-consciousness or complaint.

Staring at grey cinder blocks, "You're in the Holding Tank." Heavy iron clangs, reverberates in empty space, key turns, footfalls fading. *Silence.* Only My breathing, *alone once more.* Turning about face, grasping oil-painted flaked grey-green bars, cold, clenching firmer, *warmth from palms . . . .* back to terra firma and . . . *time.   Slowing   then speeding   then slowing.*

In slow motion. no sense I'm in trouble. *What's time?*

Observer looking from beyond.   ***Surreal***

Loud shuffling bare feet.   My own.

Later? Not the first time, flashing back to youth . . . small cells then at Juvie and County jails. This one triple in size. They come back. Other patrolman sits nearby, watching Me.

DiPetro writes on clip-boarded sheet. Reading my rights.

"Ah, can I have your attention?" he asks.

    Questions, of course.

    "Name?"

"R-O-D-N-E-Y R-I-C-H-A-R-D-S."

    "Address?" Tell him.

    "Phone?" Tell him.

    "Someone we can call?

"Janet."

    "Your wife, mother?"

"Wife."

Flash. "Where am I please?"

    "**Berkeley Township Police Headquarters**, near South Toms River. You know where that is?"

Flash. "My friends Lucille and Paul live here." Pause.

Flash. "How far am I from home please?"

    "Near Barnegat Bay, maybe forty miles."

    Minutes pass.

"I called your wife and she was upset."

"Upset?"

"She'll be here soon." *Oh.*

Hearing "**F l n g e r p r l n t s**"

Talking with the officers and having conversations *is easy now.* Chatting up the one who's rolling my fingertips in black ink, one by one. "So how long ya been on the force?"

"Oh, it's been ten years now, I've been lucky."

"Yeah, I've been lucky to be at my job with the State for almost the same time." *Truth.* We continue chatting amicably until task done.

Having an instinct for what to say next, hearing cues from officer, to connect with, or explore new topic, and *not overdo it. Can't really read his mind,* but having real sense *of knowing him intimately,* as a close friend or as an officer with a duty to perform. Respecting his office. Perfectly reasonable, rational, *both of us.*

In reality, *jumbled thoughts tumbling thru Me,* including those of escape, yet externally convincing as normal, well-adjusted person. *How do I look?*

Clock hands show 5:10. Hearing Janet and Bob's voices, walking in, **"Hey! My Jeans,"** black pullover with them. *Clanky gate* moves 3 feet. Dressing. Police releasing Me on my own he says, *but actually to Janet.* Walking thru open double doors, *held by my angels,* to Bob's car, parked 15 feet from station across white lines. Sprint now, *eager to get goin'. Gotta go.* Spud motions . . . *sit next to me here please.* Tapping back seat. Slipping in. Escaped from temporary home. Pregnant Barb in front passenger seat. *Sense, hear hushes, concern and worry.* Everyone handling

Me with kid gloves, using soothing language. "We'll get you better." Not caring what they say. Only My own grandiose thoughts and schemes occupy Me.

Continually moving. Lips, hands, fingers, feet. Pitch black out. *Mind Light.*

Janet sitting next to Me closes door, "Okay Bob." Pulling away, leaving this necessary place. *Driving . . . .*

Janet, "A neighbor heard you shouting Rod, and called the police. Do you remember that?" **Pragmatic.**

No answers. No one else existing. Mumbling in low ramblng surges, wide-eyed, straight ahead leaning ion front seats. Talking to *No One.* Bob driving to hospital in Trenton he says. Not acknowledging, *words still tumbling over words,* sometimes incoherent, others *clear and ranting,* but in steadier, lower yet high-pitched voice, all *full of energy and purport.*

Misty out, low white clouds, peering thru darkness.

Barb throwing me furtive glances. Noticing her, *Ignoring, noticing, ignoring.* Still thrusting forward, running My mouth, peering with headlights *into gloomy mists ahead,* addressing no one, *everyone;* muttering. Not hearing tender requests, "Why don't you sit back?

Recognizing **Mercer Hospital**, bright lights, 8 story building. "We" arriving at Emergency Room near dawn. Dr. Ward, psychiatrist, interviewing Me right away. Speaking in my voice clearly, sanely and rationally, convincingly, *it's a test of some kind.*

Says "Left arm please." Roll up long sleeve. Pinch next to vaccination scar . . . "Thorazine to help you relax."
Prescribes vitamins.

Feeling nothing. Saying nothing. Looking straight ahead at scintillating green sink. *inside, inside, swirling*

Not admitted, sending us home. Again, on Janet's recognizance. *Does she have* **Power of Attorney**? flashes by. Home. Supposed to rest. Cannot. No sleepy eyes, but darting, moving, *seeing words, pictures, scenes.* Saying nothing now *except to Me.* Just laying.

"He should've given you a sedative and put you to sleep," says Jan. Me *not commenting*, nor apologizing for behavior, *or try to explain. What? Who?* No hard questions.
    Eggshells.

Next morning Janet a little miffed at Dr. W because he turned out to be of no help with just vitamins..

Even new life's blood doesn't distract Me.

Next afternoon, "Who's that?"

Peering out bedroom windows. *Seeing* men in blue suits, dark glasses, black skinny ties, lurking behind tall lilac bushes. *Sure, they're* **FBI** *I'll bet,* not telling Janet of course.
    Radiate peacefulness, she doesn't question Me, or interrogate Me; *she lets me be,* bringing pills and water as necessary. Soup and crackers, salad. Pepsi. Setting me up in bed, all comfy, giving me clicker. As if I had a cold.   Janet is a rock thruout, has been thruout . . . our marriage. *Trying to act sane for her and others by concentrating, TV engrossing then pitiful;* seeming to fool everyone *into thinking I'm on the mend.* Totally self-absorbed and *no regard or feelings others, except Me.*
    Exploding thoughts and feelings hitting *rapidly.*

Three nights passing fitfully, *even with extra* **sleeping pills.**

Next afternoon Janet and Jesse out running errands. Me, watching TV and seeing commercial on "*how to make millions from new inventions.*

Spokesman announces, "Call us, and we'll turn your dream into reality!"

Dial 800 number, speak to male voice, jotting directions, knowing South Jersey, Cherry Hill Mall. *Good idea where it's near.* Quickly dressing then driving My car 30 miles down Route 295 and Route 72 to dilapidated office building in Pennsauken. Entrance hallway has dirty, dark deli, paying buck-fifty for small cup of joe. Three sips, *terrible lukewarm coffee.* Toss it. Ride slow elevator to 3rd floor and tiny waiting room of **Inventions Submission Corporation.** Four worn corduroy-covered chairs, an end table with lamp on, and pitiful few magazines. *No windows. No receptionist. Just a white door. Marked* **Private**

Idea is a moveable bathroom sink, on pulleys. Pulling up on side handle lifts whole sink up, making it easier for the elderly to brush their teeth, wash and so on, practically standing straight. Nondescript man opens **Private**. *No jacket, no tie,* asking if I have an invention idea, "Yes." Leaving for a minute and returning with clipboarded, papers and pen; hands them to me.

"Oh, brought My own," *Always carry pens, matches in glove compartment.*

"Please take a few minutes, fill out the forms the best you can, and knock when you're done." *Back to his office, closing* **Private**. *I know I have an excellent idea.*

Filling out three forms, personal info, describing moveable sink, drawing what it looks like, *in less than 10 minutes.* After finishing, knocking; *consultant invites me in.* Sit down on only plastic chair *in front of his small desk.* Barely 12" separating Me from his desk, wall behind practically touching My back. Introduces himself, asks my name, if I live near Trenton like I had said. "Grew up there."

Asking Me to sign "**Statement of Confidentiality and Non-Use**," *sign eagerly.*

He explains, "It's necessary so we can consult openly." Fascinating, *mind racing ahead thinking of possibilities and wild commercial success.*

Our Corporation.

"Like everything, Mr. Richards, this is a process. First, we do a patent search to see if your idea has been registered. Second, if not, we must draw your rough design according to established standards. Third, we canvas the possible manufacturers to see if they like the idea and we can strike a deal. Fourth, if one does, we patent your idea in your name." *Blah, blah, blah.*

Hitting me, *This is going to cost $$$.*
    Become skeptical.

Ah, finally finishing, "This sounds understandable, right?"

"Ah, of course."

"Then based on all those steps, and the incredible benefits that will ensue, don't you think a thousand is a fair price to get started for all the work we need to do?"

"Ah, well, We'll have to think about it." He tries the hard sell, *but not going for it. Even I'm not stupid enough to give him my credit card when he asks innocently*
    "Do you use VISA?"

Departing abruptly, *not bothering to close* **Private** Taking my copy of confidentiality statement.

Rush, quick now. "Good, nobody home." Never tell Janet.

Inflated opinion, knowing everything. **Idea brilliant!** [A2]

78

Home alone next mornin', writing letter, special letter, to the **President Carter.** Four long paragraphs, pointing out social ills in America; *what can be done to fix them.* Railing against him, *stupid policies;* threatening in harshly personal tones, as if scolding a child in worse way. Telling plainly what exactly needs to be done. No uncertain terms.

Addressing it to the White House. *Sneak out; mail it secretly.*

No memory of other happenings at home, except Janet, "Are you trying to hurt me?

Tried to hurt her and Myself. *She's frightened.*

Thru thickness, new malaise, yet drastic action, *needed.*

Picking the place and convincing me to come, telling Me **Princeton House** will help. At the front desk. Janet standing there, showing insurance cards.

While I Sign Myself in.

"Hi, my name's Rodney and I need to stay a few days. Can you help Me please?"   *Not knowing **its prophetic.** Much more help needed.*

Lasting only three days before kicking Me out.

1.12 Coming Down?

Stepping into head psychiatrist's office at P'House, declaring,   **"I Am the next manifestation of God."** [A3] *Brimming over* with the spirit of the Interlocutor, the Son of Man, and the Apostle, Peace be upon Him.

Overwhelming thoughts, feelings, power, omniscience, authority; absolutely no humility to moderate them. No control. **Not at all** like real Manifestations, Humble, Great. Same pre-existent Soul in the same body.

"Rodney, welcome. Name's Peter. I accept who you are and would like you to tell me about it. Can you do that? We have all the time you need, we won't be interrupted. Also, here, here's a glass of water for you in case you're thirsty."

He accepts Me. Accepting him. My friend immediately *puts Me at ease.* He's in khakis, open plaid shirt and penny loafers, and beckons Me to a large, high, curved-back wicker chair in his office, then closes door. *Welcoming.* Taking glass, siting comfortably. Pulling his sleek black desk chair on rollers over facing me, 3-feet away. Sitting down, crossing leg, *smiling wide, sincere,* caring only about *Me.* Paranoia banished, *my old self talkin'.* Sitting comfortably, squeakily, on thin print pillow. *All things seeming clear, every event has purpose.* Thoughts pouring forth as words and can't speak fast enough, tumbling out.

Cooperate fully, not belligerent, describing Our Vision, the Faith, Ideas for Corporation, World Peace.

Important now, must speak coherently.
Help him understand. **My Muse.**

Calming, focusing,

"MencanachieveWorldPeaceeasilyAll . . ."
"Rod, you've got to slow down, please. Try again"

"All barriers . . . crumbling. Soon . . . full equality of women and men; universal education a relative reality; everyone will have work and wealth; so many needs filled, and there'll be universal health care. English the international language of business and life, learned by all peoples as an auxiliary tongue. **Communications exploding,** able to speak to others instantly. **World Federal System** close at hand, as evidenced by **United Nations**, a temporary stepping-stone and . . . ." [16]

Peter looking on keenly, *nodding head approvingly,* jotting notes, saying, "I see," "Sure," "Yes, that makes sense."

Totally at ease, don't remember being sedated altho *I . . . am.* Sleeping soundly for five hours, at this alcohol, mental health, drug facility. Gradually "coming down," **Thorazine** and **Haldol** *in My bloodstream.* Thorazine powerful, acting as central nervous system suppressant and antipsychotic. Haldol, antipsychotic tranquilizer.

s l o w i n g   d o w n exhibiting My blue slippers paddling the floors, from bowed head. Drugs adding increasing *depression, restlessness, agitation* at same time. Reaching pool table and opponent.

Eyesight sharp. Steady enough to half-way-stroke.
Unbeatable. Unstoppable.

Long green shot. "8 ball, corner pocket," sinking it, smirking.

The next day sunny. *Light streaming thru large windows.* Breakfast, scrambled eggs, bacon, *Umm bacon.* After games of pool, shuffling to my shared quarters. *Roommate lying on his bed, reading magazine.*

Sudden com-punc-tion.

Loud voice, "I'm breakin' outta here." Pause. "Now."
Immediately he jumps up, rushes out of room,
To tell someone?   No matter.

Marching up close to 4 x 5 foot window, clasping hands into balled fist, raising them high above, and, in single downward motion, **"Bang!"**
Window shatters, shatters again, at its central point.

Huge rectangle of plate glass exploding outward and inward. Hopping on 2-foot high windowsill, walking outside, crossing worn sidewalk, leisurely sitting down *on soft grass.* Sunny out, clear skies. *Peaceful.*   Looking at hands before me — *no blood; not   a   scratch . . . .*

Management immediately placing me on suicide watch. Two good-looking long-haired blondes accompanying Me wherever I go. "You're my angels."   Telling Janet, Mom and Dad when visiting, "I have two more guardian angels."   *Stephen My personal Guardian Angel,*
like for Mom.

It's tomorrow. Nice black-haired nurse handing me meds and I loudly refuse, knocking pills out of her hand across room with swipe of My arm, *screaming,* "I'm not taking those!"

Shouting at her and world *for their imperfect states.*

On fire. **Rational Soul on fire.** [17]

Within 2 hours orderlies hold Me down, doc lifts sleeve, *feel pinch.* Clear liquid pushed down and in.   Within the hour:

Van speeding, bumpy.

All stretched out,

Immobile.

but, tugging, at, something . . .

M a n a c l e s

1.13 Fair Oaks

I will not let trouble harass Me.[11]

Groggy. "Where .. We .. goin'?"

    "North. **Summit Hospital**," *says pleasing EMT.*

During long drive, *meticulously,* with tiny motions, *wriggling hands free of wide restraints,* folding arms across chest, pulling up grey wool itchy blanket, *composed,* attentive. EMT in white winks, lets me lie quietly.

Thinking: *Janet had given up full-time teaching at* **Nottingham Middle School,** *while pregnant with "Pepina," after a stint at* **Langtree Elementary.** *I'm glad she's home, there for me, and Pepina, now baby Jesse. We had both agreed, based on her wish, that she raise Jesse "hands on." Any my 15-thousand salary was enough to sustain us.*

Arriving at **Fair Oaks** and far from familiar, rural, Mercer County environment. Overcast *but dry.* Bustling traffic, city streets, lots of pedestrians. Ambulance passing brick gates, entering circular drive, climbs slight hill, *brakes.* Winking attendant opening doors outward, hopping down, pulling gurney *Me,* out. Another white fellow grabbing other end, pulling, carrying til reaching ground. *On estate of some kind,* sheltered from big city, *tall varicolored, hand-sized maple leaves dotting the landscape.*

One white man untucks my blanket, *removing it.*

    Shorthaired man unbuckling leg shackles, saying, "Okay, you can get up now."

Sitting, rising, standing **in a haze.**

Another white smock wearing stethoscope, presumably a doctor, saying, "Rodney, we're going to help you feel better."

Burly attendant with embroidered letters 'Fair Oaks Hospital' on jacket, walking over, "guiding" Me up concrete steps to central doors. Multilevel orangey building looks like a mansion, 2 story brick wings protruding aside it, surrounded by spacious, thick-stalked and greeny-yellow trees, All *maples?*

*   *   *

Janet trailed in the green **Toyota.**
Going thru Admissions, have stream of doctor interviews, blood tests, EKG and so forth.   Not remembering lunch or dinner. Later   *finding Myself*   in male dorm room for 10ish bedtime.

"Bang, Bang, BANG!" 2 a.m., kicking narrow, thick window glass embedded in brick. Actually not loud, *only have socks on.* Unable to find shoes in darkness. Have had to climb up onto even narrower ledge *to get next to window.* Can't get good leverage. *No dorm mates stir.* Finally climbing down, laying on the single white bed.   Not sleeping well.

2 days later meeting Joey, big handsome Italian kid with thick black hair *who's in for doing drugs.* Becoming fast friends. His third time, *and he has defeatist yet cavalier attitude.*

"Yeah, I'm hooked, but so what?"

Shootin' the bull, *getting friendlier. He's a good listener.*

Next day attending psychotherapy session together.

Tall blonde, *Swedish therapist*[?][i]'n white coat again, sitting in rocker, *directing five of us,* "Rodney, why don't you lay on the floor?"

84

Weird, but going first, *up for the challenge.* Curling up in fetal position automatically, *comfortably.* Like bed but harder. **On My side.**

"Go back in your memories. Express how you feel."

Pause. *What does she want? . . .* Begin moaning . . . "Mommy, where's mommy?" totally faking it, but as real as I can make *what I think she wants.*

"Joey?"

Him laying down, quickly mumbling similar phrases. *Woman is encouraging, goading.*

"How do you feel at this moment? What hurts?"

"Oh, So lonely, I feel abandoned," *Fake answers, more moans . . . more   Words.*

Suddenly rising, sitting in My favorite rocker, *covering face. Hold back . . .* real tears. Other two inmates taking turns. *Unproductive except that last.*

Silent until now, Indo-American girl really crying, shaking slightly. G*ood fakir like Me and Joey.* Long pause; *we're dismissed. Do we have to do this again?   Have to . . . to earn privileges.*
Afterwards coming the greatest prize . . .
I can smoke! Recalling that much from
Admissions.

Fair Oaks, like school, *has rigid class periods.* No time to be alone, *and dwell, on unpleasant things of life,* or, how badly life's treating me. Actually, Never been that kind of person anyway, but **euphoria, energy,** *receding.* I didn't moan and groan *because God chose me to be . . . sick.* Even if it's genetics, *not blaming parents,* nor anyone else. *Never One to feel sorry,* no matter what

85

circumstances. Even as a kid, *Always happy, carefree, non-caring, no consequences,* livin' in our near-poverty.

A week? *passes,* now sitting in examination room, Dr. Gold, *always in smock with stethoscope,* entering with chart and folder, *closing metal door, speaking to Me.* He's young, good looking, shorter, thick brown hair. *We have a good relationship. Like him.* He's nice, kind, forthright. *Like Janet.* Speaking *simply yet directly.*

"You might get a kick out of what I'm going to tell you."

"Really, Doc? Good news or bad?"

"Funny you should say that because, actually, it's good news."

"Okay, hit me."

"Rodney, you have Bipolar Affective Disorder."

He's diagnosed me as — BAD !?

I hear him say it, laugh and joke, "Yeah, I'm BAD alright! Badder than you, Doc!" *Not happy or sad.* Just information, *data.* Can't hurt Me. *"BAD" would have been a fair moniker in my troubled youth, but now? Hell, I'm respectable.*

What's the good news?

"We're starting you on **Lithium**, which should help prevent this from happening again." Pause.
"Are you alright with that?"

Don't ask. "Whatever you say Doc, whatever you say." Never had fear of drugs, good or bad; *none now. Complete confidence he knows what to do.* I've always trusted doctors, even failures like 2 unsuccessful surgeons with

40-years experience removing My polynoidal cyst.
Third was the charm.

This revelation, diagnosis, whatever, *not impacting Me.* If counseled as to the signs of mania, how to handle suicidal impulses or the rest of it, *not making an impression.* Just like the multiple doctor consultations, group therapy sessions that followed, *remembering none of it.*
Dr. Gold must have filled Janet in however.

She's tells me later, "They wanted your system clear of drugs first, so they could determine your natural level of lithium — a baseline."

Dr. Gold had told me, "All plants and creatures contain trace amounts of it. It'll help you feel better."

Good, not feeling so hot. Janet also told me, getting me on the proper dose is extremely important. *Too little and I'll flip out again. Too much* and I'll be stumbling around dazed, *and toxic levels* causing dehydration, kidney problems, seizures . .

Possibly death?

Great.

At lunchtime given Lithium, *capsule form* [(?)]. Becoming My most powerful mood stabilizer, *having calming effects.* Not knowing or caring at all, how its working.

But the blood draws. Levels checked every few days it seems.

Short needle piercing the crook of my arm. "Ow, watch what you're doing please." Resent blood taking. *One good thing, not bruising easily.* Janet, just the opposite, little bumps against a desk or counter produce large ugly blemishes on her see-thru-skin.

Big, well-supplied arts and crafts room. "Tap, tap, tapping." Taking many class hours hammering 5-pointed stars into 2-inch wide leather belt, while sitting at wooden worktable.   During stay, also painstakingly topping off jewelry box with colored stones embedded in plaster-of-paris; carving a bas-relief of 1850's sailing ship, *inspiring,* and shellacking   wooden   frame   *til*   **finally   finished.** "Ahh , , , good job."

Spending almost a week on each simple project, *stupor-like, in dream-like state.*
During most of My time at Fair Oaks, *going thru the motions,* all the time depressed *and dull-witted.* At one session with Janet and Dr. Gold, others [?], finding out bipolar was called manic depression, comprised of two stages: **HIGHS (mania),**   followed by **lows (depression).**
The disease causes mood swings that range from *feelings of endless euphoria and energy*, to not being able to get out of bed.   *Couldn't care less.* Don't care what drugs I'm on, when getting out, *just **doing as directed.***
Exciting breaks at hospital *coming in chilly fenced-in courtyard.* "Ah, tasting like heaven," to a smoker standing near me. *So on edge without them. Anxious.* Janet bringing them regularly, but no matches, no lighter, *only orderlies have lighters.* Waiting for orderly outside making us all anxious. *Smoking helping moods.* Quiescent now. *Slow inhale,   deeper   exhale.*   Done.   *Light   another.*
Next week full, more psychotherapy, group therapy, family sessions with Janet and doctors, *more tests,* arts and crafts, meal times, smoke breaks and group meetings. Dr. Gold even asking Janet to speak at two combined family sessions. She relating her fears, hurts, and disappointment that it took so long, to diagnose me.

Decades later, we realize how lucky I am; was.

Second **excitement** comes.

Oh, that day we take the first field trip, riding high in big blue submarine school bus around downtown! Major accomplishment in privilege level, *only achieved with good behavior.*

I'd been "incarcerated" 4-weeks.

Thrilling seeing grass and trees and stores and homes and people walking on the streets. Not beige walls. *Oh this feels greeaat.*

Love window seat going anywhere, driving or flying.

I'm almost back to normal, never minding bouts of slight lethargy, **buzziness.** Surroundings seem fake sometimes and continuing to *act like mild zombie* at times, doing only what I'm told. But thoughts closer to rational.

Clearing.   Level.   Normal.

Do better increasing privilege levels and disposition. Mom told me how she and Dad had came up to visit one day. Dad staying reading magazines, Mom and I strolling thru town. Having nice lunch together and window shopping. At Hallmark, on Prospect Street ^(?), buying her Christmas ornament — *with my own cash.*   A tiny raccoon on a gold loop. *No idea what significance it might be.*

*On Lithium only, **releasing me** to Janet.*

Stepping outside and feeling cool. Drizzly December air. *Oh, so good to be free again!*   Pausing on hospital's front steps, raise arms in thankfulness. *Coolest mists soaking my face.* Being at Fair Oaks had been better than jail, even with restricted freedoms. But I'd been a prisoner just the same, despite the beige carpet thruout. Having known what hard floors were from real confinement was like, from multiple youthful trespasses.

Escape!

Walking to our dark green Toyota. *The invisible car.* Janet placing my bag of clothes and things on the back seat, next to Jesse's seat. We joked about that car, because we both felt other drivers didn't see it — too many of them pulled right out in front of us, or cut us off. *Too many to be coincidental.*

Opening my door, "Thanks," and getting in. Janet coming 'round, sitting, buckling up. Looks at me.

"Don't you need to do something?"

"Ah, I don't think so. We've got my things, right? Um, the doctor told us I'd be alright." *What is she talking about? What does she mean?*

"Don't you need to buckle up?" Typical Janet; alert, practical, to the point. Always a watchful eye.   I shudda known it was something mundane I'd forgotten. *My fault. Not alert.* **Never alert** *-- enough.*

"Oh, yeah, sorry." Not saying another word while Janet drives home, not that I have anything to say. Mumbling, "I'm sorry," once or twice more. In which case, Janet would have opined, "Nothing to be sorry for. Doctor Gold made it clear you couldn't help yourself. You didn't know what you were doing." Sometimes having a hard time believing that.

However, useless at home for next two weeks. Jan juggles my available paid sick time with Chris at work; and appears undisturbed. It's good to see Jesse's big smiles and hugging him, loving him. ***Cuddly. Like Jan.***

By then my memory of the hospital stay becomes fuzzy and any details escape me. *Just wanting to forget whole episode,* hoping Janet can to. Realizing, Nothing's all that simple, but adopting attitude going forward from the Baha'i prayer, **"I will not dwell on the unpleasant things of life."** [11]

Typical fall season, our millions of leaves dropping from 60-foot Norway maples and covering yards. Uncle Jackie and Cheryl are the first to rake 'em, while Jesse jumps in piles taller than him, bag them, and drag 'em to the front curb. A*s usual* *filling half its 90-foot length.* A job Janet and I normally do. Their wedding reception, under an Army tent, had been in our backyard. I had painted the house beforehand.

Was I his Best Man? I wore grey tails.

Other friends come over and help Janet with babysitting, bring food dishes, and do things around the house.

During the next weeks and months, however, other family and friends *not understanding what was wrong.* Few news and magazine articles describing bipolar.

Most people knowing nothing about the disease.

Kitty, an aged dear friend, told Jan "I don't get it. Just tell him to get over it."

At some point, conjecturing, *It must be extremely hard for Janet to trust me. I mean, with my background, having spent a week in jail while dating her, and my poor youthful drug choices. Together with other hurts and embarrassments.* **She must have known** *before marrying me that I wasn't 100% squeaky clean. Who is? But now? She knows I could flip out and do something crazy with no warning. I could possibly do something to harm myself, her, or even our son. That knowledge would create uncertainty, wouldn't it?*

But Janet never showing doubt. always exuding confidence in me, *which is another reason I love her so much. It's not that I'm a bad person, even with the label BAD.* Janet's love never, not once, indicating that.   In fact, her love — *my rock, to me, unshakeable.*

*   *   *

Janet stayed with me and supported me in everything, and thru everything. I came to an understanding and sympathized with her; *tried harder to please her.* At least, to the extent I could, *or remember to.* I've always known I'm hardly capable of empathy or forethought. *Not where people concerned.* Work exhibited no difference in me, where I could be a hard, brusque, *taskmaster.*

I resolved to make the best of my illness *by ignoring it,* especially with a wife and son to care for. That resolve would have been worthless without Janet's determined support, *which she gave wholeheartedly.* She never belittled me *or made light of my condition. She never made me feel bad.* Never reminded me of it. Her every thought and action geared toward making me better. **Normal** — back the way I'd been. *I can only hope to thank her enough in the next world,* because I've been inadequate in doing so in this one.

When stupid, bad or hurtful things happened to me I always just shrugged them off, *never holding a grudge,* whether against man or God. Well, except for those really ignorant, unintelligent and uncaring idiot driving maneuvers -- sometimes mine as well.

Twelve months afterwards Jan and I still haven't discussed the episode, *changes in me,* or consequences. *I feel no need to discuss it unless she wants to.* I'm totally unaware of all the hours she's spending submitting claim forms and cajoling Blue Cross & Blue Shield claims reps over the phone so my hospital bills will get paid.

Somehow, 2 years later, I heard that Joey, my best friend during my hospital stay, had relapsed and was at Fair Oaks again, this time for death-threatening heroin addiction.

Begin counting blessings.

1.14 Return to the Real World

"Hi Chris, **I'm back!**" I cheerily offered to my boss the first morning. "I really want to thank you for all your help.
You know Janet thanks you also."

"It's good to have you back, Rod, and Janet is remarkable. We have a lot of work to do, especially with Telex."

Having been allowed to leave hospital in December, *I'm back to nor-mal* and back to work 1/2-days. Even tho I'd accrued sick leave, it hadn't been enough and it was exhausted, along with accrued vacation time. *But Chris **has been more than helpful.*** In many consultations with Janet, had stretched my sick time so I hadn't lost my job or my benefits, even tho some time had been without pay. She and Janet had been on the phone almost daily during this period. *I will always be grateful to Chris for that.* Just as equally her mentoring and her writing skills she's passing on to me. She's a demanding boss, which I inwardly welcome. *To get this knowledge thru my thick skull.* Chris, always patient with me, but rushing in her own doings. *Never raising her voice at me,*

*And of, course, **I'm always grateful to Janet.***

So I continue rewriting our reports and memos until Chris agrees, sometimes five times. "That's good, Rod." *Hearing praise meant a lot; to my confidence also.*

My beautiful brunette assistant Alice had kept things going in my absence; she'd taken care of the massive equipment inventories.

"Hey Al, how did the inventory go with Gene from **IBM** Was everything priced?" Negotiations with IBM, and other duties. She'd filled me in on our deal with **Telex** to replace older **SNA** terminals over the next 2 years. Greg Lemieux, the Telex salesman, had been persuasive with a great personality and their large discounts. *Which usually means the* *product's overpriced to begin with.* But these were fair. They were our biggest hardware contract vendor for IBM-compatible controllers, terminals and printers — **the precursors of PCs.** We purchased thousands of 'em worth millions of dollars for installation in agencies across the state. *And Alice and I kept track of them all. A*nd other info processing procurements as well.

One nice thing about work, *among many*; no one asking where I had been *or why I was gone.* In government bureaucracies like mine, with so many employees, it was easy not to be missed *when you weren't the sole decision maker.* I didn't know if, *It just hasn't registered with them?* Or, *Has everyone been told of my mental illness? Are they afraid to ask?* No matter which way, Alice and salespeople missed me more than others.

Not embarrassed by my episode *in any way.* Just life. *Life happens. Deal with it, then move on.* No moans and groans. *Don't blame others.* Fix it or forget it, like drivers who cut us off. *Janet and I share this attitude completely.* We're polite activists, informed independent voters, trying to model good behaviors for Jesse as well.

However, as good as work is, at home we're still coping with Dad's bills. His estate's insolvent, and Jan and I have significant personal funds left over from his bequests. My brother Stephen **hires a lawyer.** *Gently implying a lawsuit for his share.* At our request, Mr. R calls Stephen's lawyer. They speak at length.

Upon hearing our lawyer's advice, we send Stephen 54 hundred dollars.

"Thank You" is written on the outside of his light blue notecard, dated March.

"Dear Rod & Janet, Sort of an apology for being disagreeable for so long — I guess it was all just too much. Get

94

little Jesse a tricycle and let me know how much. Love, Steve." *Id never called Stephen "Steve" in his life.* It was another sign of his changed adult self. *We didn't buy a trike.*

Of course, I love Stephen. *And have no conception of how Dad's death affected him.* **We were always cordial** afterwards, always friendly, *but never embraced on meeting or leaving each other.* At the time, I begrudged him those little monies a bit. W*hy? Perhaps because I'm not that close to him, and, he had never even met Dad, let alone lived with him like I had?*

I don't know much about Stephen or his life.

At the Trailways Bus office back in Santa Ana CA which had still been there, I had shipped two boxes of Dad's stuff to Trenton and they were lost in transit. "Crap." but nothing could be done except hope they turned up. *They didn't. "Inshallah."* They settled our claim with 198 smack-e-roonies.

Mr. R and his secretary Olive McDonald, a good Baha'i friend, co-Assembly member and Jesse's mentor, had been invaluable in addressing innumerable other issues, like the bogus bankruptcy proceeding. *Also, I'm very concerned about my* **arrest charges.** *Indecent exposure?* Disorderly persons? Don't remember which, but Mr. Robinson told us it was to much trouble to worry about. S*o I dropped it, reluctantly. Janet hadn't wanted me to pursue it anyway.*

We pay the firm $540 for its invaluable legal services, and by mid-February, all Dad's bills are paid. *Whoo hoo!* We do three (or four) things with the balance of funds; I buy a Honda 360 cc motorcycle at **Cooper's Cycle Ranch** on a whim, as well as a regulation **Fischer pool table** for me; we put money into the house like a new electric service from 100 to 150 amps, and other stuff; and we start a college fund.
*Janet doesn't buy a thing for **her frugal self.***

However, at Jan's suggestion we do a couple things together. First we splurge and drive to the swanky **Waldorf Astoria Hotel** in Manhattan for a single night. *Just the two of us in a miniscule flower-print wallpapered room on the 14th floor without a good view. How soft and fluffy the white terrycloth robes are.* Something we had never experienced. *It feels good to be away with my wife,* and we enjoy each other's company. The next afternoon we see *Chorus Line* to our delight. *Even tho its set couldn't have been plainer.* After the matinee we head to Carmine's for an Italian dinner, *my very favorite.* We couldn't eat their delicious salad, rigatonis and cheese-filled raviolis on their huge platters.

But we bank away the money and I **only pull** 30 bucks a week at ATMs cash for lunches, *cigarettes and spending money.* But Janet doesn't complain. Much.

Concentrating on work, the needs of the home,
family   and Baha'i;

I   am   now   a   confirmed   employee,

homeowner,   husband,   parent,

and   believer.

1.15 All Wound Up

8-months after Dad's funeral I receive a **Warrant of Arrest** for Rodney C Richards Sr from the **Sheriff-Coroner's Office** of Orange County, that contains a $268 judgment against him. I have no idea why it was issued, but we pay it without contest. *I'm feeling noble again.* We also end up paying the City of Orange 10 bucks for an old parking ticket that had been forwarded. *Now I know why people need estate lawyers, and an executor prepared for all this crap.* Most importantly,   WHY EVERYONE SHOULD HAVE **A LAST WILL AND TESTAMENT.** As an National Treasurer's Representative I was facilitating many sessions on writing wills to Baha'i adults of all ages — it's a spiritual obligation for adult Baha'is, and never to late.. *BEFORE you're incapacitated, which we'll all be.*

But we decide to use some money for a trip in May . . .

*   *   *

The stewardess asking, "Would you like a drink?"

"Yes please, Pepsi if you've got it." *Good, she has it.* **Coke** only okay as an alternative.

I know Janet can't have anything. *Not even water.*

Barb sits next to me in the middle, and Janet, curled up, hands clenched, eyes closed, pursed lips, leans on a pillow against the window — with the shade drawn. *Oh Janet, I hope you get thru this okay.* I feel sorry for her severe airsickness. It's not the airplane or the altitude that makes her so, and she isn't afraid of flying, by any means. Her inner ear is the problem, and it just cannot handle airplanes. She does slightly better with eyes clamped shut in no light. *Janet has long ago tried dramamine and other remedies without success.*

May '80 and we're on a United flight to **O'Hare**, to attend the **72nd U.S. Baha'i National Convention** near National headquarters in Wilmette, Illinois. The election gathering will take place in Foundation Hall under the towering **Mother Temple of the West.** Approximately one hundred delegate will be electing 9 members to the National Spiritual Assembly

97

(NSA), our countrywide governing council. *Except for Alaska and Hawaii who have their own.*

Barb's husband Bob is squeezed into a plane seat 'cross the aisle. *Probably giving his seatmate a fireside.* Bob might start one with, "Do you know the informal motto of one of the oldest black colleges in the United States? It's 'Wake up, Get up, Do something.'" In firesides to us he'd go on to tell of Dr. Martin Luthor King Jr. and **The Movement's** struggles, who himself had been a graduate of Morehouse College. Bob would quote from Shoghi Effendi's ***Advent of Divine Justice***, a long letter written in 1938 to the American Baha'i community, at that time less than 4 thousand members. In his letter, one prescriptive section states that relations between three groups, American Baha'is, blacks and whites is **"the most vital and challenging issue"** confronting them, and that one of the Faith's watchwords is unity in diversity. *Of which we're all very cognizant.* [18]

Shoghi Effendi, named **Guardian of the Cause** and appointed **Interpreter** of its Writings, administered its affairs from 1922 til his sudden death in 1957. *I was a big fan, fixated on his long, in-depth, epistolary style.*

In numberless talks back home, Bob would go on to **inspire us** to take individual responsibility for our actions and do something to serve our neighbors, friends, co-workers and mankind. *He could make a snake molt its skin with a poignant paragraph.* His general knowledge and memory were keen as was his wit, also like Spud's. *And he was a top-notch jokester and storyteller.* So much so that he convulsed his audiences with laughter, or choked them up, *me up,* with heartfelt empathy. *He's a sought after speaker.*

When I first met him in late '69, he had always dressed like an **ice cream truck man**, attired head to foot in white. He had a 6'2", 250 pound frame, sported a thick bushy dark beard, and wild, a little curly, thick brown hair. His hugs were ferocious but fitting. *And he hugged everyone, small, medium or large.*

Many Baha'is hug, or kiss each other on the cheek(s), even some guys and women, tho not supposed to.

After '72 Janet and I'd visit him and his new wife Barb at their Hamilton home on Nottingham Way. Barb and Janet would converse, laugh and share old family pictures and stories, and Bob and I would play chess grunting and grousing, while he shared tales from his travels. *He taught me backgammon to, and he usually won at both.*

Wow, this is going to be awesome! That's what I had thought when we had confirmed our trip.

It was Janet's and mine first plane trip together.

Coming in low over the warehouse district and then the airport hangars, "Hon, we're getting close and will be landing soon."

"The shaking will stop in a minute, I promise." *It doesn't.* It's the Windy City. *I can only offer Janet short words of encouragement.* But Barb is a big help. Janet's filled two bags.

I feel,   Love it! hard to settle down. The only way I can is by reading the flight magazine cover to cover twice, even the stupid expensive ads. *They should have a separate magazine in our coach section, with a range of <u>affordable</u> items.* Worked on the page-length crossword puzzle. *I got a coupla' dozen answers.*

*I like answers,
as long as they don't involve understanding myself.*

Stable on my meds, Jan and I had decided to go. We were stimulated and looking forward to convention. We all disembark, Barb escorting Janet closely to **Baggage Claim**, Bob and I finding our luggage, then paying for a shuttle bus, which doesn't help Janet's motion sickness, to the **Orrington Hotel** in Evanston. Ready for us, we check in, and the matronly clerk hands us our convention packets with agenda and itineraries. Reaching our upstairs adjoining rooms, unpacking. *Janet immediately lays down to rest.* We don't talk to her until she feels better, meeting in Barb and Bob's room, watching TV and conversing, much less without Janet there. Later the four of us joining 30 or so assembled friends after dinner. *And renew old acquaintances with folks from around the country.*

It will take a full day for Janet to regain her normal stomach and lose her headache.

And **this had been a good flight.** Janet was semi-accustomed to flying because she had flown 2x a year to Knoxville, Tennessee for weekend **Child's Way Editorial Board** meetings, while I cared for Jesse. *It's the **U.S. Baha'i** children's magazine.* [19] *She's a managing editor.*

While the delegates were meeting the next day in Foundation Hall, we all join other spouses and guests on a tour of the main temple structure above, the only **Baha'i House of Worship** constructed in North America. *Listed on the **U.S. National Register of Historic Places.** It receives hundreds of thousands of visitors each year.* After morning prayers in the beautiful auditorium that seats 11 hundred+, we're led up narrow stairs to the clerestory. *And allowed to walk outside carefully in small groups.*

The docent needn't have requested, "Watch your step," as we tread on the wide tarred roof. *Lake Michigan glistens from a height of 75 feet with no obstructions.*

Only hundreds of yards away, "Whoa, look at all the sailboats. Look at that tall one.!" And, "It's so clear I can see for miles." During the next few days we visit the national offices, and see first-hand how hectic the scurrying people, phone conversations and envelope stuffing going on is.

*That evening we attend the 19-day community **Feast** at a nearby elementary school.*

The school auditorium where its taking place is standing room only and conversations going non-stop, only interspersed with hugs and cries of **"Allah'u'abha!"** a common greeting. Prayers and readings from the Writings are shared aloud among scattered low chatters, then announcements and Evanston Baha'i community news. *We can barely hear and don't reach the refreshments -- to many people and families.*

Reaching outside to leave Feast. *It's pouring.*

Jan, "Shall we look inside for an umbrella or newspaper? Or look for a phone to call a cab?" Bob and Barb are still inside. *They know many more people.*

But a very nice older couple Janet had been conversing with under the school door overhang, offers us a ride. Their black car is parked right out front, and he and his wife are also staying at the **Orrington** like us. We have a very pleasant ride and talk amiably with them in their spacious car, thanking them twice when we all exit at the hotel.

After entering our room and relaxing, Barb knocks on our adjoining door, which I open with, "Hey, great Feast, huh?"

"Yeah, let's talk about who we saw," this meant for Janet of course. Barb and Jan are sitting on our bed in their pajamas. Bob lays at the foot of another, covering a wide expense, while I'm watching TV. Janet's telling Barb about the nice old couple who had given us a ride home. As she's telling it Bob jumps in, "O my God! Do you know who that was?"

"Nooo, who was it?" *Huh?*

"That was Mr. Wolcott and his wife. Did you notice they had a driver for their car?"

"Well, kinda, we weren't paying attention, but yes, they did. Who's Mr. Wolcott?"

"Mr. Wolcott is a member of the Universal House of Justice." He said it with a little awe.

Janet and I both knew that the House of Justice was our world governing body, composed of only 9 members, head-quartered in **Haifa, Israel.** It hit us that this had been a very special lift. But honestly? To us? *It was as if old friends had been discussing the weather and the topics of the day casually and without restraint.* The Wolcotts' seemed to be an exceptionally nice couple, and good listeners. I learned later that Mr. Wolcott had served on our own NSA from '53 to '61.

I have no memory of who was elected to this year's NSA except for Robert Henderson and Judge Dorothy Nelson, perennial favorites. *They seemed a good choice.*

Baha'i elections are based on a person's qualities and mature experience, with no campaigning, no nominating or no electioneering; *It had indeed been an eventful trip.*

* * *

1.16 Yea, Drugs!?

Having taken over a year to work out the right combination of drugs, *I'm wearing them on my sleeve.* Going from just below the radar to extremely alert and itching for action. **Never depressed.**

After working together we found an effective drug with my psych's help and Janet's observations.
An effective   cocktail of 11 pills daily.
Swallowing hard.

And a cocktail it is.

My meds consist of **Tegretol** (lithium), mood stabilizer; **Wellbutrin**, an anti-depressant and smoking cessation aid. *Which doesn't curtail my smoking -- wish it did.* **Clorpromazine,** an antipsychotic; **Geodon,** for schizophrenia and bipolar disorder; and **Desyrel**, an antidepressant and sleep aid. Taking blood tests at my HMO clinic every three months to check liver for toxicity and side effects. *Don't like it,* **but do it anyway.** Thus, over time, phlebotomists come to have difficulty getting blood from veins in either arm. S*mall price to pay -- stableness and rationality.*   Become inured.

Using that year to feel some semblance of true normal. Just enough pharmaceuticals to control my brain's imbalance *Not too much where I feel drugged, or depressed* me, the *true . . . me.* The *controllable me.* The *stable me.* The *safe me. With all my reality, feelings and faults intact.* At least, as close as I can tell. *More importantly, as close as Jan can   tell.*

Even so, only originally downing pills with
        Jan's constant nagging. "Rod, did you take your pills?"
            Oh, resented those words!

By this time, *feeling oblivious.* The whole thing — *forgotten,* except for taking the damn pills 4-times a day. Going thru the motions but somehow doing better than "Okay." Only concerned with myself, for as little attention as I paid to others *or to events around me.*

In October '80 Janet has great news and tells me alone in bed, "Rod, I'm pregnant." **She's pregnant!** Immediately hug and kiss with hope and joy, and   promises.

We're ecstatic! Everyone else also. Even I can feel it.

1.17 Temporary Respite

Janet and I enjoy afternoon movie matinees in spring '81, just the two of us. Watching *10* one evening, with Bo Derek and Dudley Moore, I whisper, **"Wow, she's pretty,"** Janet just smiles. *As usual, I have a crush on the stunningly attractive leading lady, corn-rowed, long-haired blonde, which occurs in every film I see.* Especially the action movies where their bodies go along with these women's gorgeous faces.

Our good friend Evelyn is babysitting one afternoon, also caring for her and Spud's daughter, Leah, cutie. With his good looks, curly thick black hair and beard, he's also an avid TV, movies and music afficionado, singer and guitarist, and knowledgeable on most any subject. *An all-round conversa-tionalist who's quick-wit, laughs and smiles disarm you.*

Evelyn, the second-most organized person I knew after Janet, held a high position in training and development. *She's even more direct than the two of us.*

When we arrive back at their place to pick up Jesse, and after a happy reunion with him in polka dot jumpsuit and good spirits, Ev asks, "Do you have any problems understanding him?"

"No, none," we bark together.

"Well maybe you should have his hearing tested? I can tell he knows what an object is, but I find it hard to understand his speech." *This is ironic, because his middle name, Kalim, from the Arabic, means "speech."*

Janet and I don't agree with her, but say nothing else there, and thank her for her concern and babysitting. Driving home, **a little miffed** *that* someone has questioned our son's abilities, *especially since* we understand his mumbles quite well. However, we love, admire and trust Ev. Knowing her, we understand she wouldn't have asked unless she had felt sure it was a problem.

The next day Janet searches for a facility that gives tests.

We wait anxiously for results from Project Child, at the college. The research doctor tells us, "His hearing is fine, but his speech is not developing as it should. We tested 130 sounds, and he's only acquired 26. Here's what you can do...." That starts speech exercises at home. After a year of promising development, *classes at **Mercer Hospital.***

My fourth joy comes **in June '81 w**ith the birth by another Caesarean of daughter Kate Amelia! After 15 hours of Janet's pushing I'm falling down dead tired. *But still there in spirit — just not in the operating room of course.* And she's born a healthy weight, with a small round bald head and twinkling eyes. "Beautiful." *Janet and I, both blessed and happy.* Again all our friends and families are thrilled when we bring her home.

"A rich man's family!" my mother-in law exclaims, now that we have a boy and a girl. *We're exalted, and little Jesse grows to adore his baby sister.*

After being home a week however, Janet's mending as well as caring for everyone, and is nursing Kate. *When **her lips turn blue and she stops breathing.!***

Seeing it myself as Janet rushes in to show me. Immediately puts her on her shoulder, rubbing and patting *vigorously*, til Kate's breathing again. Grabbing her carry-all, we bolt out, speed to Emergency at Mercer, with Jesse in the back seat. After a quick intake they roll her tiny frame to the **Intensive Neonatal Care Unit.**

I take Jess to Janet's mom's and hurry back.

"Will she be alright, Doctor? What's wrong?" Jan asks first. Petite female specialist doesn't know yet *of course. Too early.* Janet knows her because she has a good reputation in Hamilton, where she practices. She explains intravenous feeding will be required because it's serious. *Reluctantly we agree.* They gingerly stick a tiny IV into her tiny foot as she yells. Janet's doubly upset because she's concerned Kate won't nurse. Jan stays with her much of the time in a hospital bed next door, always watching her thru the partial glass wall.

Kate's extremely ill, with a high fever.

We pray, **"Thy Name is my healing, O my God, and remembrance of thee my remedy."** [20] Everyone offers healing prayers. *Us most of all.* After a few days our baby girl is diagnosed with a bad infection and doctors continue to monitor her progress carefully, treating her aggressively with antibiotics. Thank goodness, after 7 days, she's declared healthy, released, *and everyone's relieved and grateful.*

Insha'u'llah

*   *   *

1.17 Temporary Respite

The next weeks and months are super hectic, with 2 young children, growing responsibilities in the Faith and at the State, family also. *Why am I being ornery and moody?* Often cursing or shouting at Janet for no good reason. *Not that I usually do*. But also doing the same at work. This could be the bipolar acting out, so Janet and I don't let it fester. We go to **GreenSpring's** office immediately to see my psychiatrist.

He doubles my meds temporarily, and sets up bi-weekly meetings with Mark Wilenski, **a psychologist**, to help our relationship. His office is in a Ewing apartment complex off Parkside Avenue. Janet and I go. *I'm not sure we should share our thoughts and emotions.* But Mark is so relaxed and natural about it. *We're soon able to overcome our inhibitions.* Thought-provoking, mildly challenging exercises challenge us. *Even so I hold back mine more than Janet. Reliving how I had hurt her, can't help but choke up.*

Mark interjects feeling questions.

"Rodney, how did you feel when you shouted at Janet?"

"Um, mad? But nothing really."

"Nothing?" Janet asks.

"Well, just angry . . . ." *I was irate.*

In one of Mark's sessions Janet hears me say, "Hon, I haven't intentionally withheld information from you, really." I **"Uh, I just forget."** *Most often I don't give a second's thought to who I saw, or what I did or thought, or what's important enough to remember — I don't share -- nor care. Why not?*

To her everything's essential, like asking "Did you run into anybody you know at the food store?"

"Ah, no Hon," was my canned response one day, even tho I saw neighbor Maryanne,[?] the reliable dog walker. Just wasn't important enough for me care about sharing. After Jan went to Acme or Shop Rite, of course, I heard the life story of the woman next to her in line, what school her kids went to, and their grades, and her husband's profession. *I always* _tried_ *to listen attentively.* Often I heard touching stories of overcoming hardship, or achievements of their children, and what Janet had shared to encourage the parent.

Thank God Janet talks,   or we wouldn't communicate.

When someone she meets is dealing with a bipolar spouse, relative or youth, she shares about me, her. *She offer's our experience as a way to make it seem less catastrophic. Janet can start a conversation with anyone about anything.*

Mark draws us both out. He's relentless yet kind. "Here's paper and pen. Draw a line down the middle. On one side, answer the question 'I want for myself' and on the other write 'I want for my spouse' Then we'll go over it." *For every seven of Janet's answers, I have three.*

Reading our answers aloud, *few agree.* Heartfelt discussions of how each of us, and our marriage, should be — what we think it should be for us, follow. *Both of us independent and have our own concepts of what we want to do and how, and for and from the other.*

We see him monthly for two years, before we both realize together *we've overcome our major "issues."* The biggest takeaway *is cutting out unrealistic expectations.* We both come to see **we aren't mind readers,** especially Janet, so if she wants something from me, she has to spell it out, kindly and reasonably. I, on the other hand, am encouraged to share and not hold anything in. To share what I want for myself and others. W*hat I'm experiencing. Just what I think. Not a lot. Well, I do have a few wannas.*

Staying with Janet and the kids is the most important one.

We also discover: **"Make no assumptions."** Janet could no longer assume that just because the grass stood 6 inches tall that I would take note. *She thought I'd naturally cut it without her pointing it out. I've never noticed.* As soon as she mentioned it I was in ready agreement; then I'd cut the grass. This went for everything. *I don't think of these things myself.* But no more of that.

After this I found short lists on the kitchen counter of 'suggested' projects around the house. *And I don't mind one bit. A big help in fact.* Her lists are short, doable.

Also clear, always been clear between us, **'What happens in the past stays in the past.' Immutable.** Never productive to go back or dwell on it. *Good or bad.* We try to learn the lesson, *remember the good times*, the things that worked, and go on.

Except for this winter, I'm still exulting riding my Honda on the city streets to and from work. *Oh, so biting at midnight in March!* I have to wear my brown wool turtleneck sweater. P*ull it up past my chin.* Taxation who leases the building we work in, allows me to park cattycorner in the basement garage, leaving space for a vehicle, until one day, a lottery executive's car bumps it and it crashes.

A 20 dollar side mirror smashed.

Buy a new one at Cooper's and repair connections.

But Joe Mule was nice enough to leave his name on a note., After replacing the mirror myself and sending him the bill. *He paid cash after a little dunning.* However, two weeks after that my bike's kicked out of the garage, as if it had been my fault. It doesn't matter why. I stop riding my bike to work, and park my car 2 short blocks away by the **War Memorial.** I've owned more average old cars than not, other than my gold, 327, black leather interior, mag wheeled, 4-on-the-floor, **'65 Chevy Impala.** *I do the work myself on all our cars, like replacing its carburetor. Or even a motor in our earlier **Nova** with ex-roomie Mike Reilly's expertise, before we drove to Wilmette on our 2nd honeymoon..*

Also in '81, Thomas H. Kean wins the governor's race by large numbers. A Republican, Kean's fortunate to preside when the economy's humming along and times are, well, good. ***A new governor always means change,** in everything.* We see many old directors go, new ones appointed, and other fresh faces. In fact, ALL new faces in the governor's office, and these were the chiefs of staff, many deputies, and the policy makers, as well as their clerks and secretaries. *And that's what hurts most. Few of my prior high-level contacts are still in office.* Too few to call and arrange streamlined procurement approvals. Also used to seeing the best leaders leave along with fewer of the bad, some of the new guys (more women than usual), *turning out not to bad.*

In '82 Janet Joins a company called **Discovery Toys,** whose business model is home sales of educational items for children. Games, books and toys for all ages, we have the bounty of testing them at home to play and learn from. *Which we all get a kick out of and reuse often.* The **Ravensburger** puzzles are best. Janet buys plastic folding cartons which she packs and lugs to hostesses homes during the evenings.

I support her by watching the kids when she travels from place to place evenings. *And also lugging full plastic cartons.*

Her first Flyer declares "**Discovery Toys thinks you're special . . . (so do I !!!) . . . as a customer . . . as a hostess . . . as someone who cares   about   others . . . .**"

1.18 A Scare

Janet notices a large skin-covering rash on 2+-year old Kate one summer morning. *It seems to migrate on her torso, and one **looks like a red ring.*** Kate's a little cranky as well. We also know Kate's allergy to artificial coloring, which caused cranky moods in the past. A friend, Beth Bowen, diagnosed that.   *Something she ate again?*

"Doctor, do you think its from the heat?"

The kids pediatrician, Dr. Bayley whom we love, tells us it's probably from summer heat and will pass. The next day it hasn't. *It's redder. She has a fever.* I happen to mention it to Chris at work.

Eyes look right and up for a moment. She says, "That sounds like Lyme's disease. There's been reported cases near Block Island where we've gone sailing."
Pause.   "It's from a deer tick I think."

Janet has me call Lyme Connecticut's health department for info and pamphlets. Hearing enough, we immediately drive her back to the doctor, who semi-agrees and draws blood over Kate's tears. *It's confirmed Lyme's.* We administer 10 days of antibiotics and it clears up. The red "**bull's eye**" had been the clicher. *It's the first documented case of Lyme's in Mercer County.*   *It's 1983.*

We're living close to the boonies, and seeing plenty of   deer driving near home at dusk, even in our back yard.
Thank you pinprick tick, not your fault.

Another dodged bullet for us, another blessing.

*   *   *

My title's been DP Programmer II.
*Programmers write **COBOL.***
Common English letters and words,
and hy-phen are their separators.
Machines translate into bits, bytes.
So codes can run application programs.
***DOS** hidden codes follow.*
The hyp-hen is its most used character.

"Move lottery-file-tickets to sort-file. Execute Sort on sort-file." The only time I actually saw any coding done was when I had taken night classes at Hamilton Night School, strictly to better my understanding of the business. *And I paid for the course out-of-pocket.*

Never wrote a line of code except in classes, including   **RPG** report writing program. *Talk about staccato.*

A year later I've been handed a new title — DP Analyst   II, making 32k a year. Darn good. *Without a college degree.* DP Analyst signifies a requirements   writer who   inter-faces and kowtows with and to users of proposed applications, which they are not clear on, and the analyst seeking concrete answers to computer-speak. Questions to determine what's really needed and wanted. *Two different things. Highly frustrating --   and   shaky   at   best.*

<p style="text-align:center">*Ya gotta be patient.*</p>

The analyst then transmits his or her interpretations to the programmer who codes it. It always seemed something was lost in translation and took months of testing and rewriting. The "client," an agency or division, *never quite pronouncing the program 100% correct. More patience. Hence slow DP projects. No one knew when perfect was.*

Life, morphing too, just like applications.

Chris tells me she had fought for my new title because my work efforts deserved it over the prior 2-years, especially with the purchasing responsibilities I now have. At least I can claim some near-analyst functions because I analyze and write RFPs -- **Requests for Proposals,** and review vendors' bid responses.

But that's how it is in state government. Only half the time does a **Civil Service** title seem to match actual job duties. *Many of us have made-up functional titles.* But I need a good one because I'm on the phone daily with vendors, clerks, supervisors and managers. *At dozens of agencies.*

So even tho technically not doing DP Analyst's work, I ask for new business cards and they're approved. And there's supposed to be some rule or something about only being allowed a Civil Service title on business cards. *Stupid really.* The State has 25 thousand employees and only 16 hundred job titles. *And even fewer exam titles.*

There's rules and more rules. I know all the Circular Letters and the few meaningful Executive Orders. In Treasury there's only one rule. *I think it came from Rich Keevey, a great guy.* Budget Director/comptroller: "**He who holds the gold rules.**"

This means life or death to programs.

But I still learn **AAS,** Chris's baby, the State's accounting system. I like the little stick finger man in the lower right hand corner with an X thru him.   *ERROR.*

Can't fix it on my own without callin' Tech Support.

Janet brings home a school flyer in September announcing the **Hamilton YMCA Indian Guides Program (IGP),** based on the great American Indian culture. I sign up Jesse and me immediately. We really enjoy this and the dozens of fathers and 8-to-10-year-old sons who're so friendly and always participating. Monthly meetings are held on a rotational basis in members' homes, where we follow   the   same   format: Welcome, hold the talking stick for   announcements,   worki together on arts and crafts, fathers and   sons, juice and snacks. *And as volunteer chief I lead a closing prayer to the* **Great Spirit** *we've practically memorized.*

Our **Blackfoot Tribe** enjoys   the   activities   and   each other's company, even   look   forward   to   it. Never   a cancellation. The boys get along famously, *as do we dads,* with them. We don't hoop it up or mock. T*hat's verboten.* Being middle-class and white,   it's   good comradery, and *we all have   enough suburban space.* Adults have their beers, *I my soda,* unless we host at our house.
        Then it's *Pepsi and* ***7Up.***

"Hey, I bought metallic markers to decorate our vests," I   announce. "We   have   silver   and   lots   of   black, orange red & green. I've cut out an oak tag black buffalo, our symbol, for the back of our vests."

We trace the buffalo, color it in, and write our Indian names in bright colors above. Jesse's *Sunshine* and I'm *Sunblaze.* We wear our gear for tribal and nation get-together's like our annual lakeside bonfire at **Hamilton's Veteran's Park,** *a few firemen are at the ready. A dozen tribes of 4 to 8 members ring the bonfire, with long sticks and marshmallows.*

The program's a great way to learn about Americanized Indian culture. *And we have fun!* [21]

The State powers-to-be have changed our name from **Bureau of Data Processing (BDP)**, to **Management and Financial Data Center (MFDC)**, with a new boss, Blair Shirk, a really nice older guy. *What the hell? New fancy name for Treasury?* But then shockwaves hit us it's announced other data centers will be merged under single management. *What the heck does that mean?*

Our **Big Blue** shop, running the **MVS Operating System,** was initially spared. But others — Labor, Law & Public Safety (SAC), with an Hitachi mainframe, and Human Services (DHS), *aren't.* DHS's disparate Honeywell system, **GCOS,** was sold to the State by Dennis Calabrese, their top sales rep. He's the best I've ever met at getting his way.

He overcomes every bureaucratic obstacle. Sly.

We at Treasury operate hundreds of statewide computer apps for pensions, personnel, payroll and so on; it makes sense we're last. *Treasury OMB controls all budgets,* which is helpful to us, *but departments otherwise run their own affairs.* Treasury processes all the dough.

Minor changes are soon forgotten. Suddenly Governor Kean issues **Executive Order 84**, in November, mandating consolidation of State all data center operations, except Treasury, into one organization, the **Office of Telecommunications and Information Systems -** forever known as **OTIS.**[22]

Telecom stood for the tens-of-thousands of state telephones, and **Information Systems** becomes the new buzzword for Data Processing. Until this time, each of the departments had disparate types and sizes of proprietary systems. *With IBM or compatible at 3 out of 4, but the largest at Human Services,* on Quakerbridge Road. Its **Honeywell** system was the anti-thesis of IBM's OS and MVS. They had won a protest bid in '74 and gotten the business, expelling IBM. By large I mean Treasury has more than 3k employees. Labor 2.5k equal to Law, and Human Services, 6k.

What will this mean for us?

Before OTIS, departments' computer systems were outdated and barely communicating with each other. *Hardly interacted electronically.* I knew this from first hand experience; for 5-years we'd been installing dumb SNA terminals, IBM's networking architecture. That network, *mainly for the applications available thru **CICS**,* IBM's transaction processing system, for finances, accounting etcetera, holding 'em together. Purchasing was done on the technologically restricted MACS system. Bob Coyle, a Buyer I worked with, called "Overnight or never."

Bigger data centers like ours *have their own multimillion dollar mainframe computers,* and differing Info Systems, policies and procedures. **PCs** *are spreading tentacles,* 'specially for the big shots. Email thru the use of **SMTP**, a new networking methodology, *is growing.*

"Hey, watch the guy run!" someone yells. Looking at the 4-by-4-inch screen, where the only image we can get is a jagged orange stick figure. *Who's moving arms and legs around an orange oval track, and isn't that exciting.* Testing this IBM "portable PC", heavier and bigger than a **Sears** sewing machine, we thought, was the cat's pajamas.

Most agencies run their "proprietary" mandated programs with isolated, ivory tower, bureaus, staffs, buildings, funds and other resources. Departments had dozens of divisions, with tens or hundreds of employees in each. Over 25k [?] State workers filling scattered offices, prisons and mental institutions around the state. *With most offices centered in Trenton not far from the State House.* As well as in Newark on Raymond Boulevard with a thousand more.

The real surprise? The new OTIS was responsible for establishing uniform "info processing" policies, equipment, software and facilities. *Statewide. And they have the legitimacy and funding to do it.*

Technology **exploding**

Gov's pen creates OTIS;

not law thank God.

OTIS changes all fiefdoms overnight. Revising org chart after org chart, taking effect immediately. Consolidation and streamlining begins. Dr. Ridgeway, *whom we know almost nothing about*, except that he came from **AT&T**, is appointed the first OTIS Administrator. Bob Meybohm, Deputy Administrator, came over from River Road Data Center. *We often heard shouting and cursing behind his closed door.* He was in charge of operations. Ron Maxson, a handsome guy with thick black hair *and young-looking face with a convivial manner,* was named Deputy for Administration, our end. Hank Murray whom I knew from the old **DPTC,** was named Director of Planning. These men would steer the new "Office," *and set policies for the next decade.* Most administrative staffs were brought together and housed in leased offices at 820 Bear Tavern Road in West Trenton.

Alice and I had worked for years with Hank, Barney, and Ed Maute, *my buddy,* at DPTC, who approved our Info Systems procurement requests and other departments. We prepped dozens for Treasury, *and walked 'em thru the approval steps.* Literally. Even to Deputy State Treasurers.

We had had a good working relationship with Barney and Ed, now transferred also. It had always only been with DPTC's blessing that funding was approved at the fiscal level, thru the **Office of Management and Budget (OMB),** for our hardware and software purchases. Now IS approvals are being done by OTIS and OMB, *not the departments and OMB.* Relearning where and to whom to send documents and circumventing time delays in the new org, *is exhausting Alice and I, b*ecause they're changin' rules every other day. *Exciting, challenging, chaotic, scary and . . . uncertain.*

Plans were made and funds approved to build a new multimillion conglomerate data center called the **Hub** at State police headquarter grounds in West Trenton. *My old haunts.*

People moved to and fro like ping pong balls, some physically. *Others on paper only.* By January '85 MFDC had also been absorbed. My boss Chris suddenly transfers to the new org. *No going away parties.*

Back at the office, thinking, *What do I do now?* At least Lew's still here, Chris's assistant director.

So, like any good state employee, *I continue as if nothing has happened. Just carry on Rodney.*

Lew transfers to 820 Bear Tavern Road as new Director of what became known as the **Garden State Network**, a physical scheme to build high speed **T1** data transmission lines for linking the data centers, the fastest communications means. Soon after he departs, Alice takes a position with Planning under Hank. *Ah, a loss, but understanding **it's upward bound.** I feel slightly sad, but heck, it's a promo. I miss her, like Grandmom's passing.*

*What will happen to me? To MFDC? With Chris and Lew gone, who'll be in charge? Will we have the same functions? With **DPTC** gone, who's really in charge at OTIS? What will OTIS do? How do I get my procurement approvals? Thoughts swirl, but keep plowing forward.* So does everyone else. Day-by-day more bodies transfer.

Maggie goes nuts with all the phone number changes.

1.19 Home and Community Life

Our community participates in teaching committee-inspired public proclamations which are developed and executed, like the 14x30-inch ads on **NJ Transit** local buses. The posters show the white **Dove of Peace** on a light blue background next the words, **"Working for World Peace. Baha'i Faith"** Even I give public talks, as do others, at the **Trenton Times Community Room**, thru hand-holding by Frank Tyger, and also talk at the **Hamilton Twp. Neighborhood Service Center**, both institutions our dear friends.

"Hey Sir Rodness." Spud intones jokingly. *A very close bud.*

"Yep, what's up Spudley?"

"I sent a photo of you into the Times, but I have no idea if they'll print it."

"That's cool, either way."

Spud's our **PI Rep,** *a media guru,* and had sent a photo of me to the paper pointing at my chicken scratch on our flip chart. I'd spoken a few days earlier on U.S. economics and the **$4 trillion Federal debt** at the **John O. "Poppy"** Wilson Center, with whom we have great rapport. My topic, the extremes of poverty and wealth in America, *seemed appropriate.* I'd spent time at the **State Library** in town doing research during lunchtimes. As a state employee, *I had open access,* and went once or twice a month just to browse and read.

The photo and caption appeared on page 4 or something the next day.

Janet, "Rod, look your photo's in the paper!"

Spud submitted things like this all the time, for example the annual Assembly picture with all our faces, and our annual parade marches. Lots of **Hamiltonians** remarked upon seeing us. Spud also maintained our local 3-inch scrapbook, which he'd pull out for display at our **Annual Meetings.** *Some years it seemed astonishing what we'd accomplished.* One thing made our proclamations and projects easy, like monetary awards to 6 high school seniors every May. We never lacked for contributed funds. *Thanks to the generosity and sacrifice of members and guests.*
Only member donations are accepted for Baha'i work.

Mayor Jack Rafferty, beloved by residents and voters, *shepherds the township's fortunes well.* We hear not a whiff of corruption. *An uncommon occurrence for some NJ politicians.*

Hamilton's motto **"A Beautiful Place to Live and Work,"** *is ubiquitous and cherished.* Street light banners thruout the township proclaim it. The free public library, *newly ensconced on* **Municipal Drive,** is a magnet *for learning and programs.* It's also where our members construct many 12 x 6 bulletin boards for the excellent children's librarian, Sue Brozena, who loved the Braille alphabet done once, in white stuffed gloves in the shapes of letters. *Our good friend and artist Rita Leydon, from Lahaska, had made them all.*

When Jess had been starting kindergarten, Jan and I and a few neighbors that she had signed up, had petitioned the mayor's office requesting sidewalks be put in on our busy county road leading to school. *After 3-months of waiting it only took* **Public Works** *2 more to install 'em.* We were so pleased we wrote Jack a thank you letter. *He helped residents and orgs a lot.* Really we should have also thanked the homeowners along the way, since they paid most of the costs. On mild days, Janet escorts Jess to school. *She's always been a walker.*

Janet scans every page of the Times in our kitchen every morning, while having **her beloved hot cup of tea** with a little skim milk. This morning she sees a small article calling for volunteers to start **The Friends of the Hamilton Twp. Library,** so she attends its first meeting. They form, and she becomes one of its officers, Recording Secretary. She designs and has printed their first membership brochure. **Annual Membership only $2.00**   *Having started with 13 women, within 4-months they've amassed 41 members, and me.*

The new **YMCA** across the street also acts as a hub of community life, packed with family programs and a pool. Males don't have to swim naked like I had done growin' up a block away from our apartment and the Trenton Y. *I had learned Jujitsu there.*

Soon after opening, Jan and I take a **Yoga class,** and so learn the **Sun Salutation**. After which our 65 year-old Indian instructor, who's phenomenally supple and flexible, teaches us deep cleansing breathing.

With 26 public schools in Hamilton, the annual **School Board** elections in November, and school budgets, are big deals. Budgets usually garner defeats by the senior bloc. *But only by small margins. Schools are poor patch-works of emergency repairs, but educationally sound.*

One nice thing about paying taxes for schools, because of **Thorough & Efficient** standards in NJ, *special classes like speech are available in Jesse's early grades.* Jan and I had both agreed that we wanted our kids to socialize normally, among diverse student populations. *And besides, the public schools contained the best resources.* Registering Jesse in **Yardville Elementary** for kindergarten had been a conscious, considered step in those directions. *Even tho we could have afforded otherwise.*

Janet and I and kids attend Daloisio get-togethers at Mom and Dad's in Ewing. Ten of us loungin' 'round the big table out on the porch for **Wednesday Night Family Dinners.**

My sister Carleen says, "Pass the sausage, please."
Or, someone shouts, "How 'bout some torps over here?"

Two pounds of rigatoni or pencil points or ravioli, *rarely spaghetti,* dripping in marinara, steaming in its huge green-flecked ceramic bowl, together with a porcelain container for more sauce. G*ravy as Dad calls it.* Homemade meatballs, cooked proscuitto and sweet Italian sausage on other platters. Dad prepares all the pasta and meats with Mom's help, and we help set the tables, serve, and clean up afterwards. 3-hours of stories and laughing. *Some evenings a little silence.* All the kids joining us at their own smaller tables. They all love their Granny and Pop-Pop, and the pasta. *Everyone getting along swimmingly, no kids fights here. Even we adults stop arguments before they start.*

When Dad's Mom had lived with us, she made these pastas from eggs and flour on the ceramic kitchen table.

I speak Italian very well: carbonara, mostaccioli, lasagna, caio and arrivaderci.

Jesse's 3 months past his August birthday also attends the **Gifted and Talented Program** at school. He likes it all and the neighborhood kids, and has close friends. We'd known since he was 2, that he might become an artist. Especially *when he'd complete dot-to-dot coloring books easily. Numbers and all.*

Life? Always more hectic with kids, with Jan staying home with 4-year old Kate, *a darling. What a pleasant, happy child!* A lot like her brother. *yet with her own personality.* My meds are working well. And all emotional responses, *still subdued,* even after Mark's past enlightenments. I can only **"feel"** with concentration.   *I have moments of joy often, but no exuberances.*

It's during this busy yet happy period that I have my vision.

1.20 The Vision [23]

Awakened one spring morning with the promised vision. Knowing immediately, *This is what overcame me when I raised my arms and conversed with the One.*

I'm dressed as a king in long, thick, flowing white robe trimmed with ermine.

Grandiose yet humble feelings washing thru me, taking time climbing hundreds of steps on the Mountain of God to the Shrine of the Bab. Kings, queens and dignitaries following. Blue skies shimmering and the sun is shining in its supernal glory. Marble terraces are complete and gardens lush and green with brilliant and multi-hued flowers and bushes. Pools of cool water in their cisterns looking crystal.

Humankind has recognized its follies and now cooperates and promotes spiritual and social welfare across the planet. All faces are turned upward in joy and thanks, thanks to the Great Lord God in this New Day. Peace is inevitable, unity assured, wars have ceased, and civilization flourishes.

The Day billions of departed and living souls have longed and hoped for: The interests of the world's peoples are being safeguarded by government and religion, the two most powerful forces on the planet.

**The Great Day of God promised in
all Holy Books and Scriptures.**

(Please see color photograph on back cover)

2.0 SECOND EPISODE

2.1 Chaos and Peace

Pure chaos. People continually moving out from ours and other departmental data centers and populating OTIS. "I want to be part of new organization too." *I whine to Chris.*

"Do you have any openings? Can you use some help?"

"We'll see Rod, we'll see." *At least she doesn't say "No" outright.* Lost at MFDC, electrified about the possibility of working for OTIS.

My persistent calls pay off. After 5-months, MFDC transfers me in September '85. *Hopping with excitement, and raring to go!* That first day I sit at a huge metal desk, 1960 vintage, *no phone, no terminal, no PC,* in the middle of a floor long empty space, with another antique desk not far from mine. *Also empty.* It's quiet, a morgue, while others scurry around us. *Things pick up.* Maggie installs a phone, and Tech the PC. *Some days starved for work;* others can't write fast enough. Whatever RFP I write and print out on my dot matrix printer, I run over to the typing pool where they have word processing equipment.

"Hi, Elaine, good morning, how ya doing?"

She smiles. Used to my needs.   "Hi Rod! Got some-thing for me today?" A gem.

It takes a day or two to get back. Then I proof it. *A new RFP, 24-pages long.   Medium-sized, for me.* **Waivers of Advertising** *are much shorter, except for the backup.*

Chris has a tiny office. *But no door.* I'm now at OTIS headquarters in West Trenton, an easy 15-mile commute from home via Interstate 295, a Godsend for commuting the 6-miles. Bob Longman, previously an Expediter from **PerkinElmer**, a computer company, *joins the two of us a month later.* He arrives fresh from the governor's office (or from DOL?). We work well together. *I become senior man.*

By November, everyone's calling us **Technical Services.** *A name I think Chris made up.* She's mentoring Bob and I on how to write for business. *Called technical writing.* She's the real pro. *Monotone, flat, emotionless text.* **No I's, we's or you's.** We focus on detailing specifications for the RFPs, that is, bids, for hardware and software without being super r-e-s-t-r-i-c-t-i-v-e. *Restrictions cost more and limit competition.* **Hardware**'s computer-speak for equipment, that is all computer-related devices; and **software**, the programs that operate— **hardware.**

Chris focuses on correcting our drafted mainframe bid language while she also writes policies and procedures for the organization. Bob and I become engaged in compiling inventories of computer equipment. *Statewide for all agencies.* Also under her direction, we institute a **Help Desk** and have pads printed by the State House Print Shop, so we can record technical requests for information.

Phone rings. *Could be anyone, doesn't matter.*

"What's Treasury's mainframe, and how many MIPS is it running?" he asks. Write down name, number, question on the pad. *I know MIPS — millions of instructions per second.*

"Treasury has an **IBM Model 3084-QC8**, *which I had operated,* 128 Megabyte core processor, running **MVS**

370/XA Operating System. I'll call you back with the **MIPS.** Anything else?"

In situations like that, I hang up and call our Joe, our IBM rep, or the Treasury **Customer Engineer**, Mac, to get the MIPS rating. *Then call the requester back the same day.* Janet and I know handsome Mac personally because we'd also rented him our old apartment back on Nottingham Way.

*But the **3084** mainframe could fill a small room. The actual MIPS turns out to be less than a handful.* The machine had cost two mil plus.

> *Happy.   Fall back   to routine;*
>
> *distractions   from hidden self . . .*
> *kept at bay.*

Jesse's in 3rd grade. *The home of the Unicorns.* Kate's also doing well and Janet and I are active PTA members. Janet helps out at all the meetings, classroom parties, conferences, school plays and events. She's soon elected **Yardville PTA President.**

At home Jesse and I often play **Impossible Mission** on the **Commodore 64** in our basement. **"Argh!"** the spy screams. *As he falls down the abyss after an aborted high jump over electrified robots.* But the computer is so circumscribed we only use it for games. The floppy in its hard drive *is eight inches wide* and has to be whirring for each new program. **The Hobbit** text adventure with crude line drawings is another Commodore game we both like. There's two things about it: Gandalf the grey with wide-brimmed hat and walking stick on the opening scenes, *and its haunting requiem march*, which is insistent. *Ba-da-ba-da-boom, ba-da-boom . . . ba-da-boom, ba-da-boom . . . .* I don't know its title.

Kate's loves opening gifts from Granny and Pop Pop, on our **Christmas** eve visits at Mom and Dad's. Janet always bringing them a huge mum or red or white poinsettia. *She bought from school sales.* Then to Jan's parents Christmas day, and Grandmum preparing traditional **British** dinner made by Jan's war bride Mum. Her golden stuffing, cooked in a deep well on the stove, a little crisp. *Just the way I like it.* Grandmum has bought the kids little gifts, always 25 or more each. *She'd shopped all year for them. All* wrapped in Sunday funnies.

We have fun exchanging gifts at both homes. Love having duel Holidays.

At home Kate frolics with our calico kitten Whiskers, who follows her traipsing around the house *and attacks her little feet with every move.* She and I also play a **Barbie** game on the Commodore, in which Ken calls her for a date, like this:

The pink phone rings and Barbie says "Yes Ken, I'll meet you." Then she drives her pink sports car to the store and buys pink clothes, depending on where they're going. Maybe white shorts for tennis. *Whoa . . .* While shopping, Ken calls, "Plans have changed Barbie. We're going to play golf!"

She rushes to the sports store to buy a pink golf outfit. Once out of the changing closet, Ken calls again, "Plans have changed! We're going to dinner, so dress appropriately." She rushes faster to the dress shop, for a pink gown. This cycle continues ad nauseam, but Kate's enraptured. And I am too, because she likes it. However, after 30 minutes I suggest strongly, "Ahhh . . . .wouldn't you rather dress your real Barbie and drive her convertible yourself?"

Sometimes it works, (Yeah!) and sometimes not. Grumble, grumble.

A highlight of the next summer is attending the Discovery Toys business conference at **Disney World** in Orlando. *Something*

I've wanted to do since '79. Janet drives down Interstate 95 and the 4 of us stay in a Disney hotel with large outdoor pool. The kids want to swim much more than visiting attractions. *I'm fine with that.* Especially while Janet attends day long conference sessions.

I go to the keynote with Janet. *After handing the kids off to babysitting services.* In the great auditorium, Rosa [?], a dark-dark red-haired middle-aged hot tamale, and inspirational speaker, describes meeting her husband at the front door of their home . . . "Welcome home honey!"   Naked, girded in cellophane wrap! **A *tad awkward*** *for me and the other dozen husbands in -- a ballroom full of raucus women. . . .*

But the real highlight is the **Character Breakfast** next morning with Goofy, Minnie and Mickey. The kids flip out when they come to our table and pet us. *Such smiles!*

Once back, OTIS is going thru significant changes. *Organizationally and technically.* Governor Kean's been re-elected in November, which helps OTIS grow from say, 400, to 600, including more data processing programmers and analysts. We all sigh. *Our jobs are safe for another 4-years. Maybe.*

One of many good things about my job is fixed office hours. I always arrive by 8, and stay after 5 when necessary. *Plentiful work and coffee keeps me going.* My addiction makes me the de facto head of our **Mr. Coffee Club,** making sure a fresh pot is on the burner at all times, even when I'm the only one in on Saturdays.   *I drink 5-cups every   workday,* fewer on weekends. *Coffee highs become a normal part of my days.* **It's the only buzz I can get**, *because my meds tone everything down.* My reactions — are subdued and excitement doesn't come easily.
      But I have plenty of energy.   Plenty.

I'm functioning above "normal." I begin riding the cycle for hours at high speeds on curvy country roads, passing like crazy. Some high periods spent riding aimlessly for an hour out and an hour back. *Can't alarm Janet. Not afraid of a crash, I have Guardian Angels. More afraid of what Jan'll say if gone too long.*

The first spill comes when hitting an oil slick while turning at busy Five Points in Mercerville. After dropping the bike, I hear "Vroom -- Squeal . . . **Lurch.**!" *The sound of brakes that only one vehicle makes.* Looking up from the asphalt and twisting my head back . . . *Oh hell!*

The center city bus that has been following has halted . . . within 5-feet of my sprawled body. Not really scared. *But should have been more surprised.* No one even gets out of the bus. *At least the driver doesn't blow his horn.*

My increasing sense of wellbeing allows me to take everything in stride. **No deep concern** *about consequences.* Like getting run over. *Predisposed that way most of the time.* Probably explains why feelings of remorse or shame *rarely occur to me.* I take things super-casually. *Some call it a "dulling" of emotions, and to an extent its true; never feeling uncontrollable joy or deep sadness.* My biting tongue is ever present however. *To go along with my impulsiveness.* And at work its coming out. *It's become even more apparent at home.* I'm not saying "I'm sorry" enough when inflicting hurts on Janet. *Forget circumstances.*

Never have a problem with finding energy tho. From the minute eyes open ere the alarm rings at 7, until 10 bedtime. *When a wave of sleep overcomes me.*

That's my normal. **No highs, lows.** *In-between. Just so I swallow my pills.*

Spring '86 turns out to be beautiful, and when my 2nd cousin Dave Pullen has a red and white **For Sale** sign on his Honda **CB500**, *half a* **Harley,** I jump on it, *literally.* In mint condition, brown tank with black racing stripes, running boards for footrests make for very comfortable riding, and front and rear crash bars. This extra safety feature helps me convince Janet we can get it. Dave gives me a small discount. *And it only costs a few hundred bucks.*

I sell my first cycle, my midnight blue 360, for a hundred.

The buyer calls me a week later. "I want my cash back. The transmission's acting up." *But he had previously checked it thoroughly.* Had ridden it around my neighborhood until satisfied. So I firmly refuse to take the bike back.

"Look, I've never had a problem that a little cable-tightening doesn't fix."

If only I had a tightening mechanism for my impulses.

2.2 Close Call

The summer of '86 arrives with the annual **Memorial Day Parade** in Hamilton. *The only highlight of the year.*[?] Instead of banding with the Guides, Jesse and I march with the Baha'is. He roller blades around me, all of us with our matching T-shirts saying **"One earth . . . One people"** surrounding a globe. We adults carry balloons and hand out stickers to all ages, with a blue peaceful space shot on them, surrounded by "The earth is one country and mankind its citizens," from JF Strain's ***Special-Ideas. Great stuff.***

Along with everyone else, Jess and I wear big smiles striding along the route, waving and laughing with the crowds. As we spy our family and friends gathered at the end of Herbert Ave in front of **The Church Yard** cemetery, they're *jumping up and down*, yelling with delight to get our attention. Spud pops out in the middle of Nottingham Way *and starts snapping pictures*. Janet and Kate, Grandmum, Granddad and a few Baha'i friends have been sitting on folding garden chairs or are standing. *And rush out to greet us.* Its invigorating being in the parade each year. *I'm the biggest mover and shaker in its favor.*

This is the same **Presbyterian Church** cemetery in the Square, where Janet and Jesse had been walking along when jess was only 3. Its tall faded white tombstones couldn't be missed. Jesse asked, pointing, "What are they Mom?" He was always curious, taking it all in. Janet had replied, "Those are gravestones, where dead people are buried after they die." Jesse looked around, walked a little more, then looked down and stopped. Picking up a small stone from the side of the road, he asked, "Is there a dead person buried under here?"

Each year I say, "Hi, how ya doin?" *Wavin' to the cute 2-6-year olds with red, white or blue balloons tied to their wrists.* "Howdy!" I yell to an elderly married couple who smile. *Waving again to families in their lounge chairs enjoying the entourage.* "Happy Memorial Day!" I shout to a group of gawking neighbors.

Invariably someone responds "**Happy Memorial Day to you.**" *I don't know why "Happy" sounds so natural, but it does.* The purpose of the federal holiday is to remember the men and women who had died in the Armed Services. *Yet all their faces, always smiling, and watchers having a carefree time caught up in the spirit, balloons, ice cream sickles and gaudy gifts.* The little flags are genuine.

Another pleasant day in "beautiful" Hamilton Township.

Afterward, as we'd done for years, instead of all of us going to the **Nottingham Firehouse** for free hot dogs and drinks as did the other marchers, we join families and friends at Spud and Ev's for their annual picnic. *With varied summer meats, homemade salads, snacks, drinks and all the fixin's.* An annual treat for forty or so.

"Spud, how 'bout a burnt pork roll with cheese and summer sausage?"

"Of course, whatever you command, Your Royal Rodneyness."

I like my food cooked well and very hot. Like mandatory extra crispy bacon, which together with sunny-side-up eggs, is my go-to breakfast. If the bacon wasn't crispy enough, I'd send it back for more grill work.

Spud and Ev never asked the Assembly for reimbursement for money spent on all their coolers full of food and drinks and other goodies, since volunteerism and personal sacrifice are keynotes of a caring life. *After all, none of us have paid positions.*

Janet's busy with Discovery Toys, performing home demonstrations and managing her growing business. *And ten direct reports — her sub-managers.* She earns a percentage of their sales as well, in typical pyramid scheme similar to **Mary Kay Cosmetics.** *She also handles all the cash and checks and paperwork.*

In June we celebrate Kate's 5th birthday at home, and in August, Jesse's 9th. Kate's going into Mrs. Turp's Kindergarten class at Yardville, and we came to adore her seasoned teacher. *And her positive cheerful attitude and kindnesses.* Jesse, in

4th, is still in the Gifted and Talented Program, having separate classes occasionally. *To stimulate his mental acuity.* And his speech and vocabulary are great. Jan and I are proud of them both. *Well-behaved, cheerful, friendly and courteous kids.*

We had worked hard encouraging their sense of humor. *And we laughed a lot, every time we were together.* I tried to play and read with them, and helped 'em say prayers. Janet really did all the work, *out of love.* For the most part I always pay attention to their requests quickly, *never liking it when parents ignore their kids, whinny or not.* Janet was attentive every moment, naturally. *Especially as their primary educator.*

Motherhood and teaching are the most honorable professions and deserve much more respect than they get.

*   *   *

Life was good, nor-mal.

But since early fall, work was frenetic. **Again.** Assisting my boss in writing 30 pages of specs for a 7-MIPS mainframe, and its software, has taken me overtime to meet the November 15th deadline. *I don't mind not getting paid overtime, I get half the time put in as time off -- and rarely take it.* At work I'm pushing. *And impatiently punishing staff.* At home, Janet has already been commenting on My moodiness. *Nothing seems to please Me and its becoming harder making choices, even simple ones like which vendors to give purchase orders to, or, at home, which movie to watch on* **HBO**. *Not like me; never have problems making decisions, even if just an "Okay."* Becoming meaner, raising My voice at work, home.

"Rod, where have you been so long?"

"Ridin'. That's all!" Stormin' away. *Angering easily — without provocation.*

Smoking   more,   uptight,   tense.
Getting lucky once the big bid document is out on the street. Somehow recognizing jumpiness, racing thoughts again, lack of con-centration and moodiness for what they are. *The illness.*

Almost, slipped away . . . .

"Hon, I'm, ah, not feeling well . . . think we ought to see doctor . . . soon?"

"Rod, what's wrong?"

"Racing thinking . . . can't . . . control . . .

thinking . . . ."

"We   need   the   doctor."

"That would explain why you're waking up earlier than usual. Have you missed any pills?"

"Ah, not sure."

Indeed I'm not, because I'm so damn forgetful yet always **preoccupied.** 7-years remembering my meds has always been haphazard; usually Janet reminds me. My daily pill case has four slots. If I noticed   I hadn't emptied one, and was 3 or 4 hours late . . . *I'd take 'em and push 'em down the kitchen garbage bag so Janet wouldn't find them.*
"Yeah, I took 'em."

No idea why I'm being so stupid.

Missing multiple doses was killer — guaranteed mania if I didn't catch up in time.   *I hafta get that into my Head.*

Hadn't put My own head on straight -- yet.

Had I missed multiple doses?

Immediately Janet calls my psych, seeing us next day. Doubling up on lithium and antipsychotics. During next 2 weeks hardly thinking -- straight -- without jumping off on tangent, taking concerted effort on My part to focus. Seeing Me from afar, looking down at Me. Disconnected. *An observer,   aware   something   not   kosher.*

Truer, **a gatling gun spitting lead in my head,** whose crank is turning by errant brain cells and inner spirit. But my body had acclimated well to meds. *I'm a good responder. Unlike countless others   who can't or won't or don't.*

   With both he and Janet as my "doctors," coming back after 3 weeks of constant monitoring. Janet watching my every word and move, making sure I've downed my pills on time, including doubles. Also downing extra sleeping pill at night.   ***Lack of sleep's my other killer.***

Retuning. *Avoiding flipping out.* Still hearing whispered intonations. *Why don't you end it? You can't take this! You've done as much as you're going to do. Who cares? End it.*

*   *   *

First time. I know this. Mania.
Surprising in hindsight I'd had the wherewithal to tell someone about overpowering, reality-destroying symptoms. *Avoiding another death, possible death . . . .   Rationally, I know Janet, the kids, my family, all our friends, the Baha'is, even co-workers, c*are that I'm around.

Dodging 200 rounds per minute straight out of My Mind.

Janet and I not talking about what could have happened. *Another month-long hospitalization and incredible stress on her avoided.* It's over -- we move on. *I can't admit medication throw-a-ways and cover-ups to her, or to anyone else.* Oblivious to any connection between taking meds regularly and avoiding an episode. *Always in denial. I'm NOT abnormal.*

Hah! As if I'm not . . . . But I'd never known that, by how my friends and coworkers treated me. Not once had anyone made me feel different or less than, normal. Far as I can tell, no stigma attaches. No one pressing me about my illness; not even my brothers or sister, not even jokingly. No idea where these folks are getting their info. *I don't care!*

At this point, not having delved into existing literature on bipolar either. Not offended by their silence. *Yet I could be more than open if asked. No different than anyone;*
          damned if I'm a mental case.

Now supposing this lack of special attention to my condition, *even by me,* is another blessing. *A disguised blessing. Does anyone want to think of themselves as mentally ill? Does anyone want to second guess every wayward thought? Every emotion or lack of emotion? Every word and every action?*

Janet's bearing that burden. One I've never understood.

My spirit doesn't allow it. Thinking of myself as mentally ill is . . crazy. But the caregiver, them, is not, are not. *And I'm lucky enough to have one,*

Only too aware. Yet never seeing another tornado
          in the distance.

Is something close? Will it pass by? Or will it suddenly, without warning, like my others, swallow us up in its whirlwind? Whipping, tossing us to and fro, sucking out our breaths, destroying our family, our home, our lives, twisting heads, twisting truth.   *Everything thrown upside down, in one, brief, never ending day . . . in hell on earth.*

Not knowing it could overcome me.
Me not accepting seriousness.

2.3 Baha'i Community Life

It's December. I'm more than comfortable in my Baha'i skin. Fully integrated into Baha'i life for so many years. *Just as Janet and the kids are.* Our community altho small, has 20 adults, half as many kids, and functions coherently. Janet and I considering Bob & Barb, Liz & Rich, Cathy & Bob, Spud & Ev, Scott & Zeny, Cathy and ilene Von Gonten, Hamiltonians too. *And many others, all close friends. We all need friends.*

"I'm free. Freedom." *Feel free to be myself, my status quo.* We all teach the Faith in our own ways, hoping to attract others to its example and principles. *Yet new converts —* *slow to come.* A stumbling block seems to be living up to its high standards. *Having to reassure seekers that it's a natural process, an individual journey, occurring in its own time. It's their own path of discovery and we aren't about to tell them what and how and when to believe.*

The   Word of God does it. From immemorial . . . .

Foster Baha'i School's serving the region big time as a hub of community life and has moved from Hamilton to Ardeshir and Pouran Dean's home in Princeton Twp. Their pillared house, built for large gatherings; and their young boys, David, Robert and Mark are all kindhearted and accommodating hosts. Groups of adults and kids invade Sunday mornings for classes on all the Messengers and morals. The Deans also host the monthly **Meeting of the Minds** public gathering on topics of interest and Baha'i views, with 50-60 attending. Once I presented **Nature of the Soul**. *My best part was the Persian and potluck dishes before hand, and pastries after.*

The school's proudly and lovingly named after Bill Foster, *mine and other's mentor,* and his long-suffering wife, Ruth. We met them circa '73 when Bill worked as an engineer/draftsman for the University, so they lived in Princeton's campus housing. From Hawaii, they were an older interracial couple forging deep ties to our fledgling community. They changed our young lives by instilling a love for the Guardian's writings. *A love of finding the reference source for our statements.*

For almost a decade.

I asked Bill once on our many travels around the state about white's prejudice towards him. He wiped his forehead and drawled, "It's like this. When I'm in a store buying something at the counter, and the clerk gives me a nasty look or comment, I don't know if he's a nice person havin' a bad day, or a racist. So I always give 'em the benefit of the doubt." *Janet or I ask outright, "Did we do something wrong?" or comment when sloppily treated.*

Always leave a smile and "Thanks."

In a few sessions thru the school year, I lead the adult deepening class of 12+, on Baha'i books or short compilations like *Excerpts on Living the Baha'i Life.* One of its points is developing a sin-covering eye, and is difficult; *but I think I understand its wisdom. So I try hard not to backbite, or frontbite to someone's face, not withstanding poor treatment.* Especially being familiar with it from Christ's words in **John 8:7**, **"He that is without sin among you, let him first cast a stone at her."** To me, having THAT eye epitomizes a tenet of personal conduct similar to the Golden Rule. *An evolving spiritual law.*

Another's that all true religions contain progressive universal spiritual truths and moral values that will always be applicable, and these receive updating from time to time to meet the conditions of their age. **"Be anxiously concerned with the needs of the age ye live in, and center your deliberations on its exigencies and requirements,"** has always been the standard. *More so in this age.*[24]

For example, as Baha'is we firmly understand that religion and science must be in agreement, a cardinal principle. The way I look at it, *and something that immediately attracted me,* is the quotation, **"Put all your beliefs into harmony with science; there can be no opposition, for truth is one."** [25]

In July, our Assembly convenes a delegation to Representative Chris Smith's district office in Hamilton at the request of our national **External Affairs Office.** *He's well-known for promoting human rights.*

I volunteer to be part of the handful to meet with him and his aide at their White Horse Avenue office. During our half-hour session, Chris is personable and gracious. Scott reads our prepared preamble.

Chris responds, "I'm well aware of the plight of the Baha'is in Iran, and have sponsored a number of resolutions condemning human rights abuses." *I like him. I've always given him my vote since he was a youngster.* He's fully aware of these situations thruout the world. We politely ask him to support a new House Resolution to this effect, and he agrees. At the conclusion Spud takes a photo that appears in The Times 4-days later. Politicians always seem to get their pics in the news. But it's also our small way of keeping our good name in front of the eyes of the public.

Since we're not permitted to proselytize.

*   *   *

2.4 Another Departure (Condensed)

My brother Stephen's sudden death surprises, depresses and confuses us. *He's 35.* It's August '87. Little is   known about the disease that kills him. *Very little.*

Mom opened up and told me the story, of which I was a part. *Twenty years later:*

Two weeks before the sad event, Mom had a premonition. Something was wrong with her son.

After calling Stephen's apartment phone repeatedly all day, she convinces Dad to drive her there.

Dad, pounding on the brownstone door, "Stephen, Stephen, please open the door!" Mom, adamant, calls Uncle Tony who has a key, to come over and unlock it for entrance to the little row home on South Clinton Avenue. It's dark with shades pulled.

After doing so and peering thru the dim interior, Mom crying, "Stephen!" as she spots him. He's wearing his light blue robe, standing halfway down the stairway, clinging to the railing, in a stupor. Pale, eyes red, sunken cheeks; wobbly.

Mom orders, "We're taking him to St. Francis, now."

Stephen suffers greatly the short time he's in the hospital. Four nights later I see him sitting half-upright in his bed in the Intensive Care Unit, cordoned off in a clear plastic isolation tent. Good-looking and healthy just weeks earlier, *now a skeleton,* none of us knowing what has caused his obvious suffering to rise so rapidly. *Has he had an illness long?* He's unable to speak to me, with a stent in his skull, IV in his arm, and feeding tube to be put in his stomach the next day. I have entered his room up beat, as if this will be over soon. *Releasing him in good health.*

I look on his face and see his eyes wide with terror. *His dark pupils constricted.*

What do I do? What can I do? What happened, what's wrong? A wave of tenderness and hopelessness overcomes me but I push it aside calling:

"Nurse. Nurse!"   Entering.
        She'll know who I am from prior visits.

"Nurse, how about some warm soup? Think he could have some? I think he'll like it."

        "Let me check Mr. Richards."
        I'm hoping *in my eyes, in my voice. My heart.*

Re-entering with gloves on, carrying an orange, thick plastic bowl and metal spoon, putting it on his tray. *She's zipping down the clear plastic shell.*

        "Put these rubber gloves on and wear this mask."
After which, handing me the soup. *Lukewarm.* She leaves.

Slowly spooning out his split pea soup between his halting gasps.

The next night, August 30, 1987, meeting Mom and Dad, step-sister Carleen, and step-brothers Charlie and Ralph Junior, in the hospital lobby for a family visit. Finding Stephen sleeping, we quietly leave and walk a block to nearby Papa's Tomato Pies for dinner. We're somber. *But all remark on the tastiness of the thin-crust pies.*

Returning, Ralphie stops in the gift shop on the 1st floor, buying a small statue of the **Blessed Mother** to take to Stephen, since we all know he likes those things. *Devout.* We only wait 5 minutes. As we exit the elevator on our way to his room, Ralphie accidentally drops the plaster-of-paris gift, the head falling off, rolling a short distance.

Mom later tells me it had been a sign.

The door to Stephen's room is closed and window curtain drawn. Nurse tells us to wait for the doctor. He walks to us in the bland waiting room, closes up to Mom, and whispers something. *Oh No.* She comes and stands in front of me, I'm sitting, looking up, and looks down at me sorrowfully, as I wrap my arms around her waist, and try to cry . . .but . . . tears won't shed. *Stephen.* Complete shock rocks us all.

Shit, we hadn't been with him! Had he decided to leave us without our anquish too? But **I'm stoic now**, not clear. *How do I feel?* But try to show some strength for Mom. Whether because of the dulling drugs I'm on or my own sensibilities. *Not upset.* Carleen now sobbing openly, and my brothers, *like me,* not sure how to express their grief, but tearing up, all hugging and comforting Mom. Without speaking, all sharing concern for her. *She's still standing in place, shaking.*

Dad and my siblings in shock; Mom devastated. Mom however -- tough Irish, and has dealt with adversity all her life. Crying outwardly and inwardly for the boy she had raised almost single-handedly from baby to adulthood. *Just as she did for me.* We share the same father, Rodney Senior, a man Stephen had never met. *Except as a baby.*

Twenty minutes later, enter a small green windowless room and close the door. There are neither chairs nor adornments on the walls. Stephen's draped body lays on a cart in the center of the space. *Only his head is uncovered.* I have ten minutes alone with his lifeless body. I can recall every minute at will.

"Stephen, can you forgive me for all the hurts I've caused you? I'm truly sorry. . . I   really   did   love   you."

At that moment, heart twinging, trembling. I *Do* love my brother, *I Do.* "But I never expressed it.' *I wish I had hugged you all those times we greeted each other at Mom and Dad's dinners and outings.*

The **Prayer for the Departed** [13] falls unbidden from my lips. There for him now as it had been at Dad's service. Reciting it slowly for the progress of his pure spirit, holding his thin, stark, still warm hand. Slightly raised ribbons of whitish veins. *Shrunken.* Stare at the grimace of death on his young, sunken face, with dried white, bubbly spittle clinging to the sides of his open mouth . . .

> *No one disturbing my time with him.*
> *Demurely,   leave with family;   silently.*
> Except "I can't believe it . . ."

*   *   *

Once in a while, on the way home from work, driving down Hamilton Avenue to Cedar Lane and pulling into St. Mary's cemetery, I stop, get out. *Say a prayer at his grave.* A small gesture not assuaging my old Catholic guilt.

His tomb, under my mother's reserved plot, is fitting.
They've always been close,
and someday will be joined

eternally.

No one speaks of the actual cause of death. Ever. Stephen's doctor had not spoken it aloud to us -- only to my mother.

Six months pass. Mom tells me the dreaded words privately, after my constant, but gentle, inquiries . . .

"Mom, please, tell me, what did Stephen die of?"

Pause. Looking down. *Ashamed?*

"That terrible new disease."

"What was it?"

"I don't want you to tell the kids."

"Alright, I promise I won't." Janet and I haven't been sure of what took him so quickly. *But we've been guessing.*

"HIV"   "AIDS."

Once she tells me, the mystery resolves itself -- to a degree.   I understand then why he'd been in isolation, but I still know nada of the disease. I go over and hug Mom.
She holds my hand.

I share with Janet. It confirms what she had thought.

Our family holds a memorial service followed by a ***disastrous*** mass at **Immaculate Conception Church** in Trenton. Disastrous because the priest mispronounces Stephen's name repeatedly as Stefan, and because the funeral directors haven't arranged for any organ playing or singing. Luckily, my cousin Sheri, gowned in black, shakily stands without prompting and sings ***Amazing Grace*** in a clear soprano voice.

Undulations of sweetness and sentimentality pass thru.

Joe, Stephen's partner, who had joined us in a handful of dinners at my parents, had been asked not to attend the service.

"I should have invited him," Mom murmured softly years later. I had liked Joe but hadn't responded, as I realized Mom had come to terms with his and Stephen's relationship.

Remembering at the time she had told me, that Joe had died of AIDS as well.

A week after Stephen's passing, wondering, *Will Janet think I'm going to flip out like I did after Dad's death?*

I'm feelin' okay, no anxiety or racing thoughts this time.
The first signs of mania onset.

But I question whether Janet is having the same thought, "Will he go over the edge again?" I say, **"Is there any Remover of difficulties save God?"** *to myself. The very first thing that pops into my head when I seek help.*[26]

I'm desperately hoping to stay normal. *I need help.*

And received its warmth, for years.

2.5 Shaman

Schedules return to normal after Stephen's death   2-months earlier. I make an effort to spend time with Mom, calling often, and reassuring her that Stephen's in heaven. By outward appearances she's handling it fairly well, what had to be the most debilitating thing for any parent to go thru. But she misses him terribly, and starts referring to him as her guardian angel.   *I begin thinking of him that way myself.*

At home Jesse and I find ourselves in our 3rd year of the YMCA IGP, and we're both loving it. *I'm chief again and convener of our new tribe.* Another set of Richardses joins us at an open house in my living room, — Joe and his son Josh, no relation. Josh is a great kid: unruly brown hair, gangly and excitable. He and Jess hit it right off, sharing the natural curiosity and interests of 10-year olds. In the beginning, our **Blackfoot tribe** consists only of Joe and I and our sons. *The four of us play well together.*

Joe, a Vietnam vet, has had some struggles adjusting since leaving the Army, *he had told me,* and that his service years were just too painful to discuss. *He's the nicest guy ever.* Always considerate and offering to either host or bring refreshments for meetings, altho Janet's always prepared. *He's gentle, kind-hearted.*   Even his clothes belie his conflict between normality and the Army. *Joe always wears his olive drab M-65 field jacket and is easy to spot.*

I have my own struggle one morning.

On a Saturday beautiful, sunny and clear. *With a slight chill. Classic New Jersey late Indian Summer. Janet and Kate are out shopping and visiting friends.* Jesse's playing in his room either drawing or building foot-tall Lego figures as he's wont to do, *or showing me how to play Legend of Zelda on Nintendo, on occasion. One of many nice things about our kids*

147

is that they had learned at an early age how to entertain themselves.

They never caused any trouble thanks to Janet's rearing, and my following her lead. Polite, not afraid to make new friends or talk to adults, and morally and socially conscious to an age-appropriate extent. Consistency and caring playing huge roles in our success with them. My outward demonstrations of love for them and Janet's appear subdued, now that their aging. *Except for our constant interest, smiles and laughs with them.*

11 a.m. "Yawn . . ." *I'm so tired.* Lay down on our living room couch and . . . dream. Thirty minutes later the front doorbell rings. *Huh? Who can that be? No one we know uses the front door, all our family and friends come to the back door.*

Groggily, *Is it a salesman?*

Opening the door, Joe stands there in his Army jacket.

"Ah, hi Joe! Surprised to see you. Come on in."
            Unlocking and opening the screen door.

      "You are?"

"Well, yeah, what's up?"

      "Where the fu . . ., hell, where have you been?!"
Why's he upset?

"Huh? I've been right here. I was just taking a nap. What's wrong?" *What's he talking about?*

      "Rod, you were supposed to be at the lake at 10 for our Indian Guides event. You know, the annual Iroquois get together with all the tribes?"

148

"Oh shit, totally forgot. I had no idea." Still in a fog.

"Josh and I waited. Do you have any idea how embarrassing it was just the two of us trying to build a teepee out of logs and news-print in the howling wind? You were also supposed to bring the twine. How could you forget?" Joe, subdued but fuming.

"Ah I really don't know Joe. Um, I'm really sorry." *And I mean it!*

"I have to wonder if Josh and I should stay in this tribe."

"Aw Joe, please, don't take it that way. I really didn't forget on purpose."

"The chief was pretty pissed off, too. As Shaman, you were supposed to lead us in prayer and kick the whole event off."

"Oh, you're right. I was ready — but I forgot that too.   Crap!   I was supposed to give the blessing for the long life of the nation. What happened?"

"Warren spoke a few words and moved on to his opening statement. It went okay."

"Listen Joe, I'm really sorry, and I'll apologize to Warren at the next chiefs meeting. I'm still Shaman, aren't I?" *Or not anymore?*

"Of course, this doesn't change that. But you sure didn't act like one today." *Whew.*

I'm so sorry he's disappointed in me! Why so much? It's unsettling.

Spend 10 minutes appeasing him, convincing him we should stay a tribe, and how great our boys get along. Apologizing again for letting him down.

"Joe please, don't take my stupidity personally." Eventually winning him over, shaking hands. *Joe leaves.*

Jesse's been unaware of Joe's visit, and like me, has blocked out the day's event, altho it's not his job to remember, it was mine. As soon as Joe's left, I begin pondering, *What could have been so upsetting about our absence that caused him to react so strongly?* Not fully understanding intense reaction. *Messed up again, not the end of the world. A doctor for my nation but not for me.*

I can only conjecture. I*t was the embarrassment of being alone at the event, yet surrounded by a dozen other busy tribes.* Now knowing Joe takes this seriously and can get upset at my mistakes. *Unlike me, just taking mistakes in stride. I'm* not ashamed in the least, only "I vow to do better by you Joe." I realize Joe is disappointed.

This feels vaguely familiar.

This is how Janet must feel when I forget what she's said.

The four of us continue our tribal meetings after that, welcoming new members. *And never speaking of that day.* But whenever remembering how much Joe was upset, still berating myself with *"You _____ idiot!"* for letting my tribe and my nation down. The same thing happening to me on occasion *when I'm smoking.*

Letting Janet down, *and others.*

If I had a dollar for each time I forgot something, I'd be Sam Walton. Many husbands probably agree with me, because, *it seems that women remember for both themselves and us.* Including the kids, work, school, and everything else. *Forgetting is one of my greatest faults, and has gotten me in trouble often.*

Janet has told me many times, "Write it down so I don't have to remember for you," or "I can't remember my appointments and yours too." Sometimes I got angry at her for the well-deserved jibes, and would semi-shout "Okay, I hear you." *Well, madder at being reminded than forgettin', about something I'm supposed to know . . . which hurts her more.*

Jan never likes it when raising my voice at her. Despises me for it. Attempt not to even mumble recriminations around her. *Her hearing's too damn good.*

In my own mind 95% of the time. Rarely are others coming up in my consciousness. This has always been my modus operandi. *Regardless of my illness.* Reality, a fact. *Rarely think of others, their feelings, needs or perceptions.* My track record pretty much showing I only care about myself and what I'm focusing on at any given moment. *Paying attention to what others are saying or doing has always been one of my weak spots.* Usually aloof until something strikes a nerve, then blurting out cutting or cruel words in anger as a response.

Even at funerals thinking only of myself. Concentrating more on the priest's words than the deceased's life. *Sometimes catching myself laughing.* I have no idea how to handle it -- the dead body. Spirit's gone. I only miss the spirit.

Dead people don't evoke reactions in me, whether at God or the world. *Or my impotence to stop death.* It's only after prodding that my empathy meter scales upward. Only then with conscious effort — never rising to the levels I've seen in others. Stephen's death seems to pass unheralded in my psyche. *With no desire to learn about his killer.* Like Dad's,, for all the changes in my life since his passing. *Death events quickly recede.* I'm only concerned with today, never yesterday nor tomorrow. *Except in my professional life meeting deadlines.*

At work; a closet perfectionist. As a Baha'i; *I can seem to be a* paragon of virtue. *Except for my smoking.* That's one thing I'm concerned with always. W*hen and where is a good time for the next one?*

Always forgetting at home. Things like taking out the trash, balancing the Baha'i cash journal or writing checks, getting gas in my car and almost running out, buying twine to bundle the cut lilacs. *I forget to take my pills every day without reminders.* **Never intentionally.** *No, never intentionally.* Not one to blame them for dulling my senses and robbing me of life, even though I can. *No, mine mostly mood stabilizers anyway.* It isn't that I mind taking them. But it seems all I remember is Trazodone at bedtime to put me to sleep. I*mmediate unconsciousness, then forgetting all my symbolic dreams.* Not one tho, in color, when I hugged 'Abdu'l-Baha - love and warmth.

Except for Janet half of my obligations would have never been fulfilled, including the pill-taking.

Easily sensing her annoyance when she says, again, "Rod, take your pills."

"I'll do better," is my canned response. *Always the same.*

At home -- Relaxable Rod. No barriers. Able to let my guard down. *All other times taking effort to be interested, to care.*

What the hell, it's been 8-years since my major episode. It's obvious my meds must be keeping me from flipping out again. But rarely meditating on my feelings, or lack thereof, I can't tell who I'm meant to be. *Has it been my natural self feigning interest or concern? Or, the mood stabilizers that make me care less about what's going on around me and in the world? Am I normal?*

Blowin' thru every TV bulletin and news cycle. *Life's can't mean going thru the motions and placidly accepting. . . .*

Not yet anyway.

Change cigarette brands, picking up **Salem 100s**, lighter. *Damned if I'm going to pay the same price for shorter cigarettes.*

Laid back and easy going. Hardly anything burrows under my thick skin. *I know I have to learn to pay attention if I have a shot at staying human or. . . I'll fall into real depression **and care even less.** I've felt what that's like and don't want to enter it.* My diminished attitudes include poor self-esteem or hesitant decision making, the reverse of mania, but not deep depression.

I'm Shaman of the Hamilton YMCA Iroquois Nation and can't doctor my mind or intermittent expressiveness. Only minor control of moods I find myself in. W*hether meds work perfectly or not.*

When manic, every minute generated new anxiety, hope and excitement, had been ripe with possibilities, full of confidence and creating universal policies to solve the world's problems. Knowledge and insight appeared at will. *Ohh. Where's that intensity? I shouldn't want to flip out again, but, my God I was alive! Reality soooo far removed from my present easy-going state. I know it's dangerous. I know it intellectually. But in my spirit . . . ?*

Later sharing with Janet about missing the nation event, and how upset Joe had been.

"Oh Rod, what's to be done with you!"

2.6 The Assembly

Life passes smoothly and on April 20, again, we hear, "Janet Richards, Barbara Harris, Rodney Richards," along with six other names being announced at the Annual Meeting, this year at Ev and Spud's. Elected to the Spiritual Assembly for 13th consecutive year. *Potentially a divinely-protected governing council.* All voting by secret ballot with no nominations or electioneering. *We're pleased to serve.* Showing that a majority of our community members feel we're doing a good job. *Relative of course,* since Baha'i office holders aren't beholden to those electing them in any way, unlike politicians. *And we act according to our own consciences.* It's enough for me to know the friends must have some confidence in me, and that's, bottom line. I must be an okay guy. *See? I'm OK.*

This year there's a surprise electing officers. Evelyn is voted Secretary, ending Janet's yeoman 13 continuous years. We're pleased, Ev accepts graciously, and immediately she and Jan make arrangements to go over everything and transfer files.

Jan's not put off in any way . . . and all Assembly functions continue **seemlessly.**

I'm doubly honored being elected Treasurer again by a majority of assembly members, entrusted with stewardship of funds, altho the Assembly retains full responsibility and control. Contributions had been over 12 thou the prior year, which was a lot for our circumscribed group.

 Our 9 members meet every two weeks, usually in our living room. A place where all business and consultation stays, confidential, not even shared among or between our mates before or after the meeting. *Often Liz's expertise as a social worker was invaluable.*

It's been the Assembly chamber since Jesse had joined us before Jess joined in as a baby in '79. He was the first child in our group. *And it had made early parenting easier having him on the rug in the chamber playin' with toys and gooing. . . .* We'd consulted and watched over him, often chuckling or cuddling or laughing out loud; sometimes a little peeved at his noise. But then Janet or I'd remove him immediately, until his behavior improved. *No one has to ask.*

Assemblies sometimes pick up troubling "personal issues" of all kinds, from promiscuity or divorce cases, homosexuality quandaries, veiled terroristic threats to covenant-breaking — active dissimulation with the intent of subverting the Cause. However, more joys come to our stable unit as well, especially marriages, births and declarations of belief. *Like Janet and I had made 18-years earlier to the* **Trenton Assembly.**

This community is close, friendly, helpful. The Assembly oversees all Baha'i activities, meetings, personal matters and organized monthly feasts.

Most time spent encouraging ideas and personal initiative, or trying. *No lack of volunteers with good ideas.*

As far as others are concerned, *it seems I'm perfectly normal.* I consider myself so. *Never, not once, do I imagine myself as ill. Life can't be better!* And except for only having too few Baha'is, everyone in both my families, personal and Baha'i — *are happy, have jobs, and good health.*

Even tho I work hard for the Assembly and community, like taking a Baha'i political refugee up to **INS Offices** in Newark, twice. A zoo, but actually helpful.

Work is more intense, and I have a dozen stacks of project papers, files and folders on my desk and book shelves. *At home my desk is semi-organized.* Simply put, I have to see it to remember to do it. It isn't failsafe but effective. *My own advice: Never put an active file away in drawers.*

During this flurry of activity in so many areas, I'm not pre-pared for what occurs next.

2.7 Upgraded Position

In '88, organizational changes occur at OTIS, again, and I'm affected directly. Moved out of Technical Services to the **Procurement Units,** under Dick Reichle, an old-school manager who's pleasant enough and always upbeat.
No roadblocks for this guy.

He calls me into his office one day.

"Rod, I've talked to Chet, and we'd like you to supervise the procurement unit. You'll report directly to me. Bob will continue under you, and Cindy Jablonski and Lynda Bolling will also join your team. What do you think?"

"Ah, I'd like that, Cindy is exceptionally nice and capable and Lynda's pleasant and hard-working too. Bob works well also. Any guidelines I should be aware of?'

"You know what we do,

right?

Just have to keep everything

on the up and up."

"Okay, sure, that's great, anything else?

"No, if you run into problems just come see me."

"Okay, no problem. When do I start?"

"I'll talk to Cindy and Lynda, and you can start next week, sound good?'

"Absolutely, I'll do the best I can."

"Oh, and you can move into Tom's [?] old office. How does that sound?"

"Great, Dick. Thanks!"

And that's how I become a supervisor, again. *And of course, grateful, very. But no written guidelines, no description of job duties, nuthin'. Just learning what the boss wants, and doing what I've been doing, only now I'm responsible for three staff instead of one.* Bob, Lynda and Cindy all sharp, knowledgeable, and honest, perform very well, not invoking my temperamental ire. Dick hadn't made mention of a promotion or salary increase. *But that's how it's done in state government. Arbitrary and nonchalant. Not one piece of instruction. All verbal.*

As long as the bosses, at whatever levels, agree.

Cindy is an inquirer, getting into details, never hesitating to ask a question if unsure what to do, and I get to know Lynda better also. We have wide autonomy, so I appreciate Cindy's and Lynda's candor. The **Fiscal Unit** handles OTIS finances, info technology and supplies procurements for OTIS, from mainframe computers to green-lined printer paper, and so we begin reviewing individual and agency requests to spend money. *Besides handing really big deals to Dick and Jim.*

Until I receive a surprise one month, a half-slip of paper stating "Salary Increase Effective (date)." *Whoa.? Does this mean . . .?* And it's never clear. Sometimes these half-slips say, "Retroactive to (date)," because we receive 'em after months have passed. *Most state a title, or just name and SS#.*

I suppose my name moves on an org chart somewhere.

Not minding I take it matter-of-factly. *Like I take everything.* Jan and I eat out at **Taco Bell** or **Scotto's** for thin-crust pizza to celebrate. *Can't remember where it was. No biggie.* Just like Meursault in ***The Stranger.***

Events play out without much effort from me it seems. I'm not thinking this is a big career move, but grateful for the opportunity. Certainly haven't asked to be promoted, and care little about Dick's motivations. Assuming he needs help, and I'm available, *doing a decent job is all that's needed. And have to keep doing it.* I don't think of my new charges as staff but as coworkers and try to be civil, friendly and courteous.

But I can be tough, cold. A detail freak.

Just events playing out — like my mania.

At work my perfectionist streak comes out, differently from working alone filling blank pages at my computer. *Just as tough on them as myself. And 95% of the time we succeed.* Dick seems to agree, except when I miss an obvious document flaw I should've caught. *Stupidhead!*

I'm in my own office with a door, desk, bookcase, PC and multiline phone. Begin writing my own memos directly on the PC in MS-Word, and don't send them to the pool. *Elaine transfers to **Pensions.** Pool dissolves.*

Loving and appreciating my job. *And learning reams on info systems, procurement and contracting.* Dealing with vendors is fun, *challenging.* When wangling additional discounts, Dick and deputy Jim O'Connor are masters. Also fun dealing with dozens of State directors, managers, professionals and clerks, as we process and approve their agency requests. Practically all continuation hardware, software, and services procurements, require some research, interaction and consultation on our part. *Twenty mil worth for all 60 agencies on the big IP Waiver.*

The State now has $16^?$ departments after eliminating Energy. **Stupid, stupid, stupid.** Yet consolidating, is always smart. Treasury, Corrections, Labor, Human Services, DEP and Transportation are our biggest clients, so we see and hear what they're going thru tryin' to meet our deadline.
    But excuses fall on deaf ears.

Obtaining signed ownership disclosures, liability insurance certs and affirmative action certs from the vendors, really holds things up. Always interesting to see how many employees these companies have, and their splits by sex and race. **Purchase Bureau (PB)** and the Deputy Attorney Generals **(DAGs)**, froth at the mouth when these docs are missing from the total package and still "in the works." Three 4-inch binders full of agency requests. *Plus 10 reqs from OTIS.*

Try hard not to let specious requests slip in, but sometimes the word comes down, "Let it go."

We only have limited power to move documents along quickly that will save the State millions in new fiscal year costs. Too often these incredible savings on one-off deals languish, and opportunities pass with our deep disappointment and disillusionment in the system. Just shouting "Savings!" isn't enough to justify a fire under some bureaucrat's tails, especially a few at PB, *who do it their way, in their time,* and hold final approval. The PB Buyers are too overloaded to devote solid time to all our rush requests. And there are over 150 waivers hitting PB right now. *Ours isn't biggest nor as important as Utilities worth over 75 mil.*

At times I meet with PB Assistant Supervisor Henry Savelli for help moving a project quickly, sometimes it works. *Sometimes not.* But usually, if his boss Guilio Mazzone, the Supervisor, got a whiff of savings, it became a done deal, and he wrung more discounts out himself. At least no airs were put on, and we were all on first-name bases. Fair-minded, it was the PB Directors who were used to big last-minute waiver deals — most Buyers didn't seem to be, and Lana Sims was the best to work with, intelligent, street savvy, and all about either overcoming obstacles or quashing bad deals. The waivers we needed processed were just that, waivers of advertising.
The public won't ever read about these deals.

And what makes it worse are 90% of vendors with their artificial deadlines like quarter ending dates. We save big bucks by signing agreements then. It also means tryin' to keep track of each quarter and year-end date by vendor.

My best friend at PB is Mike Shifman, **Info Processing** (IP) Buyer for our statewide waiver and other IP procurements. He's great with our wishes, but needs nudges. He's swamped and unorganized. *But I love 'em* **like a brother.**

I also love co-chairing public bid conferences with him.

". . . and this is Rod Richards, **State Contract Manager** for this procurement." *I've listened to many a cassette tape after award protests, and respond in writing to Ron and Ken over their sour grapes objections. Ron and ken write up the Director's formal response.*

A month later I call Joe on Warren Street for a lunchtime appointment. **"State Barber Shop."** Walking in, sitting and reading the brash Trentonian for 10-minutes while he finishes with a lawyer.

"Okay reverend, give me a hug." Joey greets so many customers with a hug,. Gregarious, talkative, socially conscious. *White guinea T-shirt and bronzed muscles popping, this'll will make Janet very happy when I get home.* An original "Optimist Club" member, Joey calls me "reverend" cuz he knows I'm religious. We share philosophies. *Me never disagreeing.* Our Italian heritage comes out when we sing ***Volare*** together to other customers' amusement.

His haircuts are not regular. First clippers, my ears, nose and eyebrows, water spraying then scissors snipping thru my hair, clipping around all the edges, a head rub for 5 minutes with his hand-vibrator, then combing and touching up; finally a little hairspray. But that's not all. Trimming my beard with black clippers first. *Then lathering hot creamy foam on my lower face, followed by hot towel.* Shaving followed by a quick wipe and facial lotion. *Heavenly. Fifteen bucks.* But I leave 20. That's why I've been going to the aptly named **"Mayor of Trenton"** for almost 20 years.

I'm not done. The whole time Joe telling everyone in the shop his plans to make Trenton and its people come alive, how he helps the youth by promoting the Y, and gives clothes and money and finds jobs for the youth and the homeless. He rattles off inspirational sayings, for example, "Help is at the end of your elbow."

And how everyone needs a mentor and a chance.
Joe may be Trenton's greatest cheerleader.

I don't take my job for granted. *I love the work and co-workers and everyone in our* **Fiscal & Procurement** *division. Everyone's honest and immediately helpful.* Jan and I fully need the income. Never had run-ins or even small arguments at work. U*nless I created them with my own attitude and mouth.* I thought my minor outbursts were temporary, anomalies.

I did always go back and apologize, didn't I?

Summer months I'm free to express my personal freedom by riding the bike. Normally a joy. *Yet, I've learned, as all cyclists do, riding is risky.* Other drivers don't see me, even with my headlight always on, and either misjudge my intent, get too close, or cut me off.

Before I can react with "Holy crap," I lay my out-of-control cycle down, then skid 30 feet toward the rear-end of the big green Ford. She hasn't looked in her mirrors, but made her right turn in front of me going 30. *Shit. Damn her! How could she not see me?* Close calls and accidents don't deter me or frighten me. *But do pop my anger — and sometimes — **I think twice,** about riding at all.*

Recounting spills, or when Janet sees my torn and bloodied jeans, or hears my complaints about how blind drivers are, lead her to slowly and gently convince me. *The bike's not safe enough.*

"Rod, You have two children now, don't you think you should cut down on the risks?" *First time she's said anything.*

162

Never making me feel guilty for riding the bike, or the time I spend cleaning and polishing chrome.

Never nagging to get rid of it.

We have one strict policy when it comes to the bike; neither kid will ever ride it. *Not even in our driveway.*

An ex-schoolmate of Janet's had done that with a neighbor's boy, casually, carefully, riding up and down this friend's driveway. But the boy turned the throttle up with a big twist, the bike jumped ahead and crashed, and the poor boy, sitting in front, had been thrown off and killed. *An awful, incomprehensible accident.*

The following spring I sell the CB500 in a private sale and don't replace it. I ask for $300 in the paper and I let the buyer have it for $280. *After he'd countered with $240.* The bike's in excellent condition, and its running boards and special shift linkage are a big plus. Its front and rear crash bars seal the deal. So it's fun, easy to ride, and safe. *Now for someone else.*   I   don't   mourn   my   loss. *Wouldn't it be nice to rent a bike for the weekend. Cooper's trains then issues temporary license and insurance?* **Hmmm.** *I miss it on those glorious clear days.*

On so many fair-weather days if half-buzzy, I'm lost in staccato, grandiose musings. After my youth, never needing nor wanting alcohol or drugs, nor even pot, to make me "higher" than normally. *Reality challenging enuff.*

Besides, alcohol and drugs are effective triggers for another episode. *Which I don't want.* My hypo- or full-blown episodes definitely come from lack of sleep and not taking meds properly. *At least I know that much.*
And Janet is my welcome watchdog.

*   *   *

163

2.8 Career Milestone?

I hit a career milestone. It occurs at the **State Auditorium** on West State Street on a beautiful crisp, suit-jacket only day in November '89.

"Congratulations," says a smiling **Governor Jim Florio**. "Thank you, sir," as we shake hands.

I'm one of a hundred state managers, the great majority male, *from almost as many agencies,* as reps from **HRDI,** the state's training arm, and **Rutgers**, the state university, hand us Certificates of Completion in the **Certified Public Manager Program.** It's been a long haul — attending classes one day a week over the past three years. *Damn proud I did it.*

Janet couldn't be there because naturally teaching her kids came first. Janet always loving them and their achievements so much, she wouldn't think of missing school except under extreme circumstances. *Like a death in the family. Only close family at that.*

Driving home from the State Auditorium, stopping at **K-Mart** and buying a wooden plaque to mount the certificate. Janet does me the honor of framing it. The next day hanging it on my office wall next to my awards. *Alongside **Dilbert's** cartoon of **Dogbert** zinging one to **Pointy-Haired Boss.***

But the cert turns out to be meaningless. No salary raise. A hollow accomplishment. Never hear of any state management positions that require the certification. *What a waste.* But, it had cost me only 250 bucks to acquire, payable to Rutgers, and time. *Only time. And I'm patient.* I had loved the classroom info in its big red binders. Otherwise, OTIS had picked up the entire training tab. *Including paying my salary on days I was in class.*

Heck, I wud'da paid it -- it was that enjoyable.

So despite my disappointment, I also realize I'm grateful. The course teachers, like Steve Adubato, a broadcaster and New Jersey personality, had been informative and engaging. And I'd learned an important sound bite: **five organizational powers:** legitimate, expert, coercive, referent and reward. *As well as dozens of other supervision and management facts and techniques.*

And in State government, legitimate power was all that mattered. A certain position or title meant everything.

In my many years with Treasury so far, it's rare to have a training request rejected, or have travel and registrations to conferences and seminars denied. *It's another reason I like my job so much.* Because I've gotten out of the office for things like **IBM's GUIDE** conference at the huge Hyatt in Manhattan, the **Communications Expo** at the **Philadelphia Civic Center,** and periodic free vendor shows. *Right here in town at the hotel. Gov't visitors love the free giveaways like pens, pads, flashlights, key chains and more.*

Peak of powers,

serene and happy,

but dark funnel cloud

casting close.

2.9 Material Setback

Jesse aged out of Indian Guides, but Kate, who's 8, and I, join **Indian Princess** in September. Same set-up and principles as the Guides only for dads and daughters. We attended monthly meetings member's homes, and drove to **Winter Weekend** in Blairstown, North Jersey, near the Delaware Water Gap. All winter gear, sleeping bags, tubes and sleds came with us. *As usual, the guys had beer from home, and I my mud from the canteen.* The girls did their own things. And we frolicked at **Camp Mason** in snow-covered Hope, NJ. Each tribe performed skits in the **Canteen** in front of the whole **Iroquois** nation . . . *unforgettable.*

Janet and I are communicating fairly well, but I pay no attention to what's going on. *This always frustrates her.*

"Rod! I told you that!'

However, we had first established a pattern of messaging when I 'd worked 2nd shift during the late '70s. So we're using the back of **Gary Larsen's** *brilliant* **Far Side Calendar** for writing notes to each other and lists. Effective tools.
Janet wants to know where I am at all times.

Even so, I often hear, "I'm not your secretary Rod."

Notes also work for tasks around the house and in the yard, doctor's appointments and meetings . "Wed - trash." "Feast tonite - shave," "Psychiatrist Tues 4," "**CDRC**, 6:30," "Yardville (school) play - 7 pm." *They're the only reminders that work. I never had any oral retention; may not ever.*

At OTIS some of Dick's budget sob stories work on non-suspecting vendors, sometimes not. Yesterday we had met with VP Arnie Arnzt of **Computer Associates** — it hadn't worked. But they've always been hard-noses. These face-to-face meetings mean only one thing. *Try every legal trick to* *finagle price cuts, or Ts & Cs modifications, year after year, good year or bad, budget-wise. Doesn't matter.* Try anyway.

OMB, the State's financial watchdog, always wants cuts, and gave the divisions scenarios : cut 5%; show us. When that's done, cut 10%; show us. And so on. Dave Ridolfino and Bob Farber jumped thru hoops every year revenues were low. Mid-year, or definitely 3rd quarter. OMB would take every agency's unallocated funds and place them in "reserve." **They'd beg** *for some releases.* The agency's tried, every year, to encumber as many funds as possible so OMB couldn't touch 'em, usually by the end of first quarter, October 1st.

We need discounts, regardless. It would have been easy to imply to the vendors we'd bid their contracts out if they didn't come thru with savings, we never did so, or threatened.

We just did it. When we bid their services out, they were shocked, no inkling. Asking "Why?" Usually poor service or high price increases.

"Well maybe if you'd worked with us a little, we wouldn't have needed to." But actually bidding was rare; the users and the techies with their expensive software, costing millions. *Wouldn't even consider it.*

Staff and I meet with our big 10 contractors in February to determine inventories and prices for the new fiscal year in July. We meet with IBM, **Avaya, Cisco, Oracle, Honeywell** *(Goupe Bull?)*, and **Hitachi**, reps, others. *Each contract valued in the millions.* I supervise the unit, so chair most negotiiations and share meetings with Cindy, Bob, Lynda or Anne. *Before we submit the best deal we can strike to Dick. Rule: Never be alone with a vendor.*

Anne had originally come over from the Human Services

procurement to work for Dick, and was now our best discount-generator by far, next to Dick and Jim, with Lynda and Cindy not far behind. She's has a little grey-haired motherly demeanor, soft-spoken, kind, but has a devious streak in her. *A **sharp mind,** easily able to avoid contracting pitfalls.* She knows human behavior from years of experience in DHS procurement, and how to appeal to the vendor's sense of greed. "And if we met the quarter-end, would you thro in 20 thou in training?" *I get to know her and her husband Sal well. He's a fantastic artist and Maine landscape painter.*

We play traditional roles, Anne's appeasing cop to my skeptical cop.

Work's frenetic from March to December with lots of meetings, emails and phone calls. *I receive 30+ emails daily, and have 40 topical files on MS-Outlook.* I keep a log at my phone to summarize callers name, org, number, date, etc.; really so I don't forget. ***I work best giving quick, immediate responses.*** *I don't mull over them long.* My projects all in contiguous piles — most frequently used on top, older on the bottom, crisscrossed.

Again, if I can't see it or reach it easily . . . .

*OTIS begins to move the State out of the dark ages of computing into **State of the Art** configurations. An unwritten policy is not to acquire bleeding edge technology.* Mainframe computer systems, the only systems capable of handling thousands of transactions, are upgraded with abandon to larger and more powerful models. I write the blanket waivers of advertising that result in approval to buy or upgrade them. Computer database work, and dozens of reports and spreadsheets are needed non-stop. *My office is an organized mess.*

*   *   *

2.10 Solid Shakeup

Surprise hits, a common occurrence in state government. *Only the front offices ever know what's goin' down. We take orders, whether brilliant or stupid and wasteful.* **Treasury Division of Administration (Admin)**, absorbs fiscal and procurement operations for 15 Treasury divisions. *So in mid-'90 us fiscal and procurement folks move downtown to a newer office building in the state hub of downtown Trenton. I guess more effective and efficient and fewer staff needed? But there's hardly layoffs unless dire ones.* This goes for financial and procurement personnel, duties and responsibilities, files, etc. all transferring over to **Admin**; but not Systems, Management, Planning, others from OTIS.

Our small procurement unit moves to the 8th floor of 50 W. State in downtown Trenton. "Oh Yeah!" By this time Lynda has moved on to work in the **Printing Control Office** and we miss her. We're only a block from the **Statehouse** and that means speedier access to the **Treasurer's Office.** A very good thing. *Now our walk-thru approval docs can be hand-carried on foot much quicker than driven by car.*

I feel upbeat about the move. In a cubicle instead of an office, but that's okay. *Always goin' with the flow.*

This will turn out to be a great career move, and as usual, I have no control of it.

"So Dick, what do you think of Jack?" Jack Flynn's the head of Admin, our division.

"Jack's a great guy, he's been around a long time, and knows the ropes. We should do fine. Don't worry. Plus, Harry K., crazy like a fox, is in the Statehouse basement." (Harry had a gaudily framed nude hanging behind his desk.)

"He and Mike McKitish, **Chief Fiscal Officer[?]**, will keep operations ship-shape."

But Jack's older and retires within two years. A new, younger Director named Chuck Chianese is appointed, who comes from **State Use Industries,** every agency's mandatory first stop for goods and furniture. In our first interview together Chuck makes two points:

"Keep your and our name out of the papers, and do an honest job," and "don't gossip and backbite — I don't like it." From my point of view, seeing as these last are both Baha'i principles. I think, *Well, that's great. Just like it's always been.*

And I obey. After a short time I prove myself capable. Chuck put me *on the management team — an equal.*
A team player. Receiving insights into internal state operations for finances, hiring, supervision, and cooperation; among objective, intelligent women and men, some younger than Chuck, and he's like 35. *Must've had a helluva record, political smarts and personality, to get his job.*

I feel safe here, welcome; a haven.

*   *   *

3.0 THIRD EPISODE

3.1 Prelude

I'm flying **Continental Airlines**, in cramped coach seating , to Rochester NY for the weekend. *Outside it's chilly yet sunny in late March, springtime, my favorite season back home.*

"Ah, look at those long lakes. Do they have a name do you know?" I'm asking the man wearing a white shirt and dark blue tie next to me. *I've been jealous since we boarded when I saw he had the window seat.*

"They're called the **Finger Lakes** because they're long and look like slightly crooked fingers," he admits tonelessly. *He hasn't been talkative — at all.* I asked him earlier why he was going to Rochester and he replied, "Business." *No further explanation.*

I followed up with, "Oh, what kind of business?" as I 'd seen Janet do many times to promote a conversations.

He says bluntly, "With **Kodak**," *as if I'm supposed to know what that implies. I don't.* He hasn't asked me why I'm going to Rochester or where I'm from. T*hat's always a sure sign of someone only interested in themselves and not in others, or just too wrapped up in their own thoughts and non-attentive.*

I don't "bother" him again. Instead I steal glances past him out his window, marveling at the miniature landscape below, liking its tiny brown or green fields, threaded by tiny crawling cars that are barely visible. I turn back as he gives me sideways glances, and finally open the airline magazine to the crossword puzzle. *I love 'em. The Times back home is my level.*

I'm flying 350 miles to a weekend training session and meeting with 25 other Baha'is, to prepare for as a coordinator for the **Sheraton Meadowlands Hotel and Conference Center**. *I'm doubly thrilled, for flying and having been accepted as a volunteer. The whole Baha'i world is thrilled!* The time's nearing for 30,000 Baha'is to overrun the **Jacob K. Javits Center** in Manhattan for the **Second Baha'i World Congress**.

Arriving there, Michael Winger-Bearskin picks me up in his **VW Bug**. *An amiable fellow, he drives us to his friend's and co-worker's* **home in suburbia.** The Friends have already arrived to the welcoming arms of Bob and Debbie Rosenfeld. *And they greet me warmly.* I reintroduce myself to Gry and Per from Claremont California, Grant Kvalheim's parents. Janet and I are friends with and visit Wendy and Grant at their Princeton home often.

One look around also demonstrates that we've all come from across the country and we'll all be co-managing venue functions for the Congress. Functions necessary to accommodate thousands of co-religionists at their chosen New York City hotels, and the site itself. With so many believers expected to attend, from different countries, cultures, backgrounds, races and creeds. *It's going to certainly be a joyous event, one not to miss.* The last Congress had been in London in '63 attended by 6,000 Baha'is. *Now here in the U.S.— in the tens of thousands.*

Janet and I had sent in volunteer forms and had been appointed venue coordinators for the Sheraton in northern Jersey. I'm desperately hoping to learn about hotel management, transportation, event and people coordination, share it back home with Janet and our team, and make further plans. Specifically, about the Sheraton, with 427 guest rooms, two huge ballrooms, numerous meeting rooms and all the amenities of a four-star hotel, located in East Rutherford.

I expect to call upon tens of acquaintances to help, all volunteers, including friends from Hamilton.

It's all new to me. The scale is something I've never dealt with. Janet and I and friends Bob and Barb had been teaching weeklong courses to believers at Green Acre Baha'i School in Maine since the '70s, but that was only an audience of 40 adults. And I had given short presentations to audiences of 100 or more many times at our annual district conventions, or at state meetings. N*o fear of public speaking.* Luckily, based on my own nature which was reinforced by Janet, I was basically organized. *Have decent skills in those areas.*

I'm between an introvert and extrovert. But I don't know what to expect from this weekend's training other than learning administrative lists, policies and procedures on hotel and guest management.

To my surprise, Bob states in our first session, "Our purpose this weekend is to learn how to be spiritual and caring." *Huh?* The 100-page manual handed out was titled **Lighting the Lamp of Service.**

Spiritual and caring? Service? I've been a declared Baha'i since '70, I should know what they mean by now. What's this going to be about? Our hosts go on to exemplify service with home cooked meals, courtesy and lavishing hospitality upon us. Everyone has the same idea: thinking we're going to be trained in hotel management.

But it's looking like the weekend will contain none of it.

Instead, doing trust-building exercises, as in falling backwards. *Into each other's arms, strangers yet I trust them.*

Then, "Hurry Rod, hurry!" Taking baby steps, scrunching down and crawling around and thru obstacles following the person ahead.

I'm under our host's dining room table on all fours, navigating thru overturned chairs. "Crawl left, left!"

Hell, which way's left? Right? Out? What's she expect? I'm blindfolded for God's sake!

Together my group is studying and reciting a favorite prayer of mine revealed by 'Abdu'l-Baha, the son of the Faith's Founder. *Each morning spending time memorizing it as best we can.*

Then repeating in unison, **"He is the All-Glorious! O God, my God! Lowly and tearful, I raise my suppliant hands to Thee and cover my face in the dust of that Threshold of Thine ,"** [27]

The service to my loved ones of the prayer is the theme of the training, inspiring me. ***Motivating me*** *to think foremost of putting others' needs before mine.* Me and the team back home will be responsible for dealing with hundreds of Baha'is from around the world. *Service comes first.*

Example and facilitation are closer to the truth of what's expected.

Upon returning home to Hamilton, we meet in our living room. Giving team members, Janet, Ev and Barb, a briefing on what I assimilated up north, and going over the manual. *Trying hard to convey the sense of spirit and helpfulness which are to be our guides -- not our heads, our hearts.*

"It was sooo much different than I expected. Here's the guidebook, all about service, courtesy and kindness. **No logistical info -- at all."**

The 4 of us have been appointed in charge of hotel operations. *They're grasped it already.* Perhaps being women and nurturing helps? *These women, experienced and organized and personable, excel.*

We've 6-months to plan and personally select and ask dozens of volunteers needed as guides, registrars, and readers for devotional sessions every dawn, music venue helpers, ushers and more, and we begin calling and help them complete the necessary 3-page volunteer application.
If they're going, and buying into our spiel.

I'm sure there's going to be big problems
at something so huge like this,

but no need to worry,

the girls will handle it. They are capable.

*   *   *

3.2 Minor Setback

Six months have passed, and now there's **Fiscal Managers** in charge of all Treasury's accounting and procurement jobs, like Cliff Mallam for **Building and Construction**, and Mary Beth Davies for **Taxation** and OTIS, the two biggest. That mean's procurement duties under Dick have been shifted. *We're concentrating on new procurements and continuation waivers.* Mom even knew Cliff as her old boss, she his secretary, and then had moved to Commerce in **UEZ - Urban Enterprise Zones.**

I've been observing and learning work methods from Dick and others by osmosis. Thankfully, there are statewide **Circular Letters** put out by OMB and PB, that make rules clear.

Yet fuzzy too. Nothing "written," for us like a handbook or best practices. Merely fill out what state forms ask for. Some justifications are one simple sentence, others are paragraphs and pages. *Decisions made quickly. Hasty consultations often, especially when the front office (Gov or Treas), direct.*

Dick says, "Do your job quickly; always please the client. But doing it right comes first."

And sometimes, its easy to hide behind laws and regulations. He doesn't really stress me with demands. We have a good relationship.

My group has responsibility for handling many written OTIS' purchase requests and pulling agencies together for the **Annual IT Waiver.** *Now $25 million worth of responsibility plus doin' bids, and Direct Purchase Authority (DPA), orders. I even teach a class on 'em.* We were doing well til Jersey's economy tanks. The State Budget's a shambles, and more revenues hastily needed.

Layoff and salary cut rumors abound.

The **Early Retirement Incentive** package of 1992 is signed by Governor Jim Florio. *My old boss Chris Reid retires.*
So does Dick.

They knew what was coming, and were smart. We hear stronger rumblings of layoffs, followed by new policies being implemented rapidly to save many State operations. Florio and the legislature are also raising State **Sales Tax** from 6 to 7 percent, and **Gross Income Tax** from 3.5 to 7 percent, filling a $3 billion budget gap. *Can it get worse?*

I'm upset. I'd been called a week earlier by Treasury Personnel, our human resources office, to be at my desk today at 10. *I sit here dreading the next ring, and have no idea what will ensue.* The bad economy. *Two thousand workers being laid off. That also means thousands of "bumps."* Less senior employees will be "moved" out of their position by those with more seniority in Civil Service.

My watch says 5 of 10. *Nervous.* Tapping pen on blank yellow pad in front of me. As the minutes roll by, I'm thinking, *I know I'm safe. I must be. I have a permanent title and I've held it for four years. Surely I have seniority. Don't I?*

Mentally jump when the phone rings. "Contract Administration, Rod speaking."

"Rodney, this is Deb from Personnel."

"Yeah, Deb. What's up?"

"According to our records, your last permanent title was DP I/O Control Specialist. Is that correct?"

"Yes, I believe so. You should know better than I do."

"I'm calling because there are no positions for you in your current Management Information Systems Specialist III title. An employee at OMB has seniority and you've been bumped."

Uh oh. "What's that mean?"

"Well, it means that you go back to your old title and may have to relocate to OTIS Operations at the HUB Data Center in West Trenton."

What!?! "Seriously? I left that job in '79."

"I know, but we don't have any other option if you want to stay in State government."

"What about my salary?"

"Unfortunately, your salary will decrease . . . . I'm sorry, but there's no way around it."

"Oh." *Will I hafta cancel our upcoming duties at the Sheraton for a week? We'll definitely have to cut dinners out and date nights to the movies. Must we cut school trips the kids were hoping to go on?* The list of adjustments won't stop there.

"Rodney, I need your decision right now, as to whether you will take the open position or not. Do you want it? Or do you want to pursue other employment?"

Pausing a moment, thinking of my family and our lifestyle, our mortgage and bills. *Thankfully, Janet's working full time as a 5th grade teacher, and loving it.* Mentally intoning a prayer for help: **"Is there any Remover of difficulties save God? Say: Praised be God, He is God, all are His servants and all abide by His bidding."** [26]

I'm not going to resign from a job I know how to do, even if I haven't done it in 13 years. Neither am I going to retire with 23 years service. At 42 I'll take a 39% penalty.

"Rod?"

"Well, Deb, you give me no choice really. Ah, I'll take it."

"Good, you'll see, hopefully over time it will work out. I'll be sending your official notice of the transfer. Understand?"

Unfortunately yes. "Okay Deb, I don't know if I can say 'Thanks for the call,' but I'll still be here, I hope."

"Yes, now I've got to make more phone calls, so we'll be in touch."

"Yeah, good luck with that. Seriously, I don't envy you those calls."

"See you later Rod."

Inshallah

This whole deal seems like a small blue ball in a handball court being smacked from 1 wall to the other 2. *Never had been good at handball in high school. Have the last 13 years been wasted? Well, I'll still have pension credit. I'm just regressing to operations at the HUB.*
I can do it, I've done it . . . .

I'll call Janet. Oh no, can't — can't call her out from class. I sit stunned, but plotting for many minutes. Jotting notes. Trudge outside for a smoke.
Still shaky, but feeling better after.

Drag myself home and tell Jan the details. She'll want them. I took notes.

She's taking it mildly, I think, saying, "Don't worry. We'll make do." *Ah, love her positive attitude.* Depressing tho, knowing I'll be back to I/O Spec II. Janet and I discussing our finances, seeing that we'll make with belt tightening.

Agree to make the best of it. Certainly can't change it.

A few days later receiving a pink interoffice envelope. A white slip of paper with my new salary, $35,000.

$20k less.

We start making a real budget; never had to before. *And our commitment to the World Congress?* Stays in.

Every single state employee has received a layoff notice, as required by law. Everyone's morale couldn't be lower.

On pins and needles waiting for Deb's follow-up call with the date to report. By this time news outlets have reported over 1,500 state workers have lost their jobs. *DEP gets hit the hardest, as they always do.* Counting myself fortunate compared to Bob Longman and Jim O'Connor, both of whom had offices down the hall and have been laid off already. After receiving the news and exit interviews, they've lingered a week or two. *We don't have a party.*

Bob was going thru a particularly hard time, possibly losing his newly built house. *Thousands of other workers being displaced by bumping -- like me.*

But today I'm concentrating on the new Cisco deal, a $1.3 million hardware and software purchase thru **Cisco Capital,** their financing arm. Seems we can't buy from Cisco directly. IBM had started it with a separate financing company for their products in the early eighties, and now everyone does it this way, especially the big hardware and software vendors.

I try acting as if nothing's happened, but my heart's not in it. *Ugh, their lousy restrictive agreement. Just like all the rest. Everything written solely in their favor. The only doggy bone for the customer is the word* ***"Customer."*** *Want us to guarantee payment every year, as they all do. Well, they'll just have to accept our annual fiscal funding out clause, or no go.* I agree with them on striking the Purchase Bureau Director's right to cancel for convenience, but not funding out protection.

Then, moving on to the indemnification clause, and insisting they modify it so they're liable for "gross negligence." They take no responsibility for anything, even that their products will work as advertised. No "fitness for a particular purpose" warranty. No "merchantability" warranty. *No.* All vendor do this. Everything's "As is." "Here, I'll sell it you for hundreds of thousands of dollars, and you take our word it'll do what we say it can. After all, we support all our products. For a subscription fee, of course." *What the heck? Boy, the IT and* **Better Business Bureau** *lobbies must be strong.*

And it's really difficult finding a fair company. It often comes down to the candidness and honesty of the rep on how well we do.

Needless to say we don't really trust any vendor. After all, they can change their terms without notice. But for that we always fought to get at least get 30 to 90 days notice.

Just **then Chuck suddenly appears** in my doorway.

I always leave my door open for anyone to pop in, and close it only for personal matters. Vendors and staff come in all the time.

Entering and shutting the door. Black hair, trim build and handsome, this man's known for absorbing smaller units into his burgeoning division. *Chuck's an excellent Director, and we have always gotten along.* Because I hardly ever speak to him except for our quarterly one-on-ones, or my annual performance standards, that I write. Chuck signs off on my final **PAR** review. I've gotten "3's" consistently, the highest level. *Thank goodness he's not a micromanager and knows how to keep the front office happy.*

Jumping up to show respect and listen.

"Rodney, I know all about the bumping. Do you think you could hold out for a while and stay here, and continue running the unit with Dick gone?"

Could I? "Of course, that'll be great Chuck, you know I'll do my best." *You're kidding me — thank you Lord!*

"Okay, good then, that's what we'll do. Give me some time, and I'll try to make it up to you."

"No problem, you got it. I'll be here. Thanks." This is definitely fortuitous. *Wow, so Chuck must like what I'm doing for him to say that. Wait til I tell Janet!* Actually happy, and temporarily blotting out the huge salary loss.

As usual, I've never asked any superior for a promotion, it just never occurs to me. I was adept however, at taking Civil Service exams, and had, plenty of times. I'd had to if I wanted to make it easy for the big-wigs to hand me the title. *I usually passed in the top three. In '93 I got offered a Buyer position in the Township after passing a Civil Service exam, even interviewed with the Administrator. It was only testing the waters.*

Another reason I liked Chuck, no handouts. *Prove yourself and earn it, and get rewarded — somewhere down the line.*

Days and weeks pass, intimating it's not a formal promotion. *Could it become formal?* I've assumed ever since Dick had retired that they'd promote someone else or bring in a flunky for his job as manager of the unit, as they did at so many other agencies I knew of. *I don't think I'll have his position long.*

I have to carry on as if nothing's happened. but I get to have new business cards after asking Dave. Dave Ridolfino, Chuck's right hand man and our de facto boss, who's also in charge of Treasury's budget, approves my 250 cards as **Manager Statewide Contract Administration,** representative of what we actually do. I'm sure Chuck saw.

Dave's smart, quick, and easy to get along with — as long as there's no hanky panky or whining, and staff does their jobs.

Luckily my "bump" has turned into a tap.
A minor setback in the big scheme of things.
With Jan's support.

What could've been a bummer becomes manageable.

3.3 Rollercoaster

Sometime later, November 21, 1992, a Saturday afternoon, on the Turnpike travelin' north to the Sheraton adjacent to Giants stadium. I feel great. *Let's sing along to to the Stones and Beatles on **Oldies but Goodies.** Shame **WHYY** had cut out.*

Going a day ahead to set up. *Oh, so exciting! it's the day!* Janet and I lived near Turnpike exit 7A, and the Meadowlands Complex was exit 16W. Speeding along the 65 miles, *day-dreaming,* talkin' to myself and the radio, barely registering surroundings, goin' 75 or 80 like the cars I'm following. *Hummm. . . .* Barely register mile markers.

"All the Baha'is I'll meet from all over the world." ***All the hugs and tears** of gladness they'll be meeting old friends and new.*

Not picturing my own future tears.

Must check in first at Sheraton desk. "Here's my credit card." All of us volunteers are, after all, on our own dime.

Then asking for the manager and confirming with him that I'm one of the **Baha'i Venue Coordinators.**

"Yes Mr. Richards, we have a room for you and your wife, and an office all set up for you on the mezzanine. Would you like me to show you them now or after you're settled in?"

"Now please." *Why fidgety? Stop rubbing your finger tips together.*

Hotel staff along the way seem uniformly helpful, courteous and kind hearted.

Tastefully decorated facilities. Our team is to use the Derby ballroom for registrations and socializing, which holds 250 people, and the larger Diamond ballroom for morning devotions as well as evening entertainment, easily holding 600 in long rows of green padded chairs. Follow him to headquarters on the lower floor. Tucked in a corner is our 20 x 20 room with tables, chairs, phone, and boxed supplies. *Includes 5-foot tall signs in long cardboard boxes.*

Let's see, what's this label say? Let me open box, Oh, the main signs. Here's another, and another. Cool. OOPs, keeping him waiting!

"Thanks so much, it seems we have all our materials."

"Yes sir, good. Anything else you need, here's my card and number, or just ask the staff."

"No, thank Y-O-U." Our job is to follow the schedule, coordinate all the events and volunteers, all entertainment each evening, set up signs and the ballrooms, and handle minor guest requests. *All necessary to accommodate 350 to 400 Bahá'ís expected to check in tomorrow.* Also expecting to accommodate any registration or personal problems to the best of our ability. We've also been given Gry

Kvalheim's cell number. She's an *overall organizer, at Congress headquarters in the sold out Hyatt.*

Gry, Norwegian for Dawn, typical of so many capable Baha'is I had last met in Rochester. She had worked for Peter Ueberroth, the organizer of the **1984 Summer Olympic Games** in Los Angeles, at his travel company, so she was intimately familiar with arrangements needed for large venues. *In charge of the transportation for the 30k Baha'is coming to the Congress.*

Well-known in our area, even though livin' in southern California. We knew her personally having met her and husband Per, at their son Grant's home in Princeton Township, used for many local Baha'i meetings, socials and public gatherings. *Wendy's the consummate hostess, from an illustrious Baha'i family, the Kelsey's.*

Straightening out tables and chairs in our make-shift office, ripping open and noodling inside smaller boxes. *Documents, ID badges and neck-rope holders, nameplates, day passes.* Shove all under the tables covered by clip-on light blue tablecloths. *No door lock.*

Exiting to my room on the 10th floor $^{(?)}$, seeing the white popcorn ceiling and trim, bath, queen bed, desk and chair, and TV. Unpack rapidly, anxious to explore, filling two drawers, slamming shut. *Gotta find coffee.* Walk into restaurant, buying one to go with cream and sugar. *I'll never gripe about cost when there's no other choice. So what I'm really paying extra for convenience.* Bouncing up escalator to the 2nd floor, and strolling toward our "office" scanning across the broad, high atrium.

Rest of day spent moving, setting up, going thru registration materials, forms, supplies and signs. *Better put out* **Welcome** *ones on the* mezzanine. After dinner, scurry to our room, plop down and select, "Hey, *Batman Returns."* *Action flicks are the best, and sci-fy.*

Two hours long. *Michael Keaton's doing a decent job, but looks much better in costume than in a tux. Is that the point?* Switching dumb TV off at 3. Tossing and turning, sleeping in fits and starts. *Why can't I dream?*

Rising at 5 Sunday. *"Do I feel the illness?"* Coming in waves now, some small, some overwhelming, hitting me like '79 when I was . . . the Savior. *Forever long ago. Not happening. Keep control.* Wide awake, wired, antsy; haven't slept well, overly excited. Dress rapidly, no shower, leave. Restaurant. Closed of course. Roaming hotel for hot coffee, including service areas. Finding employees cafeteria, but coffee not ready. *Shit! Bummer, bummer, bummer. I need my coffee!* Love coffee with cream and sugar. !?#&$8? Why don't you just have coffee for God's sake? What's so hard about this? I should open a franchise. Frustrated. Curse hotel management aloud for the oversight.

Take the escalator from basement to 2nd floor where ballrooms are, and there, stumble upon a man in his fifties. "Hi, good morning, can I help you?"

He only replies, **"Eq-qua-door."** Dressed in native garb complete with thick woolen socks and tan sandals, colorful red and black stripped white wool serape draping his right shoulder and falling past waist to knees. Alone near the registration room as it chimes 7, long before bulk of Baha'is start arriving in 5 hours.

> *Let me hug 'em, he must be Baha'i.*
> Warm embrace., meaningful, full of spirit.
> "Allah'u'abha, Allah'u'abha."
> His voice huskier, Mine high-pitched.

"We . . . are brothers." Showing him to a seat inside and telling him in loud broken English,   "Please sit. Wait."

Jog back to our office, find **The Baha'is magazine** of glossy pictures and big type and rushing back, holding it out.

He's standing politely, unmoved, respectfully.   Handing it to him, opening to pictures of Baha'is from other countries. *At least he has something to look at.* Thanking me and bowing 3 times.

Return to our office and unpacking other box   of signs, assembling them, standing them neatly near windows. *Where are the damn girls?* Drinking   4 coffees with frequent death sticks, outside.

Waiting. Holding wrath in check.

Why aren't they here yet? Don't they know how important this is? Forgetting completely Janet had said "We'll be there at 9." Janet's never late. *I'm not either when I'm with her.* Girls arriving by 9, and *Surprise,* 15-year old Jesse in tow. *I forgot! I hope he enjoys it.* He'll attend sessions with her.

Janet asks ,"Rod what room are we in? Do you have my key?"

"Oh yeah, here Hon. I'll go down and get My own." All go to their rooms to unpack first. *Man they're takin' their time..* After coming back half hour later they look over the materials and supplies I've laid out, while Jess stays with our best friends the Yazhari's, and hangs out with multi-talented Laila. *This is takin' way too long . . . time's passing too slowly. I need to move. A smoke*

"Hey, where's the registration lists?" Barb asks.

"I have them," Ev says.

"Oh, so that's why I didn't see them. Did National send them to you?"

"The Congress front office did."

"Oh, good," they all say together.

Charged with keeping all lists confidential.

After setting up and consulting, dispersing to strategically place signs and post directions to the meeting rooms and bus loading checkpoints for next morning.

Janet says. "I'll stay and man the office." By this time Baha'is and many spouses trickling in.

Remember, I'm a floater, jack of all trades. Supposed to smile and welcome folks, showing them where to go. $100 petty cash in my pocket for emergencies.

Outside smokin', cab pulls up, 3 middle-aged, dark-haired women exit, waivin' their hands pleading with cabbie. Happen to be in lobby seeing 3 women out front by cab. *Why are they upset and waving their arms? Better see what's goin' on. . . They're practically sobbing.* Apparently because cab ride from the airport had run up . . . $45.

Baha'is arriving from all over, many on very limited means. Me looking officious with ribboned badge.

"It not supposed to be much. Told 30 dolla." Telling me haltingly they're from Italy.

"Caio. Don't worry ladies, let me take care of this, please. You've come a long way, please go in and register and enjoy the friends," waving them inside.

After kissing My hand and saying "Caio Bella," ladies leave, I turn to cabbie — *I'm hot, hot, how could he do that?* Hatred shooting from My eyes.

Screaming in his face, "What's wrong with you? Sonofabitch! How could you charge so much?" Can't . . . control . . . *anger.* Cabbie takes it, head down, explaining in between My verbal assaults it's standard fare from **JFK.**

Oh, you better not shout back! Scumbag. I don't know what I would've done If he had.

Coming to my senses enough to hand him 3 twenties, but too mad to take proffered receipt. Speeds off. Bell hop involved also hears from Me. "What the (eff) are you doing taking money from them for? Can't you see they're not wealthy?" Later grab him by the arm and apologize profusely. Confiding "I'm not feeling well."

Not telling team members anything about this untoward incident. Have another smoke. Step inside   for coffee.

More agitated as day progresses, stressing out, "Must watch everyone closely." *Miss nothing.* Run around extinguishing personal fires, burning endless energy, interrupting others with questions. Them interrupting my inconsequential missions.

"Excuse me, I see you have a green ribbon on for Coordinator. Can you tell me what time the buses will be here tomorrow?"

Belligerent. "Didn't you look at your packet? It's there."

"Well, I didn't . . . ." Cutting him off.

"8:30 sharp. See the large sign and doorway down there in the lobby?" I point.

"Oh, great, thanks!"

"Yeah, okay." *Idiot can't read.*

Going on all day,   between My rudeness

and my politeness.

Not alone, *I'm not alone, cuz on large issues I can ask the girls.* But single-handedly try to be all things to every one I run across, even tho random thoughts hitting me constantly. *Who's in the office during lunch today? Should go check the registration tables. How many Baha'is have registered?* Mental missives coming hot and heavy.

Which way do I go now? Registration? Welcoming? Torn   in   dozen   directions.

As coordinators we had set up dozens of other volunteers, materials and tables in the registration ballroom, as hundreds of Baha'is began crowding in. *Must check up occasionally.* So, move, check, everyone, everything. Periodically. *In small clumps, hugs and tears being exchanged with long lost friends, with many handshakes and pats on the back.*

Hear, "James! I haven't seen you in ten years. How are you?" And, "Suzie., I'm so glad you made it.   Tell me how Chicago is . . . ."

By early evening 250 standing room capacity in registration room exceeded; scene looks like controlled bedlam, except for patient weaving lines. Original idea, most people arrive and register Sunday afternoon and evening, before Congress started early tomorrow. *Ending Thursday afternoon at 5.*

Next phase ensuring entertainers organize/set up. 7 pm program in large ballroom. 10-acts tonight, instruments, sound systems, roadies. more. *All set, MC starts. Clapping. Hooting loud.* The 4 of us on team enjoy music and skits as best we can. *Between handling requests for information, schedules.*

"Everything's in your packet, please check there first." Luckily, this crowd friendly, cooperative, sitting or dancing *with abandon* held in check; otherwise controlled without our resorting to rules. *Look at those cute dancers in aisles.*

Over their screams and applause, shouting, "They're definitely enjoying the program!" *I hafta help if needed.* Coordinating musical acts like these every night.

After long day Janet and I hit bed at 11. *I still hear the music downstairs.* I know, Jesse tired, asleep on cot. *What am I missing?* Again, fitful. *Careful, don't knock Jan.* She sleeps soundly with little snores that never bother me. At home, some nights my own snoring causes her to go to our living room couch when she can't physically move me onto my side.

Awake again at 5. After decade plus of wearing suit to work every day, have habit of putting clothes out night before. Jeans, burgundy pullover, dark socks, loafers. *All here.* Dressi silently and hurriedly. *Gotta sneak out, too early.* "Clunk." *Crap. The door's so loud! Will it wake one of 'em?* **Ohwell.**

In charge of ballroom setup with 300 chairs. Dawn prayers at 6. *Quick, where's Rich? He'll say a prayer.*

And Sharon, I know I can ask her. Search goes on for early risers until I've grabbed a dozen readers for prayers and writings already selected. Check PA, mike, "Can you hear Me?" Appoint ushers thruout. Hotel staff easily directed, and have been timely rearranging chairs from last night's mess.

After breakfast 10 buses scheduled to arrive at 8:30. Critical. *Transport guests to Javitts.*

Eating early in hotel, Ev, Janet, Barb and I rush around by 8, resolving final registrations, credentials and hotel issues. *Occasional personal problems pop up. Solved.* Dealing with one registration issue as formidable middle eastern woman stands in front of Me covered head to foot in black burka. Gruff demeanor and menacing countenance. *Can only see thick black eyebrows and large, piercing black eyes, can't tell expression behind.* Doesn't have proper credentials, and had been sent to us, Me.

Repeating in broken English, stronger and stronger, "Where my passes? Where my passes? Let me see list." *Is this woman Baha'i?*

"Please follow Me." Escort her into team room. Hand her off to smiling face. No one can find her name on registration lists. *What am I going to tell her?* Question in our minds is whether we'll give her day passes at all. The Faith had had its roots in Islam. *Severe garb doesn't throw Me off but demanding attitude? has.*

Also, Thousands of Baha'is in Iran still being persecuted — harassed, beaten, tortured and killed. We all know this. We knew their government o and some fanatical Muslim clergy had current pogroms vilifying Baha'is. The Shiah government had made innumerable attempts, some successful, to search out Baha'is by acquiring residency lists.

One reason why National told us not to share them.

Seems Iranian gov't blames Baha'is for its social ills.

So shaken by this woman's dark belligerence. *Is she spying on us? Is she from the government?*

Girls consulting on what to do.

Picking up chair, asking her politely, "Hi again," *Smile wide Rodney.* "Please follow me?" Showing her to outside our room. Lay down chair, offer arm to sit.

"Ah, I'll be . . . right back . . . with answer."

Returning seeing Ev dialing headquarters, explaining situation, giving them woman's contact info. Ev hangs up, "They'll call right back."

Five minutes later phone rings.

"Sheraton, Baha'i World Congress, Evelyn here. "Yes . . . . Umm . . . Okay . . . Got it."

Ev's been jotting, gives thumb's up. I politely retrieve woman, Barbara apologizes for the oversight, using her most conciliatory tone, as she hands woman 4, daily passes.

Woman gives perfunctory "Khoda-hafez," [*] turns and leaves without another word. This is good sign. *There could have been a scene. I knew Barb could assuage the woman; our Assembly chairperson, very adept at diplomacy handling guests. Goodbye. Inshallah.*

Not expressing suspicions to Janet, others. *Will she come back? Did we get rid of her? What if she seeks me out? Must Keep to Myself.* Knowing many kind, loving Iranians liked and helped their Baha'i neighbors and friends. *This wide brush, suspicion, cannot, must not, be used against populace as a whole.*

Fifteen-minutes later disaster strikes.

Glancing at watch, 8:40. Hearing growing clamor downstairs. People loudly asking, "Where are buses?"

Huge problem! Morning buses to take Bahá'ís 11-miles from here to Javits haven't shown up. Not one. *What are we going to do? Do we call bus companies? How do we fix?* Worry, concern, unable to act. More people asking. *Shit, what do we do?* But girls scramble, make three calls, ultimately Gry's cell phone. *It doesn't matter we know her, can she help?* Answering call immediately. Hearing professional conversation. Ev, "She'll take care of it."

I [(?)] go down, make announcement, loudly,

"They're on their way. Just a few minutes!"

15-minutes later first bus arrives to hand clapping and glee. *Thanks Gry.*

More add up. Guests safely loading and away, team consults.

"Which of us will attend the actual congress sessions, starting this afternoon?"

I gush, "I'd really like to go if I can." Others turn to Janet.

She nods, "Okay, but take your pills before you go." Smile as wide as I can, "Absolutely!"

Morning going slowly as titillation builds. *I get to go.*

At noon, as agreed, taking joyous singing bus by Myself to Congress afternoon program, focused on Baha'u'llah, Prophet-Founder of Baha'i Faith. *Why am I so jittery?* Excess energy. *Wow, this'll be really sometin'; experiencing session.* General knowledge of what to expect. *Can't imagine being with 15 thousand Baha'is in one place.*

Disembarking shuttle bus, overwhelming hubbub, excited and happy voices outside and in cavernous Javitts. *What's it going to be like?* Visions flying. Huge dark hall, large colorful banners setting off hundreds of multi-colored mums and carnations. *Dwarfed by red and yellow roses surrounding multi-level stages.*

Professionalism and excellence permeating proceedings, singing, *(Glorious)* brothers and sisters dressed in native garb from 200 countries, aweing. *So many Baha'is of amazing diversity filling room.* Sitting facing central stage, orchestra and marvelous 500-member Baha'i Choir. *Can't see all singing faces, too many. Sea of white gowns, multi-colored scarfs flowing down to feet.* Good friends Martha and Laila in choir. *Where are they? Too many happy faces, don't see them. Did they make it?* Sopranos, counter-tenors, mezza-sopranos, tenors, contraltos, baritones and bass -- merged yet contrasted, solos and choir --true beauty thru My ears, weaving stories, feelings, in My Head. Visualizing, hearing Martha lead Sunday school in **It's Nice to be a Baha'i,** "It's Nice! " and Red Grammar's **I Think You're Wonderful.** [28] "How do ya feel?"

I feeeell won-der-ful . . . ."
Ah, My favorite best song. Love to sing with gusto.

3.4 View from a Roof

Sitting, snapping back to compelling atmosphere. Re-minding me, chilling, hairs on arms raised. *Heard this choir weeks earlier.* Manhattan school auditorium, Dash Crofts performed to our small assemblage, modulated singing from half-full choir in background. *So happy to participate.* Easily submerged. Reminded me of similar excursion and hearing Dizzie shout his trumpet and band play at **New York City Baha'i Center.**

Now 30-piece[?] orchestra pounding drums. *Each nation stepping forward.* Representatives from 180 countries announced one by one, mounting stage single-file to wild applause. *My wild applause* drowned out. Long African robes, Bavarian lederhosen, more serapes, cowboy hats, all. *How I love them! So proud.*

195

Chatting muffled in background *like my mind* as opening statements end; hush falls as Mayor David Dinkins gives short welcoming speech, declaring "November 23, 1992, Baha'i World Congress Day."

Listening, in tears, spellbound as Amatu'l-Baha Ruhiyyih Khanum recites welcoming message from Universal HouseofJustice in her well-paced, Canadian crispness.Alegend.

Reel from import of proceedings, *the rarified atmosphere.*

Imbibing deep, sonorous, male British voice, *so distinct,* narrating program thru booming loudspeakers. Strains from dozen violins fill background, intoning over and over, **"Oh, Baha'u'llah, what hast Thou done?"**

Third time penetrating *My heart,* wrecked, crying openly, unsuccessfully choking back tears. *Rod! Stop! Decorum please.* Can't stop, sobbing thru end of session, barely containing wails. A colorful, sound-filled blur. *Cover your face!* Cover open mouth. Get up, *wander,* aisles, down, near red velvet curtains on side, sitting down minutes before moving, moving, again.   *Can't   be   still.*

Pierced by loving yet forceful words, inspired speakers, urging, "Just do your part. You're not alone." Reverberations, feelings, *suddenly immersed* in final oratorio to Baha'u'llah, breaking down, putting face in hands again, muffling cries.   *Rodney. Control. Not here! Not now!*

Gotta keep moving.

Oh Baha'u'llah, what hast Thou done? Dozens of preformed thoughts crowding together. *You've released the Word of God, capable of changing a gnat into an eagle. Renewing all creation with fresh creative energy. Imbibing that Energy, drinking that energy, had that energy before . . . seen changes in Myself and others . . . happiness.*

Yes. Happy! Janet and the kids, family and friends, Baha'i brothers and sisters, coworkers, neighbors. They'd all do whatever I ask . . . .

Can't believe good fortune. How? Why Us? Just being good guy? Or solely thru Your grace . . . mercy.

Yet something wrong. *What is it?*

Not afraid to ask for help, but don't. *No.* Barely make it to end of session. Head down, eyes askew, arms at side, tight hands, following noisy crowds outside. *Wipe your eyes.* Searching for yellow tag, *Sheraton..*

Climb aboard with 40 Baha'is, conversing loudly. Bus pulls away, jumping up, walking down the center, *"Hello! My name's Rod from New Jersey. Where you from?"*

Fifteen-minutes and driver says over polite smile, "Can you please sit sir?" *Oh, I'm so happy!* **Insanely happy**, agitated.

Arrive back at hotel, standing outside by door, shake hands with cohorts getting off, *"Enjoy your time here!"*

Once inside, floating in elevator to 5th floor, get off, wondering *Which way? . . .*

I know! Up . . . They won't find Me.

Climb exit stairs, 2 at a time, pass poet friend Peter Murphy [(?)]. Last door. Shove it open, step out, bright, shocking light! *Voila!* Manhattan skyline materializing, inviting . . . 12 stories up. *A short flight.* Marveling, ***Sit.*** Plunk down on metal flue, cradle head . . . long time.

Keep eyes closed. Tight.

Darkness

Block out that Sun! Don't want to be seen.

Motion sits still. Asking God, *Is there help for Me?*

(Jan's, been searching alone?)

Knowing thing's amiss;

finding Me as I cry.

"I hafta get home, can't take it," moaning louder, overcome. "How beautiful are people, how inspiring they are; the city, majesty and brilliance of those reaching gleaming towers . . . " Raise arms to heaven, "I'm begging you, . . Peace . . Please . . . ."

"How sorry, can't help team . . . Myself . . . ."

Janet next to Me, trying, placating, hugging, whispering, "Don't worry Rod, we caught it in time."

Not cognizant, but . . . emotions . . . drowning Me.

Silence.

Team quickly consults, Janet calls Mom for help. Familiar with my condition, all having dealt with prior episode, as family, friends, Assembly members. Without going to hotel room first, Janet drives us to my old home. Leaving Jess in Yazhari's hands. She's quiet -- strong -- concentrating, on driving. I'm *Can't stop shaking.* Tapping foot . . try hard to listen between rapid thoughts, images . . .   hoping   for silence, altho radio's on . . . .

*   *   *

Laying in My brother's old bunk bed next 2-nights until improve slightly from sleeping pills, lithium, antipsychotics -- frequent, doubling per doctor's orders. At least I still have vacation days the rest of this week . . . just stay, 3-days.

Stay in bed, watching inane TV.
Words, images blurring away.

Congress plays out for its intense four days,
broadcast to 50 countries.

Thursday afternoon Janet and Jess pick Me up for home..

Think no more. Dodged a bombshell

But next one will almost kill me, and possibly others.

*　　*　　*

The State's mental health **HMO** reassigns me to a new psych. Sign says **Dr. Argueta.** A gentle Guatemalan-American, on My first visit he presents a bag of natural coffee from his plantation back home. *Coffee. Lovely!*

"Thanks so much. How'd you know?' I like him immediately. He turns out to be a fine psychiatrist and human being, who always puts me at ease and is non-threatening, like Peter was at **P' House.**

"Rodney, Can you guess what my desk plaque says?"

"Um, actually, wondered about that. No I can't." It's wooden, small like a name plate, but no discernible letters present. However, the teakwood's upraised in strategic spots, obviously meaning something.

"It says 'JESUS' . . . can you make it out now?"

199

He's hoping I'll guess his Christian faith? But even so, never preachy or otherwise intimating his devotion, nor ever making me feel anything but comfortable.

Never asking, even with Janet sitting next to me at our early sessions, about deeper issues, thoughts or emotions. *Strictly meds management; all GreenSpring will spring for.*

He's always askin', "So how are you doing?"

Same response, "Fine, no problems."

During these short visits, Dr. A also commands in a friendly, casual tone, "Okay Rodney, stick out your tongue." Looking for bumps on it, a sign of lithium toxicity. Then mildly commanding, "Stick out your arms and hold your hands out straight." Quaking another sure sign.

I never quake.

3.5 Four Year Interim

In honor of the **Baha'i Holy Year**, 1992, *feelin' obligated to make some sacrifice in God's name.* So . . . quit smoking. This goes much easier than abstaining from coffee during the annual fasting period. *Decreasing my smokes works beautifully with the patch.*

In '93 Kate's 12. Not extra frilly and lacey, she likes her femininity and female social circles. By this time she's in Girl Scouts with a great group of friends her age. Their scout leader is Jane Chrostowski, and she and her family live in a split-level home on the outskirts of Hamilton. The troop meets regularly, and Jan and I become chummy with Jane and her husband Jan, their older daughter Jamie, Kate's age, and younger sister Jill. *We privately called them **the "J" family.***

The 2 girls, yellow blondes, got it from Jan's white-blonde mane, cut short. Their family's bright, friendly, hospitable and normal, and like to laugh just as we do. *No dirty jokes here.* Jane is a subtle deadpan jokester, and deadly. At one of Jane's girl scout meetings, I show the troop how lights work on my red Civic. a hand-me-down from Hutch, Janet's dad.

"Hey girls, gather round," as I open the trunk. "Lights are most important on a car so it's always good to check. Let me show you how to change bulbs." Point them out and how to pop 'em, even in the trunk. Open fuse box, pull one out and explain basics, simply. Jan C. teaches them how to change a tire. *That's difficult for 'em, but they get it.*

Janet and I always encourage our kids in their studies, but never do any of it for them, neither will we touch their homework. *Aid when needed, of course, examples, of course.* And the Hamilton public school's are fine. A's and B's are best, and we don't flip out with occasional Cs. *Moderation's the name of the game.* High scores aren't pushed, but admired. Our standards are high, and good grades are rewarded with small gifts, like a comic book for Jesse for an "A," and ice cream for Kate. *Naturally besides verbal praises and reinforcements. **Comprehension's all we ask.*** We had read to them constantly when they were young, and Jesse was an avid reader. Also spending time memorizing prayers with them since little. *Not the long ones.*

About this time Jan transfers to an opening at Mercerville Elementary teaching fifth graders. Almost every night Janet tells me touching, mostly funny stories from her class of mountain lions, the school mascot. She also really admires and respects her co-teachers, Diane Donovan, the school veteran, and young Joan Petrowski, the meticulous one, and we get to know them and their families well.

Janet feels strongly, and I agree, that at least once a month we'll give Jesse a safe environment to hang out; better than hangin' at the wrong place, or going somewhere and finding trouble. *Or it finding him.*

By this time Jesse's 16 and has a great group of friends. Vigs, Marc, Rich, Conrad, Ji, Jamie and many others, all come over to our unfinished basement, and watch movies like **The Crow.** *Which I invite myself to one Friday night.* They don't seem to mind, and carry on as if I'm part of their crew. The Crow has risen from the dead to enact revenge, and the black and white contrasts are strikingly stark, with deep red blood.

His friends continued playing pool when I left after the film, munching snacks and drinkin' soda. *A good bunch.*

Even band member friends set up and play downstairs.

Jesse's friends really hit it off with Jan. She has an ease about her and takes sincere interest in their doings and opinions. *All of them are frank and warm to her.* They have great discussions standing in our kitchen. Janet and I retire to our room and watch TV until 11, then conk out while the parties continue.

Jess and Kate are not problems, never have been. Difficulties that can't be overcome by trying are non-existent, and even then only temporary lapses and not character flaws.

All their friends, including Baha'i kids, seem that way also . . . even the rambunctious Weber boys. *But how do I know? How does any parent really know? Well, Jan and I think we do, and treat them with respect.* We never looked down on them, not once.

*   *   *

Another year passes. *No incidents.* Except the Assembly has lots of fun hosting the *Baha'i World Mini-Congress*, almost a week past Labor day '94, for over 100 kids and their families. Our own follow-up idea commemorating the real World Congress. *Coordinated by an appointed task force.* Janet, Barb and Ev of course, the Webers, Spud takin' pics, others. Us guys handle set- up and cleanup, together with other helpers.

The all day affair is held at the **Princeton Unitarian Center,** and we're expert at organizing and delegating. It's reminiscent of the similar **Star-light Conference** for 120 children and adults the Assembly had hosted and organized years earlier. Good friends Henry and Grace Ouma had secured the **Busch Rutgers Campus** in Piscataway for us then.

For the Mini-Congress, held in the Unitarian's wonderful facilities, some of the kids wore native dress, as encouraged. In the theme of **Unity in Diversity**, Kevin Locke, a Native-American and Baha'i, wears his native garb: white fringed leather head to toe, beaded moccasins, beaded headband, and plays enchantingly on his **Lakota** flute. But the highlight's Kevin's traditional hoop dance performed with 20 or so white plastic hoops twirling round and between, over and thru, his dancing, pounding body. All of us are spellbound, hoping it all works flawlessly; and it does, even extracting himself from the body-sized hoops. ***Incredible!***

"Hey, this looks interesting, let's stop in." So I had stopped meandering on my bike on a clear, perfect New Jersey day at the **Rankokus Indian Reservation,** home to the **Powhatan Renape Nation.** That's where I had first seen Kevin in person, aside from his many pictures, performing a touching prayer to the **Great Spirit.** Seeing him later at his jewelry table, I had thought, *He might be Baha'i.* But hadn't introduced myself. *I should've.*

Most of our experience handling large events has been accumulated over 15 years of hosting the **Annual District Convention** for the election of a delegate to National. Held in October, our conventions were attended consistently by 110 or more Baha'is. Arranging for and renting a school auditorium, delegating setup, refreshments hosted by nearby Hopewell community, setting the agenda and timings, pre-publicity, appointing a **Convenor** and **Head Teller**, and arranging teachers and babysitters for children's classes. *All second nature.* As Treasurer I paid the bills, and also had responsibility for ordering and picking up 2-dozen pizzas and selling them at lunch.

"Get your pizza here, only a buck per slice," as my friend Richie slaps them down on thin paper plates, also handing out cheap napkins. *We always sold out.*

Two Fund boxes sat out on the side that I managed: one for contributions to the **National Baha'i Fund,** and the other expense donations, usually 7-hundred +. Whatever difference was needed to pay for stuff, the Assembly kicked in, usually only a hundred or two. I made announcements at the podium thruout the day as to their progress.

"Friends, so far we've raised $400 for expenses, and $200 for National. Thanks so much everyone!" Contributions to the Funds and Baha'i works can only be accepted from Baha'is.

But the real convention purpose for me had been re-greeting the friends during breaks and lunch, commiserating, sharing teaching or community growth stories. Folks came from middle and south Jersey, most of whom we only saw here. During convention, community spokespersons shared teaching and consolidation activities going on in their areas, and another pleasure was welcoming new believers.

"I'm Michael [?] from Atlantic City, and (so-and-so) taught me the Faith four months ago." And we'd clap heartily and seek him out afterwards to ask about how he'd first heard the **Message.**

At the end of the afternoon, the Head Teller announced the delegate, *usually the same person for 6 year stints,* and we'd all disperse after saying long goodbyes, hugging, then cleaning up. Relationships seemed closer than just seeing so many mainly annually. *The goal is always to leave the facility cleaner than we'd found it.*

A few weeks after this I walk into the Spanish Deli across from 50 West where I work, "Hi, could I please have a plate of pinto beans, raw onions and salsa?" [29] *Delicious.*

While paying I ask, "Oh, and how 'bout a pack of Salem 100s?" Open 'em and light up in the foyer before opening the door to the howling wind outside. *Something I haven't done in two years. God, it tastes awful!*
Almost throw it away. Almost.

Five cigarettes a day then on. Better than 10+ my usual. I also begin buying cartons from **Smokin' Joes** just 'cross the Delaware River bridge in Morrisville a month later. The savings are substantial; in Pennsy, $5.50 a pack; versus 7 bucks in Jersey and its higher sales tax. *What do I care, really, I can afford it. My one vice -- and its legal to boot.* Janet doesn't complain *(Thank God.),* when she pays the bills. *As long as I never smoke 'round her, the kids, in the house or around others.* And I don't. *Always off to the side. Not sneakin' tho, I'm not ashamed.*
Somethin' I do. That nobody else seems to?

About this time the State bans smoking in all its buildings and offices, so I bring my glass ash tray home and put it in on a garage shelf for rainy or cold days. *In public **I do try to find secluded spots.*** When walking always cupping it or tossing it when passing strollers or kids. Dad had long ago taught me to tee my butts, an old military trick, so I never littered, stickin' 'em in my back left pocket. *I feel less guilt that way.* In fact, I 've got a bug against litter, and 9 out of 10 times stoop down to pick up large pieces of trash or bottles or cans in my path.

> Janet always says, "Ugh, how can you touch that?"
> *Just like finding trash,*
> *Never know when my illness will find me.*
> *And where it will dispose me.*

4.0 FOURTH EPISODE

4.1 Deeper Setback

At Mercerville, Janet and good friend Diane still attend all school PTA meetings and volunteer to help out. Jan on **Audit Committee.** The **Mercer County Board of PTAs** nominated, and the membership elected, Janet as **President of Presidents.** Another feather in her humble cap, and eventually leads to her treasured status as a **Life Member.** "Congratulations Hon!" *Downplayed proud response.*

It gets chillier. Indian summer gone. Always colder by now, at least snow and mush isn't black with dirt, smog and soot. By 7:30 parked my Civic in the state garage on Bank Street. Try to enjoy first smoke while walking down Willow towards work.

Why aren't I feelin' happy this mornin'? Impending doom has wakened me earlier than usual. The kind of doom powerless to stop. *I'll die of lung cancer or lose my job or Janet will lose hers.* Can't shake ill feelings.

Always stop at **Town House Restaurant** 'cross the street for my usual. Entering my building lobby, "Hey guys, how ya doin"? Both female guards. Everyones "guys' to me. Wave to one who know me.

8 a.m. Alone on the elevator, 1 of 6, whisking 8-floors to mine, using keycard and making beeline to my office with head down. *Don't speak to me. Don't speak to anyone.* Utter no "Hello's" Settlin' in and gulpin' joe, turn on computer, start writin' newer RFP, in between check 20 emails, finish status report, use Google to look up def for **IBM Systems Network Architecture (SNA).**

Things don't seem -- kosher with this.

Questioning begins by 9.

"Rod, what do I tell Human Services about that request for Peter Martin software without the Disclosure Forms? Do I send it back? I already asked them twice."

"Leave it with me Annie, I'll call Lou Marino later," their **CIO.** *Thank goodness for Annie.* My right hand woman, capable of leading most jobs in my absence.

Take quick call from DOT about separate ***Application Programming Support Waiver*** I compile and review for professional services.

Interruption, "Rod, what's my deadline for getting the RFP inventory together?"

"Carl, how much is done?" spend 10-minutes going over his progress. He's smart, methodical, good worker. *Ugh, more questions. When will they stop!*

Writing specs for maintenance and repair services for 16 thousand pieces of state computer equipment is enjoyable. *Blank pages never slow or stop me.* Carl's inventory development in **MS-Access** invaluable, and altho OTIS **Operations Director** Roger Race and his assistant Regina had had the original idea to consolidate, we get to execute it. Only their legwork has made it tenable. It's time consuming, nightmarish, since to a very large degree our vendors simply know *more than we do*, about actual equipment service metrics similar to **MTTR — Mean Time To Repair.** *Knowing that stuff would've cut our costs.*

Hiring consultants to help develop specs is problematic and not done. But we're capable enough to achieve our goals. This RFP has 5 large categories of vendor's equipment maintenance and services, including PCs, printers, scanners et al., IBM, Telex, and Honeywell/Bull.

All brands in fact. Gen'l reqs in the beginning, then detailed and individualized per 8-10 sections, except for boilerplate.

"I'm tired." Depression settles upon Me like cold damp blanket, upsetting natural rhythms, dampening my confident spirit. *Was that the right decision? Or shudda' asked Chuck first?*   As day progresses becoming unsure   what's right. *This is not like me at all.*

"Tony, what do you think DEP will say when we tell them to re-justify their vendor request?" Anthony Gibbons is also handling all the state agency inventory reporting and is a whiz on Access like Carl. Tony, a real gentleman, thoughtful, never rash, always sits and stands up straight, dressed in pressed suit, white shirt and tie. *I like it when we go to lunch.* Tony even gives me his 1st book of poetry, **Dove** one day at Town House.

It's our delicious Greek greasy spoon diner — warm welcomes from Spiro, Mary and Henrietta, er, Hank. Mary and she keep up running patter of "I'm better than you." "Oh no you're not, what about that large party . . . ."

DEP's the **Department of Environmental Protection**, and I know I'll hafta call Mike Vrancik, their chief fiscal accountant. "Will he get it for us? What if he refuses?' "Talking outloud, conjuring his refusal to change his justification for spending tens of thousands of dollars. "How will he react?" Suddenly remember: Mike is the most congenial and accommodating guy at Carroll Street administrative offices.

"Sure, Rod, don't worry about it, I'll email it over in an hour," Mike says, and I know he will.

Rushing to get the 25 mil IT waiver over to Shifty and the Waiver Unit at PB, by June 1st.

Darker catastrophes popping into head, not just from poor decisions, but physical ones like losing My family to a car accident. "Dear God nooo." Fighting a house fire. Envisioning gruesome *pictures* of Baha'is in Iran being tortured by some fanatical   clergy   or   gov't   police.
By 10 out front of the building having 2nd smoke, right on time with regulars.
Breath issuing forth hot clouds in cool mist.

Next few days, feeling . . . worse -- but not sick? blaming meds for depression and insecurities, throw some pills away surreptitiously. *I'm smokin' more.*   Down mood improves. Life turning better, *ah, no . . . worse.* Wild thoughts filling Me, beginning, *losing control . . .* mind, moods, actions. *How can I possibly work.* Affecting our household. Affecting everyone so badly. *We're arguing.* Janet and I arguing — something just not done,   and never, never, in front of kids. Except now.

Usually both stopping, especially If my voice rises. Then silence, and stony, no conversation til apologizing. Jesse bringing   home   C   in   English,   real   shocker. *Is it from disruptions?*

Morning arrives misty, overcast, again. *Ground snow covers inches, but roads and side-walks just, wet.* Home sitting in living room scanning Sunday papers. Kids in their rooms doing what kids do. *Janet sitting on couch across from Me reading her required* **New York Times.** Here I am on love seat now reading funnies. Only read funnies on Sundays. *Dilbert not to funny or sick today. What's wrong with Scott?* Always try to guess what Doonesbury's saying.

I'm warm, toasty as Jan says, in white terrycloth robe and dark blue slippers. Too warm . . .

Depressed and sensitive.

Aware of Janet's voice, can't focus, *can't hear what she's saying.* slip away.   Of a sudden,   angry,   **exploding.**

"You don't know what you're talking about!" Churning inside. *I can't control this!* Raw, raw anger. Throw papers to floor, rip open front door, push outside, slam it behind me. "Thunk!" Stomping, stomping; down steps, path to driveway, out   to   sidewalk.   Hesitate,   *Which   way   to   go? Gottagetouttahere.   How   can   she   be   so   calm? Can't she see trouble's coming?*

Jan quickly opening front door, yelling,
"Rod . . . Rod! Where are you going?"

Turn back . . . glaring, "None of your business!"
 Storming, storming, purposefully up street. *Can't sway these thoughts.*

Thirty-five degrees surrounding Me, "Why am I so hot?" burning. . . inside

Tension bur**sts**. "More heat. Gotta wipe this sweat!"   Wiping   dripping.   Hands   clenching   sides, plodding   down street,   turn   corner,   continue storming block, purposefully,   onto   Route 524. "Where's the cars?" No traffic encumbers usually   busy   road. Catholics   leaving **St. Vincent's.**
        Spot   under   big   bush   with   browning   leaves, *There, I gotta sit down.* Looks inviting.   Next   to   sidewalk.
 Plop down in snow.   *Hmph.   Who does she think she is?*
 Irate.   Cross legs, robe open. Sitting cross-legged in snow, steaming, screaming face . . .higher,   screams **louder.**

Pulling up . . . black and white Crown Vic . . . pulling up.

It's a black and white. Oh, **Hamilton Police.** *Why they here?* Caring, not caring, what they're doing   *Who called   THEM.   Can't be here.   For me . . .*

Doesn't click. . . . . . .

c-l-i-c-k.   *Close mouth Rodney,   settle into lotus, hands on   lap . . .*

"Hey, how ya doin?" Young officer asking, climbing out passenger side. Lights not flashing. Officers appearing friend-ly. First officer   approaching   slowly, carefully, blue   clad a r m   out-stretched, offerin' left hand.   Right   at   side.
        Near holster

"Why   don't we go for a ride   and   we'll   get   you feeling better in no time?"

Say nothing. stare past, *Don't look at his eyes,* yet ever obedient,   standing   upright,   honorably, walking to car,   ducking in,   *tight   opening.*

(Officer shuts door.)

I'm not ill.   Not.

Quiet,   please. I'm thinking. Thinking . . . .
Not quiet Inside . . . .

4.2 Another Hospital

Ending up in **Hampton House** in Burlington County, amidst flat farms, rolling hills. Precious greenery.   Lowbrick building with 10-foot   walls.   Can't   see   inside   .   .
        Injecting heavy drugs again, Haldol, Thorazine.
Too powerful,   dulling senses,   Mind,   slowly,   quickly.
        More   drugs.   Stagger in line 3 or 4 times daily, behind zombie-like males and females dressed casually,
Like   Me, to dispensary. Mumble name,   nurse   scans wristband, handing Me small white paper cup with pills. Handing me a bigger   *Dixie cup*
        swallowing them . . . *in front of her.*

I   don't   want   problems.   Do   as   I'm   told.
I need smoke   breaks.

212

Shuffle around main floor. *Why can't I focus?*
Random, shooting, curious thoughts, moving, expanding, twisting. Gradually come crashing, yet cycling back up sporadically.

Regular group therapy sessions mornings; *I don't like this*Not going well. Meeting fellow inmates in large grey room, 25 of us seated in a big circle on   black   plastic   chairs,

doctor's   facing   Us.

Tall white smock, black hair, long straight nose, and white   smock. Trying, *Be cool, get . . . points . . .* have discussion. Looking on, but away, *Can't look in eyes*, Can't   listen,   not listening, only hearing disjointed phrases.

Him speaking softly, methodically. Me frustrated *What's this nonsense?   Get to the point.*

Becoming   nasty   and   combative,   shouting   pointed questions   answers:

"I don't care about others feelings. What about mine."
"Cindy doesn't know what she's saying! Having kids is not a burden." Doctor staring.
"Jimmy, I don't agree with that." *Is that a glare?*

Only supposed to speak after raising our hand,   being recognized.

Cut off speakers mid-sentence; *bad   habit.*

Shouting   certainly   not   allowed   .   .   .   .

Ruffled doctor trying to maintain cool head; finally says, in louder, deeper voice, "Rodney, you need to leave now, we'll see you in group tomorrow." Rising and stomping out, slamming door behind me.   Smoking privilege   revoked.

"You have to act better in group," whispers orderly after dinner. Me,   madder.   Dawning on Me, *Gotta have cigar-*

ettes, Gotta get away. What do I hafta do? Act   *nice?* Sidlin' up to girl with long green streak in brown hair,   blue jeans,   mottled blouse,   "When ya goin'   home?"

"Well, the doc told me another week if I reach the third privilege level."

"Privilege level?   What?"

"They must have told you. Maybe it slipped your mind?" *She's kind.   Slipped My Mind?*   After first day, out of it,   not remembering . . . .

"Good behavior and taking your meds every day earns points. At level two they let you stroll the grounds outside the walls. And at level three you go home."

Ah, that's it. Maybe I can fool 'em. Maybe, I can just act nice . . . **they'll let me smoke . . .** *leave.*

Not payin' attention to what anyone shared earlier, but starting to. Try to appear "rational." Begging and pleading whoever'll listen,   "I will be good in group, I promise."

Smoking — important; one of few things I have control over; but strict break times. Eventually approved to go outside with others, to same hemmed in, grassy area. Surrounded by single-story buildings on 2-sides, sliding door on other; egress, regress; opposite, tall, sturdy wooden fence, grey in tone. One sapling in small square, full branches too low to walk under. *It's drizzlin'.* Stoop under, hold trunk, wait for orderly's flickers.

Cold dropping on Me from leaves. Irking me.

Janet bringing Kools. No concern or missing her, kids, anyone, anything. Feeling sorry for Myself and playing for sympathy; more from guilt at being here than from guile; altho motivation to escape still nudging Me toward submissiveness now,   *biding   the   right   opportunity.*

214

At first half like My comrades, shufflin' 'round, head down, avoiding their eyes, they avoiding Mine. Speaking not, barely functioning. Staying in bed hours, with its rubber pad, green sheet on top and green pillow. Gradually decreasing Haldol and Thorazine. *Changing Me.* Start feeling better, *Alive.* Draw with pens at dawn on paper on table in common area. Colored papers, crayons. No sense of big overhead clock hands moving.

Tired of planning elaborate escapes. Join in their small arts and crafts in other wing, paint dull white clay pot a green glaze *that looks black.* Planter looking like bamboo on outside; 8-inches in diameter and 6 tall.

Next day telling me "We've fired it in our kilns."

See it 2-days later on shelf with other clay creations, dark green with slight yellowish highlights, *I love it. Mine!* But not seeing it again.   Earning other privileges, having meals with Janet in airy, light-filled, modern gleaming cafeteria, its long pine tables reminds Me of **IKEA.** Try to appear upbeat to her, but awkward.

Hesitantly, *"Ah, how are the . . kids?"*

"They're fine Rod, they think you're away for work."

During later stages looking forward to these kibitzes . . . immensely. Another, allowed to walk outside. *Outside! Free again.* Brick compound on the grassy grounds. "Ah, human."

Oh how to see the Sun, and lay in Grass,
*   feel it thru my fingers,*
*   run under Trees and soar in the Wind!*
*   Glorious Wind!   Free*

Beginning to care.   But going back inside . . .
*   What a downer . . .downer. . . .*

Four long weeks — released. Janet picks me up, again. None of my friends, family or co-workers asks me for details upon my return, and true to form, we all "move past it."   Sorta.

215

When I had left Hampton House, when they handed over my green planter, *joy!* Home, rush in. Place it in kids bathroom. It's a lovely, highly glazed, perfect pot for the shelf it's on. When happening to see that pot and its philodendron, *only seeing a nice-looking pot and healthy plant.*

No image of its source.   *I won't dwell on negatives.*
   Uncanny ability to forget.

4.3 European Interlude

It's a pleasing late May of '95 when Jesse graduates as a **Spartan** from **Steinert High School**, in the top group of his class. He's previously gotten good **SAT**s, and   Jan and I have never doubted he's going to college. He wants to and so do we; he's prepared himself well for this new phase with renewed energy and enthusiasm. *And he's never been a slouch in those areas anyway.*

We're equally proud of Kate, who's moving from **Reynold's Middle School** to Steinert after him, with good grades and lots of friends.

To everyone's delight my brother Ralph had previously announced his engagement. Ralph, a banker, had   met his attractive fiancee Yvonne, while both working at **Skandinaviska Enskilda Banken (SEB),** a Swedish bank founded and largely controlled by the Wallenberg family, on Park Avenue in Manhattan. Yvonne was a native Suede, and also announced they'd be married -- outside Stockholm.

Mom & Dad's generation including their brothers and sisters, their kids and grandkids, my cousins, first and second, were all attending.

What fun!

Jan says, "Go. But don't forget to take your pills."

The gang and I take a livery van to Newark Airport, 25 of us, arriving in blue daylight. By this time my salary has returned to its 1992 level, never to be recouped, but we can afford my trip. Janet feels deathly ill whenever flying, unavoidable, so she sadly stays home with the kids. Happily as well. We all paid our own way.

Sheer summer beauty of Sverige, fresh clean air and skies, friendly smiling people, the ancient city's narrow streets, its stone-carved bridges, and surrounding seas, all breathtaking. We all arrive in another van, disembark, and watch the distinguished couple, being driven to 400 year-old stone church in a 1920s Rolls Royce acquired by Yvonne's brother, Ronnie.

A car enthusiast, he's associated with an auto shop, and races his yellow **Camaro** surreptitiously late at night on deserted highways, with friends and watchers gathering on the sidelines in the after-midnight hours. I'd seen the smiling faces of excited onlookers, male and female, while watching the 3 a.m. race video played the night before at his house. *Thrilling!*

The simple traditional Christian ceremony on high platforms in its dark interior, doesn't linger. We all travel by reserved coach to the reception at the historic **Grand Hotel in Soltsjobaden.** *Well-named,* it stretches and looms over a picturesque marina packed with tall masts. ***They match its tall white walls and black turrets.***

All of us lodging at the convenient conference center 'cross the way, with dull dining, kitchen, motel-like rooms. Breakfast provided by our wonderful female servers. At 6 one morning I find myself with keys to a white van, and go explorin' alone looking for . . . *what else?* Driving, finally finding Wawa-type store on the highway 8-miles outside the tiny village. *I guess chose the right direction,* because whole area is very rural with mild sloping hills and green flush low fields. Mostly I we lounge and sip and enjoy our company, sharing stories, laughin'; cousins, nieces and nephews listenin' or absorbed in **Game Boys.**

Mentally, spiritually, tryin' to psyche myself out while in the last two days. Enamored by the beauty of this country, itching to take off . . . *Explore.* Trying to, but stymied — no car keys. This Nature's, immenseness and historicality, quaintness, *overwhelming* my being and I'm experiencing the joy of *existence*, alone; skin . . . tingling. Waking before dawn each morning and pacing, climbing the grounds and 14-foot boulders along the edge of the dark blue **Baltic Sea,** musing *"Should I cross to that small rock island?"*

Everyone's experience . . . exceptional, and the family becomes closer, happier.

It's the first time I've been out of the states; but it wouldn't be

My last.

Less than a year later,

will give in hard

to

roving inclinations.

*   *   *

In the Fall Jess starts **Drew University,** and thanks to a healthy scholarship, the choice had been easier. He and we thrilled with the small liberal arts college, located in Madison, NJ. Liked for its openness, campus trees, black squirrels, and well-known President, my ex-Governor Tom Kean.

Small but idyllic. **President Kean,** a very personable and edu-cated leader I had shaken hands with twice. *Once as   my Governor,* who has a sterling reputation, trustworthy and is   adored by   students. He has an open door policy and a rapport   *kings would sigh for.*

I had liked Drew right from the get-go when they required freshmen to have laptops. *Hey, that's pretty cool, I like that. Smart.* Also progressive, and   Jess   is   a   whiz   on   them anyway. So   we   buy   him   a   DEC   laptop at **Circuit City.** Furthermore, Treasury's Fiscal Officer Mike McKitish, who I admired, also a nice guy, was handling their finances as **CFO.**[?]

Packing our large '90 midnight blue **Pontiac Transsport,** the **Boat,** we initiated 4-years of **Garden State Parkway** treks.

Kate's voted secretary of key club and playing field hockey as she progresses, and becomes student manager of the girl's team. *Sad I never get to watch her play.* But Jan's there often, after her last class and bus duty.

Life seems to best it can be in our little township of
        80,000.

Rolling thru red **S T O P** sign leaving our development -
                              - earns a ticket.

Inshallah.

5.0 LAST EPISODE?

5.1 A New Doc

January, '96 my psych for the past 8-years, Doctor A, leaves GreenSpring and opens his own practice. Liked him a lot, would miss 'im, but not upset. *That's just the way it is.* So the HMO calls and assigns me to Dr. Wolf. I make a late afternoon appointment at 4, as I do with all my doctors and blood tests. *So not missing much work.*

Janet and I figure we'll give him a chance. On the first visit meeting him alone in new office on Bellevue Avenue. Young, good looking male psychiatrist.

File's open in front of 'im.

"Hi Mr. Richards, tell me about yourself."

Talk 10-minutes about my bipolar history, wanting to keep the session short. Rushing thru feelings whole time thinking, *okay, be normal, can't read My thoughts, only My face. Stay deadpan. Stay cool. Tell him what he wants to hear — no surprises. Everything's fine. Stop twitching.*

How come he doesn't ask to see my tongue or hold out my arms like Dr. Argueta? Don't ask or offer.

220

Concentrate. Don't slip and ask him a hundred questions about himself and his qualifications and background and what happened to Dr. A and if I can stop taking some pills. I'm wary.

I don't know you from Adam.   I can fool you.

Stop fidgeting!

Act cool.

"So, how are you doing? Have you had any racing thoughts?"

"No, none. I'm fine." Janet wasn't with me, I lied easily.

Sends me on my way. At the receptionist's window on the way out, I make next month's appointment with him.

When I get home, Janet's keenly interested. "What was he like?"   Hiding laughin' face.

"Well . . . he's okay. We talked for fifteen minutes. He's not as good as Dr. A. and I see him again in a month." Walk hurriedly but carefully to our bedroom. *Quick, turn on TV before dinner so **I won't have to answer more questions.***

5.2 Leaving Work

[Friday February 2, Day one]

Damn clock. 2 a.m. *Can't sleep* — stare at the lighted cable box, turning over minutes. *Close your eyes*. Closing 'em for 15th *time*. Time at a standstill. *Sleep for God's sake.* Hoping. Wide awake now, 6:30, Janet's back towards me, sleeping soundly; her baby snores barely audible, never hindering my sleep.   Usually.

But now it's a buzzsaw to sensitive ears.

We both get up at 7 on workdays.

Janet's alarm, "Woop . . . woop . . . ." She reaches right arm out, pushes button. Let Jan get up first, as usual, putting her robe over her pajamas, sliding tiny feet into slippers, knowing she's going outside to pick up morning paper. Then she'll sit at kitchen counter reading it page by page, looking for names and photos of people she knows, or past and present students. Of course, TV news and weather report on as well.

Now I can take my shower. "Ahh, love hot water from **Waterpik.**" "Ugh." Hate deciding what to wear in the mornings, so I've laid out my clothes the night before, as I've done every night since '79. Light grey sharkskin suit hangs on our closet door with white shirt, black belt, black casual rubber-soled shoes on floor, and red power tie hanging from doorknob — standard work attire. I rotate three suits; have dozens of innocuous dark ties, many from old yard sales. Fully dressed in 4-minutes, spray on best cologne, **Polo.** *Always on my birthday list.*

Janet comin' in, "It's in the 30's out, Rod, wear your warm coat." By then she's in the bathroom, door ajar, puttin' on makeup getting ready for school. Her school building's 85 years old and summer temps exceed its age. Tall fans only blow superheated air.

It's criminal.

222

Walk closer to bathroom door. "Bye Hon, see you later, have a good day at school."

"You too. Drive carefully," responding with ao smile. Smile knowingly back, *one of Janet's favorite phrases,* cause' she *never had an accident* and means it. **Always means what she says.** I lie.

Pull off black **London Fog,** my one nice overcoat, out of living room closet and put it on against upcoming chill. Pick up wallet, 30+ in cash and change, strap my black **Casio** before leaving. Usual for this time. *Uneventful 15-minute ride in medium traffic cruising west/north on the blessing that's Interstate195. What an easier 6-mile commute. Thank you Feds and DOT.*

Park in thousand car State garage on Bank Street, lock up, walk along Willow smokin', insert card key and enter back of 50 West. No guard in back. *Always quiet at 8. Nice not having to walk far on nasty weather days; love free parking provided by John P. in charge of all spots. It's like gold. All employees should have free parking.*

Take elevator as usual to our lobby shared with **Pensions** offices. Use key again, nobody around. *Didn't feel like steps.* Once a month walk the 8-flights up, or six, not today. *I'm in a hurry.*

Our young boss, Chuck, the canny director of our division, often takes the steps.

Rush to My office slightly rushed. I hear My head say, *Close the door Rod.* Suddenly nervous, agitated, high strung. *But wait. I'd better leave the door open or staff will think I have someone in here with me.* I have an open door policy. *Try to appear normal,* My Voice telling me. Pace the morning, flitting thru papers, notes, *debate. What to do.*

Unable to focus attention on a project, increasingly worked up, stopping . . . clearing webbed thoughts . . . *listening . . .*

Hearing one Word in the center of my mind,
> **"privily-whispered"** in a **"honeyed-tongue"**
> . . . inhaling sweet fragrance . . . [30]

H a i f a

Reply instantly. **"Baha'i World Center"**

Long subconscious desire: meet with Universal House of Justice. Not connecting to first episode. Never been to **Holy Land**, anywhere really. **Inner Voice**, only voice I hear, directing Me, *"I'll be successful announcing myself to supreme governing body and just barging in on deliberations."*

But here, now. Co-workers will think . . . I'm at lunch. Bolt from building to garage, race home — *Janet's at school as are Jesse and Kate* — run to den, grab key from hidden spot in desk drawer. Race to **Yardville Bank** 'round corner. Sign in, open safe deposit box, retrieve passport, return box, then, to teller, "3 hundred please," from our joint account. Speed home.
Gotta put key back. Jan won't know.

Time. Don't have much time!

"Crap." *Glasses at work next to computer. Without 'em, I'm nearly far-sighted.* Grab old aviator pair from bedroom dresser top drawer. Remembering, remembering, *Left over-coat at work too.* Decide. It's *sunny now, don't need London Fog.*

Not . . . going . . . back to work.

Hop into My jet, Granddad's banged up jalopy, drive to . . . *Plane. That's how I'll get there.* Newark Airport . . .

straight shot to Exit 13A. Forty miles, hurry up!
Drivin' 85, 90, jetting smoothly on and off fastest lane.
Possessed, determined, plotting . . . .
Turnpike over, on highway, watch ubiquitous parking signs.

Easily find long-term lot. D94.

Thrust car

into slot.

Knowing where I'm going . . .

5,000 miles away.

5.3 Surprising Rejection

Waiting. *Impatient.* Standing, climbing up shuttle, then hopping off at international terminal. Pick up mounds bar, flashy spy novel, $5.89 at small stand.

"Thanks, eat this now and read on the plane." *She's paying no damn attention. Have to explain Myself or she'll think I'm weird.*

Find terminal; walk quickly to **El Al Airlines** desk, almost running, compelled. *Got to buy ticket to Haifa for next available flight.* Knowing flying Israeli airline is safest. *Slow down.* Casually stroll up to female clerk at empty counter.

"Can you please tell me next flight to Haifa? I'd like a ticket." Asking in politest voice.

"Tomorrow evening – **Tel Aviv** is the earliest. We're closed now for Shabbat."

Vague idea . . . *Shabbat . . . holy day?* Don't clarify what that means.

"Do you have any luggage?" *She can see I don't.*

"No."

Nearby well-dressed man joining her, asks me, "Can you please wait sir?"

Wait . . . an hour. *I'm fidgeting again.* Sitting in row of cushioned chairs, beside myself. Wondering . . . *what's going on?* After all, *He asked me to wait.* Hopes to obtain flight still high. But shakier the longer clock ticks. Jumping . . . subject to subject, not once feeling negative about my chances of buying one.

Smiling middle-aged woman in navy skirt, white blouse, crossed navy tie, and a dark swarthy man in suit and long tie call me back to the counter, asking, smiling, "Passport and driver's license please." Hand them over. Man walks away with them.

"Why are you going to **Israel**?"

"Visiting the **Baha'i Shrines on Mount Carmel.**"

"How long are you staying?"

"Three days." *Only because had heard many Baha'is visited Haifa and received 3-day passes.*

"What luggage do you have with you?"

"None." *Again?*

"Do you know anyone in Israel?"

226

"No."

"Okay, please take a seat, sir, we'll call you."

Sitting in same spot, half an hour; anxiouser. Shouting in My Mind, *Hey, I'm losing time! I need to get moving. . .* Neither all the passengers and people going to and fro, nor novel, distracting enough from *worry . . . my new . . . worry.* Determined, *need fly El Al for direct flight. Try other airline? Oh can't, they have passport.*

Reservation clerk calls, "Mr. Richards?" *Finally!*

Calmly walk up to same counter/stall.
Handing back passport, license.

"I'm sorry, we can't accept you."

"Why not? Isn't everything in order?" *Why not?*

"I'm sorry, we just can't," nearby man reiterates firmly.

"Thanks for nuthin'," *SonofaB,* stomping away, *What? Why? I'm perfectly normal!* Not sure what to do. *Dammit! Wasted my time. They've made it clear I'm not getting a ticket.* "Humph" Leave to look for other airline, *they looked jittery about something.*

I don't look odd, do I?

I do.

5.4 London, On the Way

How get to there? What's heading there soon?

Threading My way thru masses, see big board — regard **BA** direct flight to **London's Heathrow** leaving just after 6. *Hmmm* Book passage on **Jumbo Jet,** My first, using credit card. *How cool is that. . . .*

No questions, simple, "Thank you, sir, for flying **British Airways**." Waiting area. Remembering, *I've never been on such a jumbo plane. Wow, that's going to be so neat.* Eagerly anticipating. *I need somethin' to eat.*

Find assembly line café. *Sandwiches look terrible, old, stale, leftover from lunch.* Buy large coffee and pastry. Cream and sugar at side counter. *Umm, coffee.* Gulping. *Tasty . . . for an airport.*

Spending hours sitting, eyeballin', people and kids and bags, bags, bags. Chat with strangers, two young girls, best friends, stopping over on way to school in Switzerland, visiting Manhattan.

Even businessman, returning after 3-days of "bored" meetings for new business startup. Then, *I'm alone.*

Methodically laying script out. Dozens of scenarios checked off. "*Dear members of the Universal House of Justice . . . . "* Dozens . . . ..

Wholeheartedly -- looking forward to this. Thoughts racing, not staying on single concept more than 30-seconds, propelling me -- into structures -- of advanced civilizations. . . . Having flown domestic numbers of times, inter-nationally to Sweden. *Not fearful of unknown. I can handle Myself.* Projecting ahead . . . *difficult now* . . . no concerns about outside U.S.

I'll be okay regardless.

. . . Feel entirely confident . . I know, sense, abilities . . .
capable of overcoming any obstacles placed in my path,
power . . . coursing thru me.

Mission . . . *clear.*

Check onboard with 300 others for 6 hour flight. Told to expect to arrive by 7:00 a.m. London time. *Better reset watch.*

Jetting off, *pushing Me into seat* as behemoth rises. No need to grip arm rests.   *No fear, in God's Hands.* Calm, looking out.

Amazing yet so familiar. Relax, **you're fine.**

Don't know I'll try to jet off Myself . . . at 30,000 feet.

Enjoying flight tremendously. *So high! Love it.* Looking out window as We skim above eastern seaboard, dwindling sunlight, smiling at it, laughing "Heh, heh, heh." Quickly gaining altitude and settling in, darkness, clouds, obscure further viewing.

Try reading spy novel; *I can't get into this. . Should I be on alert?* Reading flight magazine cover to cover. Passenger sleeping next to Me. Open magazine again, skimming pages, find crossword. *Good.* Always carry pen, begin fairly difficult one for 15-minutes. Loving puzzles, always, this, no different. Finishing, but for 7-letters.   Trying again, thumbing back, reading ads, scanning images of islands, scanning, put back, open spy novel;

Hmmm . . . for a period;   harsh   thought —

Should I sleep? Try sleeping.

Bor-ing.   Nod.

5.5 Renaissance Man

[Saturday February 3, Day Two]

Intermittent dreaming, colorful, glowing, til first light, fully waking, gazing out oblong window again. Used to fitful sleeping. *Reinvigorated . . . more alive . . . .*

Skimming over green **Emerald Isle** at dawn, home of our original Cavanaugh clan, Mom's family surname. [31] Hoping, wistfully. *Would like to visit someday.*

Not thinking once about Janet, kids, work, the past — only Me, moving forward.

Hearing only one **Voice**, none others.

Not looking behind or thinking ahead . . . moving . . . dodging . . . connecting — axon to synapse, thought to thought, impulse to impulse.

Standing up, gliding up aisles, looking for a smile, giving nods and greetings . . . . *Happy.* ***Flying   high.***

Approaching Heathrow, *Ah Ha. I know who's here.*
Must visit. Expects Me.

*His gravesite on city's outskirts . . . **obligated** . . . to go . . . part of mission now, My Mission!*
"Make this My private pilgrimage."

What do I know of him, leader of the Baha'i Faith?
Recalling his history . . .

Called **Guardian** by his grandfather, 'Abdu'l-Baha. Appointed by Him in 1921 sole Interpreter and **Head of the Faith.** Shoghi Effendi's sudden death, sad and dramatic, London in '57, well-known by Baha'is. Not understood at time, confusion.

His writings enthralling, since Bill Foster originally taught us, smitten by Guardian's command English,

British, Arabic, Persian prose, sentences as long as a page, letters as long as books. Tremendous stress he was always under; directed fledgling faith for 36-years.

This renaissance man's physical heart just gave out, but his astute mind, spirit . . . and real heart . . . with us forever . . . .

7:30 a.m., disembarking, converting 30-dollars to pounds. *Ah.* Sipping from large cup of coffee, sitting, lounging, thinking, thinking, taking in lay of the land. *Think.* See sign pointing to London tube, realizing *can get around anywhere* . . . . Following moving throngs, arrows. Cemetery on outskirts of city. *What town is grave located in? Better call information. Must be on best behavior. Or they'll send me home.*

Tube entrance Phone booth, dialing

information, asking operator.

"*Number for Baha'i National Center please?*

Write on palm. Connects us. . .

Cheery, bright young woman answers.

"Good morning, Baha'i National Center. May I assist you?"

"Hi, ah I'm a Baha'i visiting London and wondered how to get to Shoghi Effendi's gravesite?"

"And your name sir?"

"Rodney Richards." *Might they know who I am?*

"Yes, Mr. Richards, thank you for calling. Will you be staying in London long?"

"No, just to visit the grave."

231

"I see, and where are you now if I may ask?"

Why's she asking that? Who is she really? Why does she want to know where I am?

"Yes, I'm at Heathrow and I can see a tube connection here."

"Correct, you want to take the **Blue Line** to Arnos Grove on the other side of London, almost at the end of the line. The site is now called the **New Southgate Cemetery** and is just a short walk from the station on Brunswick Park Road."

Immediately at ease,   *Oh, she's giving me directions, not turning me in!*

"Ahh, it's not **Great Northern Cemetery** anymore?"

"Oh no sir, they changed that name many years ago when the suburb of New Southgate was established."

*Well, glad I called. **I WAS going to find it.***

"Great, thanks a lot, and you have a great day."

"Is there anything else I can help you with Rodney?"

"Ah, no, not necessary. Thanks a lot." *Now to get there.*

"You also Rodney!" hanging up.

As we do, terrifying thought strikes. *Is she reporting my name to her superiors?*   Passes.

"I was divinely guided to London, I'm convinced."

Buying round trip ticket at kiosk, standing on platform 5-minutes, smoothly silver-white cars pull up, stops; people herd on, quiet, unremarkable. Polite. *Don't shove and squeeze like Manhattan.*

I can go anywhere. Do anything. Nothing going to stop me. The Path . . . clear.

Long riding thru green low countryside, 9-kilometers on **Piccadilly Line**. Traversing city limits. Car reminding me of New York subway only fancier, cleaner, *altho, they're not bad.* Plastic seats seem, feel, oddly familiar. *Just like subway?* Closing eyes . . . hearing whooshing, conversations, crisp announcer's voice . . . for next 40-minutes. Nodding. Flat green fields, wheat, *dream,* bushes, plentiful. *Dream.* Quaint cottages.

Hear, "Arnos Grove."

Spy watch, 9 30. Emerge underground exit, view wide street with few shops. *Tight 2-story brown-stones.*

Circumscribed newsstand, green tarp sides and top. Sundries and flowers straddles station. "How much?" Pay young man pences for bouquet of pink carnations, ask, "Do you know the way to the Southgate Cemetery, please?"

Pointing to his right saying "That way chap," as if he's done it a thousand times -- which he probably has. *I thought that'd be the way and I'm right.* **Confirmation** once more. **Guided.**

Walking north 2 blocks, sidewalks neat, planters on windows. *Hey, clean too, not like American streets and highways.* Past well-kept low row homes with no front yards, nearing busy lanes and 2-sides of broad, round, *traffic circle? No light, crosswalk. I thought we only had these in Jersey?* Sign says **Betstyle Circus.** *Does "Circus" mean circle?* Wander thru oncoming traffic.

Impervious. Ignore those damn horn blasts. Pedestrians have right of way. Focus ahead. Continue next block following long low stone wall . . . *cemetery wall,* spy

233

entrance on right. Main iron gate filigreed on sides, arching over narrow macadam drive.

Reaching right place. *Knew I'd find it; no doubt in Mind. Not a problem.*

Seen photos of gravesite; dignified. Single 9-foot white marble column, supporting Corinthian capital and white marble globe. **The golden eagle.** Perched so proudly atop, wings open. *Head held high.*
No clue where it might be located in this sprawling place, look for visiting mourners to ask; squinting atop multi-aged gravestones, up winding little road. *But, It's early.* However, notice enticing caretaker's stone and wood cottage on right. *Try there.* Tentatively approach, knock on old thick wooden door.

Opened immediately -- showing stout, casually dres-sed Engishman, broad toothy smile, "Welcome! Wel-come," with right hand thrusting out. *Hey!* Smiling back, grasping tightly calloused aged hand and entering. Grey interior, consists of main room with miniscule kitchen to side; small **Toilet** in back. *Pay attention to sign, Must go soon.*

Adjusting eyes to darker light, noting two other
fellows in room also,
standing to the side chatting . . .

Lo and behold . . . Recognize one as Baha'i acquaintance, *Mark.* Persian from North Jersey, recognizing Me easily, "Salaam, Rodney!"

Called My name, giving Me warm embrace as we say "Allah'u'abha!" -- like old friends, just as most Baha'is do *when running into each other after a long time. The last time seeing Mark, years earlier, when our state was only one District, and had our annual conventions in a Jersey City school auditorium. How fortuitous. Running into Mark 3-thousand miles from home.* Even if connection tenuous.

However, sense of relief seeing someone I know -- short-lived. Mark immediately shoving large bound coffee table book under My nose and turning pages, showing Me gorgeous color photographs of Baha'i Shrines. In   Haifa.

Exactly where I'm going after this.

"I have a few copies of this marvelous new book about the Shrines. You can see these beautiful photos, some never before taken. It only costs 75 dollars and part of the proceeds support the World Center." Handing me open book, thumb thru more. *I'm not interested in this. But better act it.* Two inches thick; weighs a pound +.

Knowing what's coming next, "Wow Mark, awesome book. It's certainly beautiful! But traveling light, not even staying here. On way visiting those very Shrines. Sorry, just can't lug around that book right now, but it looks fabulous." *Ya gotta be kiddin'. You're holdin' Me up.*

Mark seems crestfallen, mumbling, "Uh, can I buy it from you some other time?" I feel bad for him, just trying to make his quota.

Politely desisting, catching up on other Jersey events   5-more minutes, telling him again, "Family's fine."

Morning closing and haven't even left Janet a note where I was going, nor called home. Caring nothing except for Me -- and goal. Excusing Myself, giving Mark last hug, make bee-line   for   **Toilet,**   quickly   doing   business.

Wash up. Look in mirror.   *Gaunt, wide-eyed, unkempt.*
Straighten up, wet hand thru hair.

Mentioning Janet and the kids, *guilty.* Interrupt caretaker and friend, asking, "Is there a phone I might use? I'll be happy to pay for the call."

"Of course, we have a phone. Just leave some pence in the can," showing me to large grey box on kitchen wall. Follow typed directions above the phone.

Stay calm, focus now. D e e p breaths.

Choose words carefully.

Is there any Remover . . .

5.6 "What the Heck . . . ?"

Home number rings 5 times. "Hello?"

"Ah, Bob, it . . . it's, Rodney."

"Oh my God, where are you man? Everyone's worried sick. Just got home from work, so glad you got me."

"I'm...I'm in London, visiting Shoghi Effendi's grave."

"What the heck are you doing there? You never came home from work yesterday! Janet called and they didn't know where you were. Janet's beside herself!"

236

Don't think. "I know . . . having to do this, now."

"I don't believe it. I just don't believe it . . . . Well, are you coming home?" Demanding to know. *Do I tell truth?*

"Don't know yet, . . . Still on way to Haifa."

Silence.

"Bob?"

"Rod, look, you really need to come home as soon as you can."

"I know, but can't, I must finish this."

"What should I tell Janet?"

"I'll be back in a few days."

"Are you serious?"

"Yes, I'm Okay. Tell her not to worry, Can take care of Myself. Listen, hafta go."

"Just tell me you'll be careful, and call Janet will you?"

"I'll think about it, but will stay in touch."

"Okay, you promise?"

"Yeah, I'll let you know where I am."

"What else can I tell Janet? She needs to know."

"Just tell her the truth: I'm safe and will be home soon."

Pause. "Oh, ah, okay, but . . . you better stay in touch."

"Okey-dokey, will do."

"Bye Rod, and please . . . be careful.”

Phone call . . . *I imagined worse* , but not nearly courageous enough to . . . *call* . . . *Janet.* Leave 2, pound notes in the jar by the phone . . . . *She's a damn good wife: loves me unconditionally. Has strong will and is independent; strong enough, smart enough, handle anything. Good wife -- incapable of not worrying -- about me, children, even on most mundane days. Ever since early days in Hopewell, we have pact, always let each other know . . . whereabouts . . . .*

Not now . . . hafta do this.

Mind, heart, can't focus on family, not work, nothing at all, except one thing. *Right now.*

On way to . . . Haifa. *Won't be stopped.*

Saying goodbyes to friends in cottage. Ask directions to gravesite.

"Not far up the path, **on the left.**"

"Bye gang, have a nice day!"

Mark saying, "Khoda Fez, Rodney."

Head out towards grave. Shut large wooden door behind Me, meditate on Guardian's life. *What a sacrifice! Yet I know he laughed.* Walking up driveway.

See column on left. 15 x 20 foot plot, bordered by rows of mums, tiny bushes, turning onto 10-foot walkway up middle.

Hear feet crunching small white pebbles. Surrounded by low marble railing supported by thin columns. Main column and eagle standing tall in center on speckled 9 x 9 tiered white marble base.

No one else here, *deserted.*

    Cemetery deserted. Me. Corpses.

Alone.

Brisk air, watching wisps of increasing breaths.

Heart lightly pounding.

    Bending, tenderly place carnations on base. *Wishing I knew what flowers he liked.* Stand in respect, meditate more on his life's writings. (Long minutes pass, until . . .) begin . . . to . . . cry. Tears rolling down, within seconds collapse, head on arms, at foot of steps, sobbing for Shoghi Effendi: for his great burdens carried from a youthful age, his sacrifices made for the Faith, his eye for perfection in all his doings, his planned gorgeous gardens in Mount Carmel photos.

    Feeling shock his sudden death caused handfuls of pioneering believers, when few institutions established to shepherd Faith thru obscurity. "Oh dear Shoghi!"

Minutes passing. Rise slowly. "I'm sorry Shoghi Effendi," many times over, wiping eyes with fingers, and wetness on pants. Feelings and tremblings. Tremblings and feelings welling up.   More . . . . *too intense* . . . to maintain.

Realizing, *Stop,* **he's gone too.**

    Clearing mind . . . stepping . . . backwards. Without glancing, leave holy gravesite, turn left. *Don't stop at cottage, straight ahead* . . . . head back to train station.

    Strangely, doesn't seem incongruent at all, dismissing contact with My distraught wife one minute, sobbing   for   Shoghi   Effendi   the   next.

    Inability to care for others, been my greatest flaw from earliest years. Sadly, usually taking conscious effort to express any type of empathy. *Is it my true nature? Or drug cocktail? How feeling at birth- days and funerals? Miracle Janet knowing I love her, and kids too.*

Walking firmly along street, brick and cobblestone paths, finding station easily, waiting mere minutes, boarding train back . . . seeing quotes from **Dispensation.** . . *revealed according to capacity of the age . . .* .Finding it hard to contemplate his prescient statements, with lack of attention paid them. Only struggling group of believers scattered on islands, small towns, few big cities -- even adhering fully. *In Guardian's mind, Baha'is cannot build World Order fast enough; mankind, persisting in its misled directions, misread opportunities, continuing told and untold sufferings, harms.*

Tube running back to airport.

How soon can get to Mount Carmel?

5.7 Roma

[morning continued]

Returning to Heathrow looking at terminal screens, *Flights to Haifa?* Walking up to new El Al counter, pausing. *Will they turn me away again?* Clerk seeing me, looking down . . . looking up. *Mind playing tricks?* Is *she recognizing Me? Can't be.* Blowing past, hiding behind walkers.   Flitting   away.
Energy coursing thru Me. Noticing everything: colors, tones, shapes, vectors, clothes, shoes of passersby. Focus on nothing for longer than seconds.
Find earliest schedule on **Alitalia Airlines**, to Haifa. *It's first one out, hours away.* Approaching their counter res-er-va-tion-ist with trusted credit card again. *Or has Janet*

cancelled it? Has she cut Me off our joint account? Showing passport, sliding card over. *Will it work?*

"Please sign here." Only one stop, then Haifa. *Yes. Is clerk like a "counter revolutionist?"* Pay $250 with stopover in Rome. *No questioning, but no thank you from revolutionist either. Crap! Would've paid anything to fly direct.* But not willing to risk failure. **Move Forward**

Outside. Smoking. 20-minutes later, another. Finding airport McDonald's. Eating small cheeseburger, fries and Coke, ugh, but gulping caffeine. Seeing bobby standing alert by Mac's exit. Big brown and black-striped **German Shepherd,** sitting by his side at the exit-entrance. Him in dark blue uniform, wearing black holster with handgun. Me growing up thinking bobbies don't carry weapons; this dispelling myth. Dog looking friendly, open jawed, long thick pink tongue hanging down, panting moderately. *Hot in here?*

Not aware, **unafraid.** *Protected.* Bending down to pet his head. A growl -- not from dog. "Please don't sir," immediately straighten up. *Don't look back, move off.*

Outside. Must smoke after eating. *Satisfying. Always satisfy.* Welcome nicotine . . . cooling Me.

Back inside. Window shopping back to Alitalia awaiting plane, blaring signs, prices, duty-free shops, or goods being hawked not least bit interesting.
Finally boarding, sit down, kicking up, whisking 890 miles to Rome. Too wound up to sleep much, staring out window. *Wouldn't it be nice without crime? What if nuclear fuels smaller, lighter, only used for cinder block-sized fusion reactors? What if they're safer? What if there's no stereotyping, judgments, false impressions? No crime or poverty?*

Or no . . . . Plotting dozens of utopias.

Thinking on these for 2-hours.

Engines whining's *louder, closer.* Plane setting down at **Fiumicino Airport.** *Might as well see the sights.* Impatient, no luggage, waiting for others in the crowded aisle. Moving out with flowing mass semi-orderly.

Must get to Haifa.

The pilgrimage of every **Roman Catholic** — **Vatican City,** *the* **Basilica.** *Part of My journey. I'm still Catholic.* Universal.

Facing green screen wide-eyed, exchanging pound notes for Lira. Moving on to announcement board. Hours of waiting til next flight. Seeing "Express" sign for "Roma," proclaiming 26-kilometers. *Maybe 20-miles. Too far to walk. To far for cab, too much money. How?* Back into terminal. *Ah.* Follow green **"Express"** signs to train, reaching terminal, but *not there.* Purchase round trip ticket at near-by kiosk. Must wait. Under tall, wide, aluminum canopied expanse. One track, starting and terminating right here. Sitting and fidgeting on green hard metal bench, gaps as wide as its flat metal bars, no one to chat with, lonely, pacing nearly an hour, finally, train pulling in. Last car closest to Me, worn black iron rungs, handles, hop up. Taking window seat on right, fourth seat in, big windows. *Good.* Facing front. Lurching, rolling, *Better.* Peering thru the glass to another land's landscape. Hand conductor ticket. No questions, no odd glances, no "Grazie."

Never been to Roma before. I can do this, easy.

Only 6 bodies sharing car with me. Seeing right thru them. Average people excepting greying Armani suit man, darker than mine, no tie, purple shirt, open white collar. Italian countryside appearing mostly flat with hills in backgrounds as speeding by. Occasionally seeing tall pine trees, looking odd 'cause they're 2-stories, straight up, then green, thick, sprouty branches at very top. Sporadic sentinels, forming large, spread top-growth. *Eerie looking.* **Surreal looking.** Not swaying. *No wind?* Homes low, tannish, bronze color. *Stucco?*

Make another local stop as train fills. Young man 20-something sitting facing me. Not saying "Hello." Handsome youth, shoulder-length thick black hair, olive skin, wearing black leather jacket, black pants, dark shirt. Peering out window like I would normally do. Ignoring Me.

Create big smile anyway. "Buongiorno and good afternoon. How are you?" Easily starting conversation. "Me, part Italiano." Chatting rest of way, understanding his halting English, asking about America and especially baseball.

"Phillies?"

"Nada"

"Yankees?'

"Si, yes!" We talk. Tell him I watched Mantle and Maris. Never heard of 'em.

"Your country, here . . . beautiful like U.S." Gabbing in general terms about My homeland. Not politics; anathema.

Asking him, "St. Peter's Basilica — Vatican?"

"Metropolitana di Roma. Posters." Assuming that means Metro, the subway, like in D.C., having ridden it many times to **Crystal City** and IBM classes. Loving that metro, that city. *Hell, I was born there! Oh, and just follow "signs."*

We continue chatting. Transport to Rome, loudspeaker, Italian, English.

"5-minutes."

Quiet now, smiling. Stop.

"Caio my friend."

"Caio paisan."

Easy.

Exiting drab, large, **Roma Termini Station**, with huge imposing silver portico and glass wall, finding hawker cuz drizzlin' out, paying 3-**Lira** for compact black umbrella instead of black polka dots on orange background. Traffic, confusing, short, blaring, high-pitched beeping. Desperately searching for Metro entrance like Manhattan. Rome looking similar, but low, ancient; few tall buildings above. Seeing no entrance, *Must be inside.* Spending minutes lost in subway catacombs, looking at . . . confusing posters, until deciphering one pointing to **St. Peter's** platform.

Leary of pickpockets . . . . For years carrying wallet in front left pants pocket, feeling it's safe. Dr. Balletto, long-time **chiropractor,** telling Me not to put it in back pocket, make me unbalanced while sitting, making bad back worse. Work, sitting on **Reader's Digest** she'd given me, on opposite cheek, straightening spine.

Entering first car stopping, getting off near Basilica. Seeing small signs, 9-inch square, interspersed on walls, pointing way, follow. Navigate narrow cobblestone streets and stop at **Deli** which has eight tables, ordering, eating provolone and prosciutto panini. Drinking **Perrier**. *Ugh.* Good bubbles. Tasteless to Me. Pepsi or coffee, iced tea when nothing else. Shud'da got coffee. *Roman coffee good?*

Leave, standing out front, cup hands, strike match, inhaling.

No idea of appearance. Cheery-faced, looking for smiles to return. To converse. Not one taker. Finding no good candidate.

Continuing walking 10-minutes til stumbling upon famous Saint Peter's Square before me. *Magnifico.* Halt. Behold round open space before me. Impressive ringed grey-streaked stone columns on sides, and **Egyptian obelisk** standing 80-feet tall, in contrast to particularly tiny and rust-colored **Stations of the Cross**; yet all imposing and significant in   different   ways.

Walking beneath each station, stopping, looking up, visualizing their ancient scenes; knowing them well. Sympathizing with Christ's suffering, feeling it much more acutely in next moments of **New Testament** episodes remembered, carrying the tall metal cross as an alter boy.

Piazza itself, floor of stones, high facade of dirty white circle of ribboned Italian marble.

Basilica, massive from the front, intaking breath "Hhhh." Semi-golden gates into Vatican on left. *Should I ring bell?*

More marble inside, huge columns, shiny and imposing, scattered randomly. Marble floor glistening. Remembering 9-formative-years in Catholic Churches, Latin masses, schools; not feeling attached to trappings, dogma, ceremonies, sermons. *Distant, yet visceral.*

Awe-inspiring and grandiose; *immense, much bigger than **St. Mary's Cathedral** on Warren back home; a lunchtime stop occasionally. . . . 40th anniversary of original St. Mary's burning down. The church I attended every day.*

Treading lightly afoot, not making eye contact.

Tomb in front, tombs below.

Hardly anyone here alive with Me; an empty shell.

Dim lights approaching heartbroken **Virgin Mother**, off to side behind acrylic panel. Cradling Her warm **Son**. Reminds Me, picture on Dad's funeral card. Look down, whisper prayer.

Look deeper at My clasped hands, then at nestled Christ's marble body, coming alive in Inner Eye, adding colors, heat. Light blue robe for **Her**, white for **Him**. Rosy cheeks. Breathtaking and striking. Crying inwardly, then gently, tears trickling,   for **His** suffering,   all   the   **Manifestations'** sufferings.

"Hail Mary, full of grace, the Lord is with thee; blessed art thou amongst women, and blessed is the fruit of thy womb, Jesus. Holy Mary, mother of God, pray for us sinners, now and at the hour of our death. Amen." [32]

So blessed to know of **His Return.**

Heavily moving backwards, a few people not far, continuing on, darker inside now, as if cloud hovering. Many frescoes and statues — *Heavenly.* Dragging me back. *Devoted souls. So few saints and fewer saintesses. So few champions in beginning.* Peering towards heaven, the glorious dome above, a hundred feet above, immediately wonder, *How can I climb that catwalk?* Strolling around gilded and plain walls, scanning, searching eye level for door upstairs, for 10-full-minutes, circumambulating, seeking. *Must be hidden in a wall.*

Forsake my heart's desire, turn abruptly, head outside.

Meditating while walking, barely noting darkened sky, blundering clouds. Blunder upon the papal post office on My right and it's smudgy bronze doorway.

Entering, select and buy two postcards, postage. Writing address I know well, "Hi everyone, Mom. Do you ever visit Rome. The Basilica? Vatican? I'm seeing it with your eyes, Love to you and all.

Be home soon. Rodney"

Not concerned,   care,   for loving   ones.

Oblivious.

Dreaming, billions of champions now.

Exiting, meandering back thru square same way I'd come, once again gazing up upon rusted **Station XIV.** Sadness again, pulling Me into long ago past, yet ever-present.

Threading narrow sidewalks, pay attention to the close-knit, short domiciles and storefronts, not deviating til finding Metro. Riding subway car back, quietly. *Look down and black rubber shoes. Inconspicuous.* Sit and glance at packed passengers, dressed so conservatively, mostly jeans and tops, some light jackets, noticing the blues are thicker. Nearly silent, *What's their stories?* Sympathizing with many downcast faces and, *feeling connected* thru throbbing Italian blood. Too quiet. *They're so close to grand memories Realities.*

Preoccupied . . . contemplating . . . *destiny* . . . *mankind's glorious future.*
   Seen by the **Three Central Figures**, Shoghi, others.

Make Our way to canopied train station, buying ticket, enjoying un-eventful ride, sitting on opposite side now, surveying the peaceful and surprisingly clean landscape out the large window.

Hmmm. Meditating, nodding.

Eating dinner, drinking cola, *Ugh, hate anything but Pepsi, but Coke or* **RC** *next best.* At Rome airport cafeteria, standing and searching announcement board announcing flights to Haifa or Tel Aviv. Buying one-way ticket with credit card on next one, not daring, going, to El Al again. More waiting, waiting hours, waiting all night. In and out, many smokes. Cat-napping slumped on hard grey chair, little padding. Lolling left, right, staring ahead, lids fluttering. More cigarettes. Thanking God for outdoors, clean rest room. Next morning boarding.

   Smaller, dark green and white,
   Alitalia jet heading to Tel Aviv.

5.8 The Holy Land

Passengers filling seats, cramped, 3 seats per side, narrower than usual walkway. Long, wearying, burden-laden, overly crowded noisy trip with active toddlers, crying babies. Parents shushing; no avail. *14-hundred miles. Read, think, plan, meditate, snooze.*

At Tel Aviv, stewardess handing out declaration forms we all must fill out.

Still have black ballpoint pen from work. Fill out card in bold block print.

Man next to Me seeing this, holds up his card, looks at Me quizzically. Heard his **Eastern European** speech earlier, merely smiling, saying, "For **VISA**. For **Customs.**"

He's speaks up, "Slovakia", then, "do . . not . . unerstand Enng-lish."

Politely smile, signaling, *Give me your card.* Handing it to Me with broad grin. Using his passport, fill it out completely, block letters, checking "No's." Handing it back. Shakes My hand vigorously.

Rush, crush and braking pushing me down and back. Landing intact, powerful. Hard. Man thanking Me til reaching gate. Ignoring thank you's, only nod. *Don't want attention.*

Rush, crush and braking pushing me down tighter, back. Arms loose on grips. Smiling out window, My opening to the world. He's made it. Like pressing an easy button.

Walking down long wide ramp at **Ben Gurion International Airport**, thru customs, into great concourse. Only 9. *Only two things to do: Find ATM and directions.* Fiddling with machine, receive shekels. *Card still works.* Asking passersby how to get to Haifa. Someone raises arm, points with forefinger to glass double-doors.

Under broad silver canopy. Train tracks on right, but not there; line of colored vans on left, at curb. Look like taxis. Sunlight streaming down, light blue sky, small puffy clouds, inhaling slight cool breeze deeply. Acknowledging, *The Promised Land.*

Smiling skinny youth approaching, "Where to, sir? Haifa maybe? My sharoot leaves in five minutes. Parked right here, just six dollars American." *Does he know I'm American? How? Should I ask?*

No. But he looks expectant.

Paying, jumping into back of the white van streaked with wide dark scratches, 2-other-passengers already sitting in middle. 20-minutes passing with 4-added; van full with luggage stuffed in the far back, so drive off on Highway 2.
Conversing at once, discovering two other Baha'is heading to Shrines. Conversing eagerly, like long lost friends, sharing hometowns and early declaration stories, where, with whom; personal circumstances . . . *when they became Baha'is;* I'm oldest.
Driving, north . . . 100-kilometers[?] on black 4 lane highway. *As good as home.* Driver weaving in and thru traffic like the pro he is.

Okay, where am I going? Ask, "Anyone know a cheap hotel?"

Driver chirps, "Tower Hotel on Herzel Street be good."

Tower sounds appealing. "Great, please drop me there."

Fifty-minutes to hotel Haifa, giving warm goodbyes, kiss on cheeks to one Persian women, handshaking, two people heading to fancy **Dan Panorama** I've always heard about from pilgrims, looming atop the mountain.
Registering inside with card and passport, clerk assigning Me room on seventh.

Entering, bathroom with porcelain sink, commode, and tub/shower on right. Shrieking, "Bathroom's half the size of room." One low twin bed, thin grey wool blanket hiding it; matches walls.

"What's wrong with using colors of blankets and walls?" One end table, lamp, clock showing 11:00. Looking, watch shows 10:60. *Heh, heh.* Wooden dresser, 4-sticky-drawers standing along main wall with TV on top.

Drawers will remain empty.

Just able to navigate around bed; room cramped and   stuffy. Open curtains a little and one sliding window.

Spending day thinking, conjecturing. *What do I say to the House members? Will they appreciate My company. What name?* **UniCorp?** *UniTcorp?* Rehearse elements of corporation I had written in '79.   Directors, departments clear as day.

Reading, watching TV, hotel movies ^(?), smoking. Open curtains wider. Staring out 7th floor window, turning, purposeful, putting on wrinkled suit jacket.

Must look nice. Remember key, leave.   *Adventure.*

Riding elevator alone down to lobby/foyer,   enter restaurant/lobby, sitting at empty table surrounded   by dozen empty tables, even tho dinner   time; ordering kabobs and rice, safe.   Having no trouble being understood in English by anyone. Ground meat patty, long rectangular shape, semi-tasteless without usual coating of pepper, but what I'm used to at Persian dinners, only those longer grilled   kabobs   on wooden skewers, or cooked half- sized.

Thirsty.   Tolerate   cold   Coke.

Back upstairs, long deep drags, down to nub, hot, burning throat, last one.

No cigarette machine in the   lobby. So?

"Wish there was a balcony. Want to go outside." Striping down, taking long, steaming shower. "Ah feels goood."

Drying with thin white towel, turning right, cold water   off. Turning hot water left, steaming sharkskin suit, shirt,   by hanging them on shower curtain rail, hot water gushing out of silver-plated spigot. Rinsing black socks and grey jockey's in hot water, scalding, barely feeling hotness; hang them on rail as water . . . steam, pouring   out.

 Notice plastic covered cup on counter. "Need   soda and ice." Grabbing coins, room key, grey bucket.
 Opening door.

"Oops!" Nudging shoe into door jamb with big toe. See ing hairy legs. Down long hall buying 2-Cokes, then ice machine, filling to the brim, some "plop, plop, plopping," onto tiled floor. Picking them up, plopping into bucket. Seeing no one. Shouting, "Anyone else on   floor?"   No response.   Kicking   shoe   inside,   returning.
 Hall silent   behind Me.
 Wasting half-hour finding English channel on TV, going in, turning faucets right, steam slowly dissipating, clouded mirror. Write **H A I F A** with finger. Have no sundries. Wiping teeth with forefinger and aqua. Filling cup, ice then   soda. Rinsing. Taking both, placing on end table. Bucket full. Chewing ice, a hard habit. Swooshing swallows   of cola. Chewing more ice.

"Loving curved ice cubes." Laying down. Suddenly a thought. *A thrill!* Jump up full frontal toward double window. Dark out, black, except twinkling   lights   and   tiny windows framed in yellowish glows.
 Unsteady,   swaying,   **"OMMMMMM"**,   open curtains wide, standing looking out over what lies before Me. Spreading out before Me   for   miles.

"Why not push thru big glass like Princeton House?"

Peacefulness waiting. Meeting Dad. Body resting in Haifa. New home. Not mattering where it falls.
 Contemplating body tumbling thru the midnight air, down 7-stories, taking in several minutes of new   vision.

251

Tumbling. Serene,   limbs jerk-ing   swing-ing   slow-ly.
Orange cover of novel catches eye.

>Changin' gears. Open, read on the bed but
>can't . . . concentrate . . .   on words. *Vague.*
>Fuzzy.

TV late shows blurry, abominable — mostly Hebrew. Being
Catholic and Baha'i, knowing few words in Latin, Arabic and
Farsi, but that's all of those skills. Had French in 9th grade.

"Will 'O eh ala bibliotheque?' help me here?" Pondering
freshman class. Pretty dirty-blonde teacher, mature, bright
flaring dresses, yellow, blue. Calling me, "Phillippe?"

>Lighting cigarette drawing in smoke. Ashtray on table,
glass black bottom full.

Mom choose Philip for My confirmation. He'd been one of
Christ's first apostles, she had told me. A   miracle-worker.
Mercilessly crucified upside down.

>*Gone too, to next world.*

>*Eternal . . .   Invulnerable.*

>*Dream . . . of completing . . . miracles.*

5.9 Garden City

[Monday February 5, Day four]

Up at 3 a.m. Pacing more, TV on, hearing words, shouting, clamoring for attention. Anyone's attention, not Mine. Ignoring, then pausing to view. Nowhere to go. Restaurant closed. *You know what that means.*

"Why not a dang coffee pot in the room?"
Write it off; or do somethin'.

One thought . . . stands out . . . *Need car.*

Now 8, trolling downtown thru streaming people, darker skinned, and I'm dark skinned, what shows, looking like Me, many dressed like Me, in jeans. *Yet different? Not really.* "What da we need? Security, jobs, healthy families, education, friends -- that's all for darn sakes!"
Peering in mismatched small shops, searching for . . . coffee, cigarettes. Center-city streets teeming with walkers of all ages. *Could just as easily be Manhattan without skyscrapers.* Find distinctive red Marlboro sign. Store space inside, *jammed.* Standing without, next to open glass door, packed, and open glass window.

Reach thru window, shout, "Marlboro!" Handing bills to an open hand. Not waiting for change, lighting up. Stop at corner, light up. **All good again.** Deli, buy medium black coffee. "Oh, lovely." Content. Doesn't take much. Continue, follow flows. Turning left.

Up the block, enter dark tunnel under rail-line. Coins in case in front of grey scruffy man playing. *Oboe maybe? Haunting echoes.* Step closer. Toss bills into case. Backing away. *No time to help in real way.*

Must keep moving. Big day today.
Meet Universal House of Justice.

Find cheap bookseller, drugstore, snatching an orange brush, toothpaste, black comb for back pocket. Seeing used paperbacks. Pick up Mickey Spillane dated '86 [?] to read on plane home. *Too bad, haven't finished other story.* Grabbing nut bar. Buying the stuff, pleasant clerk, smiling, friendly. Receive change, *What'd I give her?* Continue trolling.

Walking, chewing. Spying yellow sign, black lettering, **Discount Clothing**. Large corner store on opposite side of street, reminds me of shop in the States. **Red, White and Blue** downtown. *Bought clothes there in late '60s.* Sailor's navy wool pants with 13-buttons around crotch, favorite dress pants, always received "oohs and ahhs," especially wearing Navy blazer to, with gold sergeant stripes adorning left sleeve; for winter special events.

The age of wearing something I'm not.

Casement store blarin' lively Israeli music streaming from old black loudspeakers. Hummin' *Time* by the Stones. Select black jeans, plaid red flannel shirt with black buttons. Squeezing into 3x3 fitting room sitting exactly in middle of the shop. *Visible by check-outs.* Thin black curtain, 3-unmatched yellow paper thin walls, trying clothes on. Black jeans match black casual shoes.   *Ahh.*   Changing back, pay and return to strolling, fascinating signs in both Hebrew and English. Street signs with strange names, but also English alphabet. Walking, waving, saying "Hello" to any eyes pointed my way, like Mom always does. *Smiling, always smiling to strangers,   and   kind   words.*
Returning to Tower, taking elevator up to room, changing into relaxing clothes, elevator back down, asking desk clerk, "Directions to the Shrine of the Bab and Baha'i Gardens, please?"

"Gladly, just up the mountain."

Many blocks downtown of them, so also handing Me bus schedule, pointing out uptown line. Waiting outside on corner, riding one to the old **Western Pilgrim House**, next to Shrine, which can't be missed from, ah, well, anywhere, especially   lit   at   night.

"Ships sea across ocean and bay."

Finding and entering Pilgrim Centre, going up to low counter. Welcoming, smiling middle-aged woman looks up.

Blurt out, as she's opening her mouth, "Hi. My name's Rod. I'm visiting from the States."

"Are you Baha'i?

"Yes."

"Can I see your Baha'i ID please?"

Why? But taking it out of wallet and handing   it over. *Why take My ID? Can't I just be a a visitor?* Taking it kindly. She walks to the back office. *I can see her.* At a computer screen.   *Is she checking up on Me?   Have Bob or Janet told them I'm here and that they should send   Me   home?*

Coming back with ID and tan card, handing me   both. Card reads **Baha'i World Center** in top left corner, near the rounded edges of 19-pointed star in middle. Assume the same in Hebrew on right corner. Big   bold letters **VISITOR** in very middle. Line with my name, printed "Mr. Rodney Richards." *Can't tell I'm a   mister with name like Rodney? Ah, the three day pass.*   Date,   *"5/2/96."* Typed   on   back

Visitor Identity Card even bolder.

No indication I'm a Baha'i.

"Oh, thanks." Glad I'm not caught. *They're not El Al.*

"Enjoy your visit, and please have some tea in the next room before heading to the Shrine — if you'd like."

Dark tea tasting strong, viewing others sitting   on carved wooden benches along walls. Some obviously couples, both male, both female and mixed; all animated, some mothers trying to appease their young with sugar cubes; husbands chatting with men next to them. One trying to engage me, but defer with verbal acknowledgment; just a nod. Not sitting, gulping tea from bone china cup. Put it down on white lacey linen. Backing out. Can't tell if people have come from Shrine or preparing to enter.

Leave, trodding white stone path to Shrine. *Must circumambulate Shrine, round and round, this time reddish stones.* Three times. *Oh My poor Bab!*

Another sufferer, martyr, for the One True God.
God of Light, God of all!

Entering His room in reverence, the **Prophet** named the **Bab**, the **Gate.** Persian carpets covering floors, raised platform with low black iron fence, multitude of kerosene lamps, reminiscent of His era, very old,   cover . . .

one of . . . holiest spots on earth.

Kneel   on   haunches,   *Pray Rodney . . . .*

No expectations. No wishes to wish for.
No one to pray to . . . but God and Holy Messengers.
Entralled to be here.   Shallow soul penetrated.

Praying for readiness.

In a one-time Qiblih, like Jerusalem, Qiblas like Mecca   and Medina,   now   Haifa and Akka.

Next   door, 'Abdu'l-Baha's   room   white   like   the Blessed **Bab's**, but plainer still, light taupe Persian carpets. Left front wall, hanging in glass frame His **Tablet of Visitation.** Reading aloud from wall-hanging, **"He is the All-Glorious! O God, my God! Lowly and tearful, I raise my   suppliant hands to Thee . . . ."** [26]

Reminding Me of spiritually cherished times. . .

in Rochester.

Both sacred Spotless rooms with dome above. Exiting respectfully,   from under gold-scales which can be seen mid-way on Holy Mountain across wide **Bay of Haifa,** seeing images when   lit up at night. Crossing thru white

256

columns, buildings, grounds spotless,   *nothing out of place,* plain red terra   cotta pieces or   white   stones   for   paths *thru crisp blushing greenery,* full of short dark green hedges and multi-colored   flowering . . . .

Gardens --   white,   yellow.
Geraniums red; brilliant.
Like Their Martyr's blood.

Later in day, stopping, plan returning, walking slowly down   hill to Tower, lost in spiritual world. *yet not*   Reach hotel, approach counterman,
"I'd like to rent a car for a few days."

"If you don't mind waiting in the lounge Mr. Richards, I can have someone here shortly," in a friendly tone.

Good. He trusts Me. They know Me.

No   distracting   TV   in   lounge,   twiddling   thumbs, reading Hebrew paper. Unsure what to expect. *I need to do this.* Determined. Two well-dressed men in white suits, black skinny ties appear within 30-minutes, walk purposefully to clerk, a few words, then to Me, smiling, shaking hands, papers in one hand. Sitting together on adjacent tan couches with plain 3-foot square wooden coffee table between us, blue-lined, red-lined, papers spread. Show My passport, DL, they explain, I scan the contracts, and sign on the **X** line. Hand over credit card.
Cost means nothing. Scrawl signature in
three places. *As usual, unrecognizable.*

Success! Renting   white   late-model   sedan.   So   easy. Again. *Trusting Me.*

They haven't asked what I need it for or where I'm going, or why.   Nuthin'!   Boy, drivin' round here'll be fun.

3 a.m. maneuvering Audi out of its very tight   space, inching back   and   forth,   turning   wheel   in   opposite

directions, til clearing   white painted pillars. Taking longer than it does to interpret directional signs and navigate   traffic once outside. Driving on right side of the road.   Wide   awake. *Perfect out here, rain meaningless.* Left glasses in room.

"Seein' fine." near-and-far-sightedness merged. Super alert.

Driving to Tel Aviv in the early morning hours enshrouded in fog. Road winding, but longer stretches   where speedometer glows green 160 km. Highway eerily deserted. Handful of cars pass in the opposite direction.   Freeway beautifully paved asphalt road with concrete dividers.

Lose sight of road ahead in low fog, "Don't crash into embankments." Goin 90. Loud   crunching   gravel alerts my ears. . . "Damn, rode off the side agin'!"

Is this where I'll die?

Arriving in center-city Tel Aviv, traverse streets, stop on   high hill, slowly exiting car, carefully examining the area for movement . . . sounds.   Hearing dogs barking in distance . . . nothing else.   Silent,   deserted,   nothing stirring.   Great   white   grey   fog   has   lifted. *Can't hold it,* pull zipper down, peeing in middle of street. Barely make out big building far to My left, 5-or-6 stories   tall, held up by thin dark columns around its girth,   eerily silhouetted in dark sky.   Clouds passing across yellow-grey moon. Absolutely no one around; 4-in-the-morning. Untold energy. Eyes *alert.*

Streaming wildling thoughts, *Where to next? What to do?*

Size-up city . . . command . . . **You are done here.**

Mission almost completed. Today. Leaving immediately,   turnin' 'round and without passing any cars or stopping, speed back way I came. Turn off headlights, drive by yellow moon's hazy glow.   Turn them on.   Off.

Hour passes in . . . *series of blurs.*
"Have I seen another vehicle?"

Hardest part of night journey . . . the Return. Maneuvering Audi back into extremely tight space in underground garage. Leave keys.

Reaching room, sit on miniscule bed, curtains   still thrown open on large-framed window.   Peering   out, contemplating glowing city lights as they are . . .
world   megalopolis.
Remembering all of Louie Armstrong's
What a Wonderful World . . . "Oh."   "Maybe."

No books or images
can visualize   world's   glorious future.

5.10 The Seat

[Tuesday February 6, Day five]

In the early daylight hastened to the **Baha'i Monument Gardens** on side of Mt. Carmel. Quiescent, receptive, submissive. Wide heavenly vista above and world below, cream buildings ahead, Babylon's hanging gardens surround, all laid bare before and below, laid in front of My anxious eyes. *Today.*

Ten, a wave, filling my being with balm, absolute serenity. **You're here.** Filling Me with awe that only comes from seeing the truly magnificent for   the first   time.
The Faith's come so far in only 169   years.
Dispelling conflicting thoughts and images of doom for mankind. Walking up steep mountain, into more gardens, guided   stone   pebble   paths,   low   rows   bluish-green

hedges, ^{suspended} at three encircled short marbled pillars, cap-stoned, gravesites of the **Holy Family**.

Scaped, built, planted for their honor by their true lovers.

Buildings tower above and on sides, yet reality is these smallest towers also.

Reverence penetrates anew:

Tread straight up mountain steep
past **Parthenon . . .**
Holy Sepulches below.

Middle Path.

Trudging, grinding, digging in feet, climbing the 90-degree mountainside to *The Seat!* Our supreme council chamber, bigger and more impressive than the Parthenon nearby. Girded by fifty-eight massive three story tall, fine Italian marble pillars, *The Seat,* and their broad fluted Corinthian caps.

Trudging further on loose burnt sienna stones, climbing harder, puffing slightly, more than half-way up steepness.

Pausing near single sapling, alone, middle of thin burnt walkway, not really a path. Right arm outstretches, grasping tight to tree trunk, full-fisted now, catching breath.

On Fire

Staring upward, imposing edifice, white dome crown; visible from horizon, clear blue overhead, colored earth beneath.

Oh, Where God passed by. [33]

Janet and I helped build this house, I urged believers to donate towards its construction. Stunning in its grandeur, magnificent, superb. Worthy.

Do I dare knock uninvited?

Moments in meditation.

Mind ascends, examining twenty foot high,   wide,
        closed   bronze doors.

Hearing   intonation   .   .   .   low   ,,,   deep,,,
Tree . . .Beyond Which. . .There Is No Passing [34]

The symbol . . . time slows . . . stops.

"No" *. . . can't . . . can't knock . . . can't go in.*

welling inside, surging out . . . reality

Not worthy.

      Gripping   trunk   hard,   pivot,   shakily,   carefully,
peering   down   at   footholds,   concentrating.   Stepping
vertically, backing down   from **Mountain of God** . . .
at peace   . . .   wayward thinking dissipated,   heart
enlarging,   spirit   floating   in   **Abha**   **Kingdom**
brief   minutes, transported to next world . . . *not first time.*
      No person accosting me, no one asking Me, ask ing,
"What   are   you   doing?"   Teetering,   descending   wobbily,
walking pebbled paths. Hearing blue birds, red birds, chirping,
calling   one to another,   gloriously   singing.
      Leaving, opening and closing the short gate I entered
thru.   Reaching   street   sidewalk.   Walking   blocks,   only   a
short   mile   downhill   to   downtown,   obeying   crossing   lanes
and   traffic   signals   for   once.
      All   fresh,   spring   like,   but   now   . . .   racing   returns,
interjecting, scattered conjecturing. Abruptly, serene.

Coming faster

Pontificating . . . To the masses;   only I hear?

not   the   good   ones?
*   Many   more   good   than   not.*
*   Oh. Must apologize!*

Zoom! Must speak, get it all out. Burning inside.
String of planning   projects, then . . .
berating My laziness.

Zoom!

Singing praises, highlighting   achievements.

Dramas, one minute,   ease and peace on its heels.

Up, down.   Sideways.

Euphoria not abating

glancing North, South, East and West.

Energy for everything. Have faith . . .

*   *   *

My Tower, eating kabob again for dinner, alone but
not. Only meat I trust here, kosher, blessed blood, salty;
not familiar with words or dishes on menu, other than hard
boiled eggs, yogurt in the mornings.
     Not forcing myself upon strangers as I'm wont to do,
altho tempting. One pair of older Jewish marrieds in dining
room, speaking pleasantries in Yiddish[?], mixed English,
friends,   companions,   intimate,   smiling,   laughing,
four tables away.

To   far   to   shout   a   greeting.

That evening, man checking mileage number,   settlin' up for rented car. Check out of hotel, riding sharoot back to airport. *Time to go home.*

Dressed in dingy white shirt, wrinkled grey pants, dirty socks. Carrying jacket; jeans and shirt in brown store bag. Wanting to, , , to look presentable to others.

Must seem normal.

Middle-moon in night sky, quiet. Arrive close mouthed. Place practically closed. *Where are evolutionist clerks?* Plopping in another grey, hard, padded seat.

More of this.   Wasting My time!
Home now Kato. . .
Eyes fluttering, head rolling . . . .

*   *   *

[Wednesday February 7, Day six]

Dawn's light. I don't dissolve.

Open **Men** door. Walk thru and do business. Splashing water four times on dry stinking face. Swishing three mouthfuls of water. *Did I bring brush,   toothpaste?* Check bag. "Crap." Wiping teeth, smoky tongue, inside mouth with index finger. *Wipe cancer cells away. Should buy toothbrush again?*   Put on jacket.

Trepidacious. "Why am I fearful?"   *No, so what.* March briskly to El Al   counter revolutionist,

"Excuse Me please, is there a direct flight? America? Europe?"   Searching passport, computer. . .

"Sorry sir, denied."

"Can I go anywhere?"

263

"Sorry sir, not now. But <u>if you'll take a seat</u> I'll   check for you."

Sitting. *Did Newark call them? Did London or Rome?* Three hours . . third-class waiting area.

    Later, 'You must wait longer sir." Telling Me must wait . . . longer?! Wait. Don't get pissed, upset. *"Good things come to those who wait."* [35]

No rush. Home soon.

Mission accomplished. *Went as far as humanly possible, as far as I humanly could. Going as far as I could. Making it to the Holy Mountain.*   **Satisfied.**

    Spent.

    Into **Men** again, deserted. *Good.* Lock Myself in stall. Rushing, emptying pockets, undressing, emptying bag, tossing it together with suit and shirt into upright trash can.

    No luggage still. Donning jeans, flannel shirt, beginning to feel at ease. Casually peekin' 'round, step outside, further outside, outside. Standing, scanning, road, *Ah, smoke. M*odern glass and steel restaurant 'cross the street.

    Stroll casually   inside bypassing hostess and empty tables, sidlin' up to attractive woman with long, light brown hair.   *Like Me.*

Mustering politeness, no fear of rejection.

 "Hi there, name's   Rod,   here   from   the   States. Would you mind a little   company?"

    Evaluating Me, smiling, waving Me sit across from her, "Okay . . ." Hesitant. Sit down.   Introduces herself.

    "Brigitte, . . . from Stuttgart." [(?)]

Waiter hovering, "One turkey sandwich with lettuce, tom- ato, onion, no pickle, on a hard roll, no mayo, with coffee and cream. Oh, ah, please, and We need   sugar on the table as well." She ordering more black coffee.

Waiter staring briefly, turning.

Asking her more, "Coming or going."

"Returning home."

"Me too, back to Jersey, not far from New York City." She's never been. Telling her the sights, showing with my hands, subways, skyscrapers five feet apart, ten thousand yellow taxis, **Central Park**, museums in the city, altho I've only been to the **Met and MOMA.**

She telling me of, "... green wooded beauty of home." Cottages, chalets. Slower hustle and bustle, *as I call it.*

Central Park. Statues, lake, castle, circus. Ah, nice. Green varied plants, trees, remind me of home.   I love home.

Say to her, "Your English is quite good" Bringing smile. Always bringing smile, complimenting others on their English, meaning it. Too bad she can't, compliment Me on German. Sounding the expert. Between eating, she sipping, listening, chatting amicably twenty minutes. Stealing long looks at her firmer Barbie prettiness, fair skin, and *feeling . . .*
intimate   tension rising.

Flirting openly. Touching hands.

Coffee tasting smooth, thick, hot, like my mood.

Five more minutes, she stands up slowly, excusing herself to check onto flight.

Saying, "It was pleasant to talk to you — Rod. Have a good trip home."

Pushing chair back, stand, offer hand, mildly shake   hers, "Alvederzane," one of four German words   I know. Turning, walking away toward terminal. Peruse her hourglass shape in tight jeans and tight light yellow blouse. *Would she like company on her trip?*

Glancing left out floor to ceiling windows.
Nothing   else of   importance.

Rushing away to pay our bills as she promenades thru double glass doors.

Rays shoot in.

Twenty-five years of wedded bliss
        scattered like wind-blown ashes . . .

5.11 Athens

"Brigitte!"

        I'm   back   inside   terminal,   not   seeing   her, encounter blurred from My Mind . . . forgotten.   Move on. Always move on. Becoming clear from Israelis again they'll have nothing to do with Me.

        Sequestering Me when first applying for ticket   home. Leading Me to three-walled room

        Private —   Do   Not   Enter.
        Alone, sitting on hospital cart,   green   curtains drawn. They open, twice. First, interview by well-dressed man, one woman, both wearing spotless, starched, white smocks. Man flashes penlight in eyes. Ask lots of questions. "Yes," "No,"   "Doesn't   matter,"   "I'm   OK."   So   forth.
        Forty minutes? Leave Me.   Whip curtains.
Whis-per-ing.   Hearing low   "manica."   Twice.
Never to   My   face.   Speakingnothingdirectly.

Only, "Please wait." Streaming thoughts *comforting,* butcautious.

Another hour alone, huge white crystal rockets in head, hundreds, taking off from far flung silos. Then,
Done. *Need to go. What's taking so long?*
Where are these people from? Who are they?

Bare minutes passing.

Finally! No words, only silence. Escort Me back to tiny airport waiting area, rundown, hard plastic seats, grey, only grey . . . . *Where's colors?*
I'm not afraid of them. Mellow now. *Act rational.* Potential consequences of situation . . . never . . . entering consciousness.

Petite attractive woman approaches, bends down close to ear, "Be patient." **Am I dreaming?**

"They're arranging transport."

Patient, oh so patient, yet itching with scheme after scheme of changing the world to its better.
Rise, head to small sundries store, buy two postcards and postage one last time, writing to Mom and the Harrises. A bucolic scene of a wheat field with rolling hills, rolls of cut wheat sheets, sporadically placed in the now flat field, short forests in the back- ground. It could have been a scene in France. Thinking it's France. Mailing them.
Finally next woman comes closer, motioning to follow, escorting Me to **Olympia Airlines** tickets, saying a few words to clerk, Me overhearing Greek. New one showing Me behind counter, knocking on door, opening it, 7 x 8 disheveled office. Lone paper scattered desk, book shelves overflowing, grey file cabinets.

"This is Mr. Richards, who requires transportation."

Grey suit man like Me, his rounding bulky frame, belly, sitting behind sloppy, paper-strewn desk. Standing, introducing himself merely as

"I'm a Manager for Olympia Airlines."

"Hello."

Woman leaves, closes door. He offers cigar. *Should I take it? Put him at ease?*
"*No thanks, don't smoke.*" Pause, decline. Sitting now in loud metal chair, shaking legs tipsy on parquet floor.
Finally out of here? Do they know Who I Am? No trouble understanding his English, obviously Greek descent, like Spiro. Smiling at My Face. Smile back.   Hopeful.

"We will help you."

Meeting together 30-minutes, joking, filling out forms, IDs, credit card, handed one-way ticket for plane to **Athens.**

No other flights allowed. *I don't care, that's great.*

*   *   *

Air streams rushing by plane window. Evening ride uneventful, except gabbing to disinterested dark-haired woman next to Me, whole way. Texan returning home; long haired musician, who sings and plays guitar for living. Plying him with questions about music, Texas, not speaking of Me. Dislike aisle seat, never again.   Invigorated. Invigorating!

Upon arriving late to Athens airport, severely hassled,   held up by another gosh darn clerk I barely understand and is no help.   No explanations.

Trying to get a plane to London or the U.S., refusing to sell Me pass, saying,

"You must wait for papers."

What papers? I have My papers. Waiting. *Did the   man at Newark Airport call here? Did the woman at Ben Gurion call here?*

Speaking with or checking in with officials every few hours. The same.

No Progress. No explainin'. **Hate that more than all!**

Physically bored but mentally alert so entertained. Full of anxiousness. Pulling on knuckles. Unsuccessfully because never cracked them before. Rubbing my eyes with clammy hands. Wandering expanse of terminal. Finding new **Men**, washing as best I can in the filthy cold white and light blue basement room. Returning, waiting area one large room, possibly *40-feet wide, 25-feet high?* Few doors, *Where are restaurant, shops,   coffee?* Nothing but black-handed clock on one end, plastic seats in middle, flight board on side wall.

Few flights listed.

None going home.

Ten or twenty people, waiting quietly, barely talking. *Is Greece totalitarian?* Observing, always observing, mentally noting dress, movements, ages, talking, not talking. Seeing black bold text, **AEGEAN**.

A Gean?

Find safe, unreserved hideaway in deserted L-shaped section, crouching alone on top of white metal table, in smaller wing of building, open, nothing else, no one else. Stretching side to side, meditating, talking to Me, stretching. *Do jumping jacks?* Still no magazine stand, coffee. Just   Myself and swirling, flinging thoughts at each other, til they and time pass in passing. Energy levels fluctuating, dozing off and on;   suddenly wired, awake.

Woman in navy skirt, "Don't leave building." *Huh?*

Not even for a smoke? That must be okay. Where can I grab one? Perennial question. Managing to find side   flappy door to loading dock, and sneaking cigarette when   no one's watching. Nobody hassles. Guards posted by single gate; guards — **Uzi's.**

Watching as 30 departing passengers blow past them and guns and enter greyish canopied corridor. Walking close by. *Can I pass in to it?* Move away, *No.*

Tentatively visit woman at Olympia booth again -- *fifth time.*

Looking up, shaking head, "No."

All night gnashing teeth. Feeling irate . . . desperate. *Make a run? What will they do?*

[Friday February 9, Day eight]

5 a.m. Dark, Light, same Lights, same Dark. Stumbling to **Men** to crap, wash up. At 7 hidden doors at other end magically open to much bigger terminal.

Never noticed. Coffee shop's open. *Oh thank you God. And for baklava.* *Melting.* Going to counter again, to morning woman and telling My story; receive blank stare, half-smile. Leave for smoke. Return to **Twilight Zone** prison, sitting on top of My reserved table.
Weary body, disquieting Mind.

Move World-Center to World-Megalopolis. Move Manhattan-to World-Megalopolis. Move LA to World-Megalopolis. Move Silicon- Valley to World-Megalopolis; and so on for dozens of world sites . . . Institute world system of uniform weights and measures. Use existing auxiliary tongue -- English, learned by, spoken by all peoples, in addition to native tongues. Institute universal health care . . . International Job Banks and training . . . Rebuild crumbling water pipes, infrastructures in cities, bury electric wires underground. .

All planned out. In Control.

Noon, three, five. *What did Israelis   say?* *Inaudible bastards.* Quietly,   new   clerk finding Me in half-stupor, semi-arousing Me with, "Follow   me."   Doing so expectantly now, thru another rear door. Hadn't noticed smaller waiting area and another counter. This time dark blue uniformed men again, no guns.

Where are Uzis?   On shelf   below?

Standing   15-minutes   answering   questions, keeping cool -- as long as I can, *don't blow up.* ask for window seat,   finally -- receiving approval, paying for flight to . . . London,   **No problem, been there.**

Shown   to   open   lime-green   shuttle   bus   with 20 passengers, four standing, mostly jeans like Mine on women also. *Everyone wears jeans. When we were hippies they laughed.* Sitting alone, feigning   disinterest, seeing   furtive   glances. Tram running in very wide circle to rundown terminal some distance away. Pushed to my left touching woman's jeaned thigh seated next to Me, as we make even wider turn.

New terminal much smaller with ring of tan hard orange plastic   seats in large circle, middle of room, *forty in all?* Majority of seats taken, bearing brothers and sisters of all ilk's and ages.

Enter **Gift Shop**. *Memento.* Search shelves, pick up small boxed white and red chessboard, white or rust   on pegs. Pay for it, coffee, cake slice. Walking slowly, gently, kindly, around inside ring, looking for chessmasters, asking potentials, old men, alone . . .

"Hi? While we wait,   care to play chess?"

"Pawn to king four," opening. Safest. Always liked games. Bob had been on two-year-long chess kick; we had played   weekly   back   in   the   80s. Always loved this game.

Games pass between four of us, win all. Chat   little. *Flight's announced!* "Thanks." Up and out.

Athens: brown scorched hills dotted   short scrub bushes surrounding this desolate place.

Back to London, *so tired*, can't enjoy scenery out window. Dozing more, or otherwise conversing with seatmate. Asking the middle-aged guy, "Have the time?" Seeing he has watch. Mine long gone.

"Midnight" *Ahh, midnight and I'm not yet there.*

Without joy, without sorrow, without pain.

5.12 London, Home

[Saturday February 10]

Thrilling touchdown, taxi, waiting patiently, letting others go ahead. Disembark. Heathrow . . . practically deserted. Walking up to short pretty black-haired reservations clerk, ruddy cheeks, asking general questions regarding London, mainly where to stay. Flirting shamelessly. Ten minutes later, making two phone calls, setting Me up in nearby hotel, and calling cab. Continue chatting.

"So, what time do you get off?"

"You'll be gone long before that, chap."

Lovely but won't give her number.

Thirty minutes from Heathrow, **Marriott's** six stories pleasant-looking enough, light brick and tan stucco, *like Roma;* far distance from airport, *as far as can tell.* Check in by 1, use faithful credit card. No one else in lobby. Bellhop called, showing Me to small room; big compared to Haifa. Under some spell; after half an hour, *hafta move*, pacing, mentally battling, stripping to nothing, throw glasses on bed, walk into royal-red carpeted hall. Loud click.

Impelled, strolling nude through deserted hotel corridors, carrying nothing, not even hotel key this time.

Opening random unmarked door on right, sauntering into ballroom with cocktail party of fifteen people in play, standing in small cliques or tete-a-tetes, drinking white wine. *Or is it champagne?* Men in suits or tuxes, women in long, almost see thru bright dresses of differing pastel hues, some short skirts too. All good looking, a few white-haired gents. Medium-sized room, thirty tables covered by off-white linen tablecloths, no glasses, silverware, cloth white napkins.
They don't see me.

Some turn. *I wonder if they know I'm American?*

Hear "Bloody hell, what's that bloke doing?" and a few "Tsk, tsks." Buzzing becoming quieter. Hearing whispered derisions of flaccid penis, not a little laughter, but no one calls out or comes near. Meandering towards middle, slowly turning, leaving out different door. *Ha, these folks aren't impressed. So what?*

No rush. All the time in the world.

Once back in hall, "Shit. Where's My key?" Coming to minor senses, trying . . . to figure out . . . **how get back?**
Short walk thru long corridors, hide behind small counter in corner, clerk's cubbyhole . . . *with house phone!* Pick up, dial "0," ringing front desk. Telling man simply, "Locked myself out, lost my key." Giving My Name, where I am by looking at closest room number.

"Someone will be right up sir."

Upon finding Me, without saying a word or giving dirty looks, bellboy in candy striped uniform politely leads Me back to room, passing no other guests, letting Me in and handing over new key. Not embarrassed. **Neither of Us.**
Of course, everything I need in room anyway. Dressing quickly, no socks, shoes, laying on bed, watching abominable

273

snow TV show? Switching channel after five minutes of insanity. One reason had forsaken room — no decent programs/movies on "telly." *Ab-so-lute-ly terrible, producers need do something. U.S better.*

Having long conversation about it,
　　　　speaking with 'Abdu'l-Baha . . . .

Hard time sleeping most night; even **BBC** turns me off but leave on.

Too scary calling Janet but had mailed postcards　　　—
feel better.

　　　　Paranoia briefly grips my heart, but not over-whelming me, just a concern. Of course, Mind　racing, impossible to　stop . . . but . . . focus.
　　　　Just　go with flow. Skipping　thru　probabilities and possibilities . . . .

Before dawn, call front desk. "Can you please call a　cab for Heathrow?"

　　　　"We have a service sir, I'll call them now. About fifteen　minutes.　Is that acceptable?"

"Absolutely."

　　　　"Thank you sir, he'll be waiting for you."

Gathering　things,　chessboard,　darken　room,　take polished　wood-paneled　elevator　to　lobby.　Paying,　not looking at cost. *Don't care.*
　　　　Wayward thought, *A credit　card　can　be　a dangerous asset in a　mentally ill person's　hands.*
　　　　Not Mine.
　　　　Talkative and friendly well-dressed cabbie with　black chauffer's　cap,　opening　door,　driving　to　Heathrow　in pouring, black, blowing hard rain, obscuring road ahead from

other cars' sprays. Arriving. Only five pound note, and   he not accepting card. *Shit!*

"Let's go inside to an ATM, I'll pay extra." Both maneuvering, running, skirting between pelting drops. *Smart cabbie, coming with   Me.* Ditched a cabbie in Ewing that way once.

Pass into shelter, main entrance looking for ATM, pounds. Using one, gladly handing over ten pound tip. *Awfully   nice   person.* Instantly clear Mind of his name say,   "Thank you so much, sorry for trouble." He nods.

Eight a.m. Easily buy ticket on **Virgin Atlantic** 747. *Only a few short hours wait.* Visit same Mc-Donald's, large black   coffee, which I can't stand, but too sleepy at this moment, *need   it   strong.*

Smoking outside under another canopy, white   again, waiting. *Now I'm happy.* When in airseat, love playing video games with controller and TV screens built-in front of Me. However, soon move, empty seat to empty seat, trying five . . twenty, trying new controller each time, since all break within minutes of manipulations.

All ministrations fail to resurrect them.
Mumbled   prayers   fail   also.
Finally $#!&%$!

We must be flying above 30,000 feet.

Searching, trolling unhampered, few   lights   on, covers on passengers, heads on pillows. Searching for new controllers. Large white door with big red letters calling Me over.

In far back of plane now, on starboard side. "Umph, umph, umph," Grunting, pushing door handle. Unsuccessful, half-hearted, even tho idea stronger now.   *Just   go.*

Cute-looking, young blonde stewardess happening upon Me, rushes over, nonchalantly,   "May I help you to your seat sir?" Distracting Me, halting My efforts.
Stand up straighter for her.

Showing Me to assigned seat, alone, no one else in row. "Please remain in your seat sir, I'll return shortly."

Four minutes later, coming back, sitting down   across aisle,   maintaining   constant   vigil,   pitter-pattering speech, staying beside Me.

Go to   head   once   —   she's   waits   outside. Inside,   throw house, car keys in tiny trash, hear "clink" thru hand   towels. *Someone might steal and use them.* Debating. *Should I throw wallet, wedding ring away too? Throw 'em away. You don't want them to know   who You are, do You?*

Better not. Think of hassles getting new ID. *Ugh.*   DMV.

Tug   wallet   out. Passport   out. Twisting   gold   band   off. Placing on aluminum sink. Staring down.

Looking   at   wild-eyed,   red-eyed,   disheveled   Self   in   mirror. *Will they get Me?*

Back and forth full 5-minutes.

Light knocking, "Sir, is everything alright?"   Leave.

Stewardess   saying   nothing,   just   smiling   showing perfectly   straight   white   teeth   framed   against   equally beautiful, piercing hazel eyes.

Like Mine.

A glow around her,

My guardian angel . . . .

5.13 Jersey

While sitting together, chatting, she taking out pad, verifying name, address, phone.

"Do you have any luggage? Can I call a spouse or friend when we arrive?" *Who will meet "Us" at NWK?*

"No luggage, travellin' light. Call Bob at 609-555-1212."

Enjoying pretzels from cart. "Cream and sugar please," and her attention. Rushing of landing -- energizing. Landing smoothly.

Home.

Young blonde female friend, and another, escorting Me off plane. Striding easily through what seems to be shortened customs and entry line, up to booth encased in clear plexiglass. Beautiful escorts showing their badges.

"Sir, can I please see your ID and passport?" Pause . . .

Pull wallet out, hand over passport, license. Inspector scanning them, peering at Me, handing back.

"Thank you sir, you may proceed."

Put them back, back in front jeans pocket, jeans from Haifa. Feeling ring. Taking it out, slip on wedded finger.   Goddesses showing Me thru   **ARRIVALS**   to circular drive in front of Virgin. Bob and Barb parked out front at curb, expecting Me. My angels leaving with sweet goodbyes when seeing big Bob.

Standing there waiting. Arms at sides.

Noncommittal.

"Thanks girls!" They're heading inside.

"Bob, you SOB! I shudda figured you'd be here." Wrapping arms around his wide girth, reaching up into warm familiar embrace and kiss on My cheek, then one from Me. Usually Bob also pinches my ass; not now.

"Rodney, I can't tell you how good it is to see you. You must have had quite an adventure."

"Yeah, it was really cool . . . glad I went . . . but gotta have a smoke. Gotta!"

Bob standing aside and looking on. Light up, he's waiting patiently, . . . finish. Tee my butt, stomp out ash. Butt into back pocket. Barb staying in car, on cell phone.

Except he's saying one more thing.

"Rod, do you know what day it is?"

"No, not particularly."

"It's Saturday February 10th. You've been gone nine days."

Pausing.

"Oh. The highest number. I wudda never guessed that long."

Bob opening back door,
For me? Yes.

Climbing in, sitting, squeezing Barb's shoulder, lost in thinking ahead. Not thinking.

No deja vu of '79 car trip.

Not recalling much, except, *We hafta appear normal — important.*

278

Bob drives directly to Trenton's **Helene Fuld Hospital Emergency** . . . **resident Psych Unit**. Meet Janet. Stoic and solicitous. Strong. May have hugged? She's demonstrating absolute concern, furrowed brow. No raised voice, no screaming, no snide remarks, no questions. Soft voice. Only concerned with My well-being. Laying down on a cart-stretcher in small green room by Myself. *Have they given me a sedative?* Janet next to me, urging Me to sleep. Falling head, down on miniscule pillow, but tossing, turning . . . . trying to lay still for her, eyes closed partway, her arm around My head . . . for a time.   Arm gone.   Sitting up   later calling "Jan?"

Immediately, we're talking, semi-rational. Then see same white smock and stethoscope,   professional Indian doctor, kind-hearted.   Janet hovering.

Coming close, very close, convincing him and her I only need sleep.   All will be put back to normal.

"Sleep will help me a lot doc, just need a few more pills for awhile."

 Rational. Almost convincing him, everyone else I'm fine.

"Please release . . . Me." But in end, not falling for it.   Back to room, laying on high cart, metal arms down. Janet going to doctor,   long   interchange.

Hearing murmurings.

5.14 Carried away, again

Tossing, turning, kicking thin green sheet.
Given a shot . . . two? Trying to sleep on skinny padded cart with tiny pillow while Janet comes over, soothing Me, in fact, gently begging me to sleep. Again.

Blurry, little except ambulance ride.

To where? Don't care if shackled, umpteenth time.

Not recalling much about **Carrier Clinic** in Belle Mead 35-minutes away.

But, a few incidents stuck with me:

Again with shuffling and bowed head. Feeling semi-parochial, paranoid, hemmed in. *Gotta escape, get back to MY Mind. Losing it.* Again with the smoke breaks, in a large courtyard out back with high fences. Small dining room of wooden tables with a single white vase in middle holding single red plastic rose. Six of us sitting on two opposite benches. Thick dark red table spreads on top, dark red plastic on top, white cotton on bottom. All meals salads and meatloaf, except for breakfast with scrambled eggs.

Like that.

Patient lounge down hall has 3 short wooden book cases, 3 shelves each, 3 books, maybe 3 games.
Large screen, black-framed, color TV mounted on wall, with faux-leather, tan couch facing.
Splayed out, alone, watching one stupid show after the other til hafta get up and walk . . . somewhere. Pacing open room, halls. Looking in half-glass doors. Waiting for Janet's visits. Dinner together. Bringing smokes. Foggy . . . but . . . pleasant now.

Kids never visiting, can't see Daddy this sick.

Awake. Five. Before anyone else. Regular orderlies haven't appeared. As soon as one shows up, begging   him to put coffee on; wait near their empty station. Nice   young man gives me some.

"Ohh, thank you sooo   much." Milking it 30 minutes til next cup. In interim pacing in front of it, coffee place, in white wool socks, waiting for more hot joe.

   Live for coffee and cigs. Day growing long,
      no arts and   crafts to distract.

   Group therapy sessions have 12 patients in a   circle and doctor, leading . . . discussion?
      One day   become . . .   nasty . . . in group.
      Not supposed to. Extremely . . . nasty.

"Don't talk at me! I don't want to answer your questions. Stop it.   Stop it!"   Begin banging walls with fists.

"Bang, bang . . . bang, bang . . . ." Two strong men rushing in and   manhandling Me. Flailing. "Stay off Me." "Get your hands off!" Terrified of what they carry with them, something recognizable from other hospitals, and   TV.

   Thrusting   arms   thru   straightjacket,   lacing   and snapping as fast as they can, *struggling,* dragging me thru hall.   Socks   slipping   on   linoleum   floors. Watching sunlight streaming thru windows in   slow   motion. Sharply, sunlight gone, horribly bright   bulbs.   "Off, off"

 "OOmph!" Throw myself at white-tufted   padded   walls, bouncing   off.   "OOMPH!"   Then three more ever harder, pushing but socks still   slippery. Can't wiggle   them off.   Feel frustration.   Hopelessness.

   Finally collapsing in middle of room on thick grey mat and sobbing,   "We're sorry. I'm sorry!"
      Spending full day in that . . . cell. *Where will I sleep?*

Once out, sweet as honey. One morning pretty, young   teenager, long hair past shoulders, sitting on Army cot, alone in 6x7 room, crying, rocking. Seeing her clearly thru long half-wall of glass, watch her from outside a few hidden moments, she's sobbing, cursing   herself.
Brown army blanket laying disheveled at foot of bed.   Her head down on knees, arms   tightly around   legs,   knees, rocking, and constant moaning. Rocking and softly sobbing, cursing. Thick wooden, half-glass   door   closed.

Turn   handle   softly,   enter   silently,   on   thick woolen socks.   Sit next to and slightly behind her,   close, but not touching. Gradually raising grey blanket and   covering shaking shoulders care-fully.   Gently, wrapping   arms around her body, loosely, feeling   tremors.   Lay   head on hers, on messy black hair, seeing   irregular   streaks   of black mascara running down her   cheeks.

Whisper "It's alright, it'll be alright. You're going home   soon." Holding her full ten minutes while she slows, slowing moaning now, softer. *Oh why is she moaning?*

Her, unresponsive except crooning. No one coming.

I back out the way I found her. Her lips still twitching
   only softer.

* * *

The Carrier "program" had down time with nothing to do. Vaguely remember group. No windows to look out of; would've been pleasant distraction. Always feeling *enclosed*, *stifling*. But, allowed   regular   smoking breaks, thank God.   And . . . coffee   flowed.

I think I even went to an AA meeting in another part of the hospital. I   had   intoned   their   wise   mantra   years earlier. Loved their mantra.

Doctors, building, mind, confining Me . . . three sad weeks.

We is changing to me.

5.15 Aftermath

When we got home after rehab, I had just shut the kitchen door and was emptying pockets.

It's March already. I hug Jesse as a father does his grownup son, and kiss Kate's smooth cheek, offering not much more than a smile in response to their grins. They're soon doing other things.

Jan and I are still in the kitchen. Of course, she had been very upset, because she hadn't known exactly where I was or what I had been doing, or anything at all during those many days — halfway 'round the world.
    I hadn't communicated a word directly.

    She turns to me, on the other side of the counter, and breathes aloud, rationally and appealingly,
    "Rod, you know I love you right?"

Nodding, *Oh thank you.* "Of course. . . ."

    "But I can't take this again." It's her strong tone, forceful tone. One I don't often hear.
    Only when she's upset.

"I, understand. Hopefully the drugs will help."

    "I hope so . . . because if they don't . . . if they can't . . . we can't live with you. I would want a divorce."

Aw Geez. I didn't know what to say. *Heart dropping . . . So unexpected* . . . but . . . reasonable.

Janet doesn't quibble. I know she means it. I understand.

R-e-a-l-l-y understand.

Over the next few days Janet calls GreenSpring, and lambasts them over how I had been able to fool Dr. Wolf so easily, and how this wouldn't have happened under Dr. Argueta's care. She wrote them a letter sharing her vehement frustrations with them as well.

He only perceived lies for wellness.

We give 'em credit, because shortly afterwards they authorized eight sessions to see Dr. Argueta again.

First weekly, then monthly.

This would last until 2008, when he closed his practice.

I search the Yellow Pages. *What do I look for?*

Six months testing new ones . . .

til finally finding one I like . . .

a Ms.

6.0 EPILOGUE

Look at my friend's son, John [?]. At midnight he stomped down the stairs of their home and rushed out onto the snow covered ground, hopped the neighbor's fence, opened their unlocked garage door, stole a pair of skis (no poles), and rushed back home. He has on nothing but a flannel shirt and jeans.

As he gets to his driveway, he attempts to open my friend's car, going to all four locked doors and pulling mightily. He drops the skis, tromps thru the house up to his room and starts dumping everything from his dresser drawers and closet, frantically looking for an object of great import. He stomps back downstairs taking car keys from his mother's purse.   And tries to flee.

He's forgotten the ski's.

He's sixteen with no driving experience nor license.

Whether for me and my family or multi-millions of Johns or Janes, their caregivers, employers, children, families and friends, that's how "living" can be.   It doesn't have to be.

Bipolar is virulent from teenager to young adult. Remember the **Forward** on page 13? NAMI said it takes ten years ON AVERAGE, to diagnose bipolar and begin treatment. Episodes taper off with   age. Now at 63, sometimes I think, "I'd be fine if I didn't take any of   these meds." That's My mentally ill self talking; my normal, nicely   average self knows better.

Thank God Janet and I had solid beginnings, trust, caring family, friends, co-workers and others.
Thank God I was diagnosed early and have good doctors.
Thank God there are proper medications for me.
Thank God for a normal life . . .

Affordable healthcare, counseling, clinics and facilities, half-way homes, doctors, psychiatrists and medicines must be available to all mentally ill Americans. Hating our President musn't be confused with one of our greatest need. It's 50 years overdue. Might   it finally be time to care for our mentally ill as well as we care for our children, seniors, servicemen and women?
In fact, without exception, care for EVERY American?

Miracle drugs, care, watching, helping, reminding, laughing, doing, going out alone, together, kids -- great again.

Except for waking up so early every morning since retirement.   And smoking.

Recently I asked Dr. Fuchs:

"What if we try stopping the Perphenazine? I've read about it on the Internet and it treats psychosis, and I'm not psychotic. I think it may be deadening my emotions and feelings some. What do you think?"

After a little discussion, "Okay we'll give it a try, don't throw it out; but you'll have to keep close watch on your moods. Call me immediately if feeling shaky."

Great. "I'll be sure to tell Janet." She doesn't comment.

So meds change like all good things, getting better.

Discontinuing it . . . **no noticeable effects.** This had been no minor decision. I learned my   lesson   the hard way when I missed or stopped my regularly doses because I felt, "I don't feel like myself."

Then I ended up in episodes and hospitals, feeling dull, but Haldol and Thorazine were much worse, actually putting me into depression. Not caring. Not aware.   So I've been fair-to-middlin' since '96. Seventeen years of interspersed mania, followed by seventeen years without. A cicada. An insect. A nothing.

Note: I am not a doctor. All I'm saying is that these meds work for me. There's others as well. Check with your physician/psychiatrist.

At the end her story, my friend told me, "John said he was compelled to drive to the   **Poconos** and go skiing, 100-miles away.

I'm sure he would have driven fine; he was invincible.

*   *   *

Wide-awake between 3 and 4 a.m. every morning while writing this. Sleeping til 4 is a deep sleep. If I wake up and get out of bed earlier, at 2, I hear Janet mumble, "O God." I feel bad for her, because my lack of sleep affects her sleep, as she has too many   fears of what could happen to us to let it slide.

If it's 1 a.m., she'll get up, walk to the top of the stairs leading to the basement where I'm typing, and shout down, "Rod, what's wrong with you, come back to bed!"

I asked Dr. Fuchs about my sleep pattern because it so bothers Jan.

"How much solid sleep are you getting? Are you tired during the day?"

"Minimum six hours and not tired. I'm fine."

"Well that must be enough for you, that's your pattern. You'd have to disrupt it — force yourself to stay up longer in order to wake up later."

So instead of prescribing more Trazodone or something else, I'm forcing myself to go to bed later. Basically lasting til 8:30, 9 at the latest, and I'm out, with my jeans on asleep on our bed in front of . . . what else.

And summers I absolutely hate missing **Big Brother** at nine. I'm glad they got Amanda out tho, I wonder if she bullied the jury house.

Before retiring I was happiest when I could last til 10 and watch Simon in the *The Mentalist*, and *Castle,* both with great casts and stories.

A few of the (currently) 132 well-known people (Wikipedia) who were/are bipolar: Edgar Allen Poe, Mel Gibson, Florence Nightingale, Vincent Van Gogh, Earnest Hemingway, Patty Duke, possibly Britney Spears (according to some reports), and recently, Catherine Zeta-Jones. Oh, and Russell Brand. But I already knew that. I like him a lot except for bad conduct.

That's just a few celebrities, of many notables, not to name numbers of philosophers, artists, entertainers et al.

I haven't seen much written on affected business people or government employees except a few sad postal workers. They all get a bad rap.

All, all, government employees do, especially from the general public, how ever many that is. On my Civic I had a bumper sticker praising **Public Employees.**

At any given time an estimated 5.7 - 10 million Americans may be bipolar, at least 50% (from what I hear), not knowing what its that that makes them so creative, or sick. There's no blood test for it yet, only behavioral history.
Or outbursts. episodes. After they occur.

*   *   *

A few months ago I asked Jan, "What was it like for you during my episodes?"

"Horrible." She looked away, signaling no more questions.

I could never bring myself to ask more, no matter how relaxed she appeared. I realized I don't want to remind her of my episodes; too upsetting, even tho its ironic when I tell a guest, "Yeah, I've been to Rome; the Basilica's amazing," or something similar about London or Grecian landscapes. I speak at length with Baha'i pilgrims. Like the photos in that big tome.

Understated of course.

I've never thought of myself as mentally ill, or as a "sufferer." Bipolar is just . . . a convenient label, a beginning, and it doesn't control me. Taking my meds at the right times has become second nature, and I use pill cases when I'm away.
I'm still very impatient — and still impulsive.

Sometimes I actually pause before speaking and think. My words still get me in trouble, especially my postings to FB and my blogs (I change many for Janet — thank goodness she catches the worst ones), but it's usually minor and I can recover, or change them easily.

My friends all know me, so momentary flare-ups go uncommented. I'm happy and grateful but don't jump for joy for much, although our family loves to laugh more than anything else, and so do I. Usually it's just a snicker on my part The joys I feel now come from not feeling hyper, and from other normal humans.

Janet's the "fizz" in our relationship; always has been.

This is the end of the Episode stories. Thank you.

This book is a small shout out, a personal howl,
for the mentally oppressed in America, everywhere.

On October 7, 2005, celebrations marking the 50th anniversary
of the first reading of the poem (Howl), were staged in San
Francisco, New York City, and in Leeds the UK.

7.0 BEST WISHES

Six pillars saved me from my precarious,
uncontrolled   Self:

Love from a deeply supportive and capable woman; family;
sources of spritualty; a good job; community;
hospitals, docs and meds.

Any one of them can help. We may not receive them in a
pretty package.   And good health care is a big part of it   —
a right every American, nay every human of every age,
must receive.

If you're bipolar, I hope you've recognized and accepted your
own pillar or pillars,   and feel the hope,   and reach out
and hold on to it.

I was fortunate, and thankful every day. I did my best.

There I go, pontificating AGAIN.   I apologize.

It's always been these continuing internal monologues
that trip me up. I talk to myself a **lot**, especially while driving.

In 2011, I went to Meetup.com and started Hamilton Area
Pool Players for $12.00/month. A bunch of friends and
strangers. We get together monthly, shooting pool, swap
stories and jokes, and scarf down Janet's prepared
refreshments, or whatever the guys bring.

I think of my Dad as I use my/his 33 year-old pool table,
recently refurbished. I like bank shots best. I thank him when I
make one. That's me — as the true Trenton street kid and
hippie I am, shooting pool on the back cover.

Best wishes and thanks for turning pages;

now please go write your story.

Caio! Rod

8.0 HINDSIGHT AND INTROSPECTIONS

After returning from Ireland with my Mom a few months ago (May 2013), and reflecting on our experiences, I started writing about our weeklong vacation. Rereading the outline, it came to me: *What's the point? To experience first hand the Irish people's friendliness and hospitality? It was incredible. That we had a "good" time? Couldn't have been better. Touring Dublin and the stupendous Cliffs of Moher? We did; both in clear skies. Wonderful. Was it my mom's lifelong dream to see the town of her centuries-old Cavanaugh roots? We did. To meet our Irish cousins? They are a blessing. Or to taste the Guinness draught?*

It was all sweet.

No, that was ALL well and good, but the real point was to get Mom there before she passed away without touching her roots. The story I write about it will be anticlimactic.

But when we sat on the tour bus looking out the window by chance one afternoon, a huge arching rainbow stretched across Galway Bay. They're constant in Ireland. Like its people.

Mom looked thru the large bus window with awe in her voice, "Oh Rodney, Look! Isn't it wonderful?"

She spontaneously grabbed my hand and held it in astonishment and joy, as if their were no window, and as if this rainbow had appeared solely for her. That's the story of Ireland for us. It moved her, and that moved me.

The symbolism and reality excited and filled her soul. I was very pleased, very pleased indeed to have received such a bounty — for her. And that is true happiness, seeing others happy, even if Ireland Railtours, Janet, I and siblings (who gave the needed cash), Olive at Glasha Farmhouse, Maureen and Sean our hosts and cousins, and even more native cousins — or I — all had small parts to play.

Fated good weather, airplanes, trains and trams, cabs and tour buses, did the rest. Would love to go back.

While there I didn't remember my earlier wistful wish to visit Ireland, made in '96 while manic and flying on to London.

I knew I could enjoy Ireland's enhanced reality more by <u>not</u> being in a semi-stoned state.

And the "taste" of that one Guinness was particularly sweet and refreshing . . . .

And hardly anyone who met me, knew I was a Baha'i.

*   *   *

How Jan, family and friends, coped with my erratic behavior, I don't know. One minute I was a true servant, setting up chairs at Sunday School; the next, snarling at a good friend causing them to cry. After episodes I hardly noticed friends stopping by to drop off casseroles, or raking leaves in the back yard and doing other helpful chores. I also found out Jan had been on the phone with Blue Cross/Blue Shield, for many, many long hours trying to whittle down or understand their partial payments. We're grateful.

We surround ourselves with normal people who have purpose, families, jobs, friends, and problems — these folks who know how to solve their problems for themselves, or ask for assistance when needed. (That's what governments are for, laws and fairness, security, education, and to protect the poor and weakened. And so much more.)

We all converse about life, friends, family, acquaintances; we chat, we consult, we have breakfasts; meetings, parties, refreshments and outings -- together.

We eschew rose-colored glasses, but have positive worldviews. Always. We don't tolerate complaining, whining, gossiping or worse. No one blames others. This Movement in universal values is shown in Jesse's book *The Secret Peace: Exposing the Positive Trends* © 2010.

Of Jan and I listen/watch news, read papers, **The Week, Time, and Consumer Reports**; especially **WHYY-FM.**

Simple needs and wants.

Since 2009 I drink my beloved Dunkin medium coffee every mornin', eat my **Broad Street Diner** breakfast at 6; two small cups there. And every Saturday enjoy an **AMC** action flick with pal Richie, then onto **Quakerbridge Dunkin**.

They are my rewards for having a solid week. And talk about the hot actresses.

Being who I am and also being mentally ill, I struggle with my Baha'i ethic to be of service and exhibit honorable values. Sometimes thinking beyond myself, beyond what I want, what I see, what I taste, what I hear and touch, what I feel or don't feel. Performing small actions. That's why I love to facilitate two memoir writing classes every week also, and mediate dispute cases monthly for the Hamilton courts.

Retired after working 44 years, Janet longer, our ultimate comforts doing nothing significant, just watching **Ellen**, **Jeopardy** and **Wheel of Fortune**. Solving Times **Jumbles** every day. Eating out once a week together is great, and **DQ Blizzards** every Friday.

Moderation works well for us. Balance is helpful.

For me, reality is interesting and more than enough.

*   *   *

Un-Reality Is

I don't know all the words.

Not capable of expressing adequately.

A shadow, a mirage; easy in hindsight,

to describe **my** mania:

one Voice, *My Voice*; omniscient **I, Me, We, Us, Our**;

no self, no self-awareness, none;

undaunted optimism; positive worldview;

untold energy;

invulnerability even when suicidal,

unfailing belief My Rational Soul breathing,

now and forever; [17]

paranoia from my old normal self;

caring only at moments, otherwise uncaring,

aloof;

few flashbacks, but informed of all past knowledge and
experiences, drawing upon them instantly;

100% future-oriented, moving forward not back;

nothing can go wrong — every intuition, thought, feeling word
or action: exactly right for that precise moment;

projecting outcomes and being confirmed.

My mother always saying,

"There are no coincidences."

No barriers that can't be overcome;   patient
                    until outcome unfolds;

no need of djinn or Guardian Angels, although, I believe;

unaware of Inner Force always directing;

rationality when needed; bidden or unbidden;

unbounded imagination, thoughts, scenarios, plans, objectives
— fully formed, one moment or hour to the next, flowing
uninterrupted until distracted to meaningful tangents;

Noun, noun then verb, or verb, verb, verb, noun,

words shortened, sentences collapsed, no pronouns,
prepositions;

knowing full meaning of thoughts, events, intuitively;

outgoing, playful, conversational, hopeful;

crossing over into spiritual world;

feelings, thoughts rising, combining, together;

one;

*

ever nonplussed;

appear normal, one with humanity.

Look like crap.

*

If there was one outstanding modus operandi, it was fully accepting change; going with the circumstances I found Myself in; bending, flexing, patient but not always; creating a necessary new flow around Me. Mostly? Thoughts, thoughts, thoughts. Fully formed phrases or sentences, as I've described, completing the initial idea to its conclusion. Perfectly reasonable to My Mind, all actionable, whether thru My speech, writings or concrete actions.

One example:

take train Rome (millions of thoughts) . . . visit St. Peter's (millions of thoughts) . . . Holiest statue in Christendom . . (millions of thoughts) . . . drink deeply (millions of thoughts) . . . return . . . hundreds of thousands . . . tens . . .
until normal is needed.

Five phrases out of millions stuck and were deeply connected. No control over which "stuck" and which didn't. All stream of consciousness without a conscious stream. Something my psyche chose for Me. Each one of us has our own psyche, no matter appearances. Like hypnotic trance?

Writing *Episodes* is conventional writing, trying to show unknown things in terms of what is known. Incapable of writing the actual manic thoughts themselves. Even I can't recall all of THEM. Blessedly don't remember 99.99%. Never tried until writing my autobiography. Then this book. Slowing down memory brought it back, not rushing, meditating, rewriting, pondering, musing . . . feeling.

Not knowing, not feeling, can be a kindness at times.

An interesting scientific experiment would be to have two fully manic people together in one place discussing their plans and scenarios. Certainly someone's captured this already? Geoffrey Rush's ***Quills?*** **Charenton**'s diaries?

(The name of my roommates mansion on Berkeley Avenue in my youth.)

Memories, feelings, images; some extremely clear, others fuzzy, some impressions only, good memories, <u>none</u>

bad for me. Informing me as I write these stanzas over the last 16 months.

To me manic is an actionable world, certainly one we'll all achieve with control, perceiving and piercing higher realities that we were made for. When manic, only the next thought stops execution of the first. Each directed action purposeful, meaningful, except for the mundane which are rote.

While manic I was a new being, fully integrated. Myself. True Self?   Yes . . . and No.

However, there's one person whom you now know, who could not love the real me except for hope of normality and   not   chaos.   Another   story.

In this regard, pleasing Janet means survival.

And I wish she could sleep thru the night. In fact, it's my greatest wish. Until that early October morning in 1979, she slept peacefully, not on alert (for me). Since then? Pushing and shoving me over when snoring thru the roof, so bad she sleeps in the guest room or, in the past, on the couch, and still wakes at my every movement.

"Besides, when you're tired your not nice."

I want her to sleep, to trust me; I trust me, always have, even when manic. It's been 17 years now.

But after October 1979, she's never been sure. Never sure, of that inner psyche will I flip out or take off for no apparent reason. Or do the unexpected . . .

Trusting a lot, but unable to 100%. No.

Avoiding mania, at any level, takes conscious effort. Living normally takes focus and purpose. Staying healthy. Not awakening that hidden being.

And yet, in the same breath, she loves me unconditionally.

It's been 46 years.

At first it took me a decade to accept I needed a nudge here and there. And that receiving correction when I erred was good; I just had to remember it was.   I don't get angry or begrudge the "nudges" anymore, like "Rod, take your pills," or from a friend, "Rod, shouldn't you text Janet that you'll be late?"

For me, anonymous Ginny stated it best describing her (and mine) medicated moods:

"My moods leveled out" . . . . "But I felt like soda **without the fizz.**" [36] (**Emphasis** added)

And God's plan for me, us, is, well, His. I cudda killed myself, been killed, or done severe damage.   Luckily I didn't. Yet I did hurt hearts. My fate's being written.
     I   have   free   will?   Or   .   .   .

That's the true story here.

I've encouraged Janet to write hers. She could write thousands. She's a much better storyteller than I. Her memories are crisp, like her keen hearing and eagle's sight. I only have to say something once and it's enough, she remembers. If she does write her story, I'll probably be her spellchecker, since that's a thing I help with. And I like to help, not hinder her. Whether she writes or not, that's up to her.

Thinks for all of us.
Together our story isn't fully written.

*   *   *

Melodramatic, I know, but there I go again, you caught me on a train of thought, and it comes non-stop. Must be expressed.

I really do need a filter.

Jan always provides that when we're together.
*   *   *

Prophet

"I think I'm a prophet or a sign." That moonlit night in '79, when I screamed at the peoples of the world and had my Vision, something unbelievable happened. They heard me. I was **"the lion of indomitable strength."** [8]

Roars **P E A L E D** around the globe, waking spirits — children, youth and adults, from their slumbers.

Rodney had died and a new name had been manifested.

*   *   *

I have a clear dream, if you will, of those moments.

"Our world, a blue-white globe in a huge dark expanse outlined with glowing stars and planets. A lion, three times larger than the earth, is straddling it, standing on his hind legs, paws raised, head back, roaring so all creation can hear.
Is that Me?

At that instant I know that everyone else knows . . . who I really Am. That I came, as others before Me had come, will come again, ***"to make the limbs of mankind quake."*** [37]

I know they heard the roaring, and life on Earth was changed forever. But no one tells Me the truths of who I Am and what I've done. They hide it from Me. Everyone has gone to elaborate lengths to convince Me I'm normal, no one special. That's why I'm allowed to smoke.

It feels like I'm in a time warp, living in the 21st century to outward appearances, but actually in the 25th. Altho in my world, where I go and who I meet, and Janet and my friends, everyone I know, keeps the truth from Me, yet, they know.

It's not the right time. "I must do something, I'm unaware of, before they'll tell Me the truth."

*   *   *

That kinda energy and authority was what I thought and felt during those immediate days in Princeton House and Fair Oaks, which had been forgotten entirely until 4 a.m. November 20, 2012. I was enjoying my pre-dawn smoke before leaving for Dunkin.

In the hospitals, each time I had egoistic thoughts it took me days to disabuse myself of grandiose views and feelings. I put no store in them now, altho they can and do still afflict me unless I'm alert and say aloud,

"Who the _____ do you think you are?"

Philosopher

I'm not a theologian, nor any kind of spiritualist nor expert in anything, but -- I do believe in an Unknowable Essence, and the soul's life after death as it progresses, ever forward, reaching newer levels, bigger mansions, never going backward. But it may be the black or the bright starting point that matters.   That's up to me, for me.

As to my revelation direct from heaven? Four Words infused Me, the scenes in that clearing etched in memories. I don't let them affect me, after all, I do forget easily. I had forgotten.

Technically, My Christ complex was short-lived,
          but it was . . . authentic.

Inspiration may fade, feelings may diminish, thoughts may normalize, but remembrance always brings . . . incredulity. *Was that really me?*

No one has ever told me what to make of my bipolar episodes beyond the simple "It's a chemical imbalance." Its life — much worse and much better happens — time to move on.

It was impossible to predict my first episode; subsequent episodes were caused by a combination of missing pills and lack of sleep. They may have been avoided if I'd been more diligent, but I'll never know for sure.

Not until . . . .

However, I know there's much more to it. Just from my own experiences, I can attest to being one with the universe and its all-encompassing vastness; being prescient, all-knowing, all-caring and . . . angry. I also felt the intense groans of human beings, brothers and sisters, calling for the Kingdom of God on Earth. Will mankind reach it only after <u>another avoidable cataclysm</u>, caused by Man? Affecting all its peoples?

Or can our leaders find the political will to unite and put an end to millions of told and untold living sufferings?

I have hope and faith they can, or . . .
new champions <u>will</u> arise.
They have arisen. They've always arisen.

The words **"He should forgive the sinful, and never despise his low estate, for none knoweth what his own end shall be,"** has taken on new meaning for me. [6]

I <u>need</u> humility.

I say my Noonday Prayer every day, or at nite.

Thought:

He has an all-encompassing Plan. Two Plans in fact:
A Major Plan and a Minor Plan.

Janet has plans as well. The first, survival — under the best possible conditions — for me, Kate, Jesse and Rachel, and our recent granddaughter. She thinks of her own needs last. I trust Janet's plans more than I trust mine, which is just one day at a time.

I've learned important lessons. First, I only have limited control of myself. Second, humans can do anything that brain chemicals, the heart, the seat of the soul, and adrenaline can direct the body to do. Those complex combinations of head and heart, nurture and nature, and our own natural, individual spirits, and more.

I think I'm learning the basics -- the five outer powers of man: sight, touch, taste, hearing and smell. But also the five inner powers: imagination, thought, comprehension, memory and the common faculty, that links them together.

I view the episodes I've had as long, unrestrained, heart and mind impulses. Inner powers exerting their deepest, and most compelling influence over the outer powers.

Their balance, to me, means my normal.

I was impulsive before being manic, and have mellowed little as I've aged. I can force myself to be patient, but it's hard. The Writings say, **"the tongue is a smoldering fire, and excess of speech a deadly poison."** [38] And how well I know it. Being both a know-it-all and poor listener, doesn't help either. Uncontrolled, angry outbursts at a member of my staff, cost me a managerial position in early 2008.

But those stories are for other works.

Being Special

"You're Speccialll." Jan's saying the words, in only her tone of voice, drawn out as only those who know what a putdown by someone really can burn like.

Burn, as in knowing another intimately.
It stings. The truth stings.

*   *   *

Had another vision, can't remember when.   Another forceful,   memorable,   vision.   I remembered upon waking;   but its not like a dream . . . this has been . . . experienced . . .

In back seat of a long black limo. Turn to see who's sitting next to me because I feel a presence.
Turning . . . no one.   Its night; with moonlike glows. Can't see driver, but swing both ways, looking out tinted windows.
Turn head forward, face ahead, and seeing, feeling, speeding along one side of four-lane highway.

302

North or South, East or West?

Seeing no vehicles, but perceiving them.
Limo's lights only illumination. Striped, crisp white   lines
flashing under the vehicle.

Must be four or five a.m., no other cars are on   either
side. *On the Turnpike. Must be.* Vaguely   sensing
entourage of   blinking lights, other dark vehicles — no
sirens. Behind me.

Eerie "whooshing" of tires along the surface only
sounds.

Where can we be going?
Sensing all hell's breaking   out.

Feeling as if traffic's been diverted entirely.

*We   must   be   going   to   The Seat
and they've   cleared -- everything.*

I'm going to meet Them, be told the truth, will know reality.
"Time" is Now.
Can I really be someone special?

*   *   *

Recently Doctor Fuchs told me,

"Your twinges of grandiosity will never go away."

She's read an early draft of *Episodes.*

She has an even better idea of how I tick now.

We were exploring my illness.

Then, a shock.

She stated something to the effect of,

"Rodney, what-ever is in your makeup, your genes or your determination not to let this illness rule your life, perhaps even your own effect on your epigenes, I don't know. But in my experience, what you've achieved, and the marriage you have, is not common for bipolars. In fact, just the opposite. I know of too many that have a manic episode, we stabilize them on antipsychotics, and then they cycle down to severe depression. And then we have to treat for that. Weeks or months later another manic episode follows and it starts all over."

Oh, how I wish I could help them! Are there enough Janets out there? Family members? Friends? Are there enough good doctors and hospitals? Rehab centers?

"But, but Doctor, you saw how I admit in my book I must have a mild form of bipolar, since I've never had severe depressions. Moodiness, yes, often. A little paranoia, yeah. But nothing so dismal that overcame me like mania did the opposite way. That's another reason I've been blessed. I think they should change my BAD label to 'Somewhat BAD', the new term for great highs and not so bad lows."

"You're a 5 or 6 for sure." Simply stated.

Always learning from Susan.

Fini: This book first completed during Mental Illness Awareness week October 2013

9.0 NOTES and SOURCES

9.1 General Sources

9.1.1. Wikipedia is heartily recommended. If you think I've spouted some facts, they are either from anecdotes or Wikipedia, or otherwise referenced in Notes. My family does not like me using Wikipedia as a reference, so I listen to their objections. It's not life and death. On 9-21-13 I came home from errands and there was a card on the kitchen counter with only my name on it. I unsealed it and read the cover: *"Wikipedia said you don't exist."* There's a picture of Lincoln below it and the words: *"But NOW it says you shot Abraham Lincoln."* *What's this?* Inside: **You're welcome,** with a hand drawn smiley face with curly cue. From Janet. I show it to her and she laughs heartily, saying, "I just couldn't resist." Very unusual for Jan to give me a card other than our prescribed days. So, I get the point.

I like Wiki stuff anyway. And besides, at the very bottom of their articles, they do list refs and sources. Up to you if you want to believe 'em.

9.1.2. Baha'i Faith Contact Information: **1-800-22-UNITE** and U.S. Baha'i website: **http://www.bahai.us/ with contact info.**

Baha'i World website: **http://www.bahai.org/**

Free online Baha'i literature: **http://reference.bahai.org/en/**

9.1.3. Recommended reading: *Baha'u'llah and the New Era, An Introduction to the Baha'i Faith.* J.E. Esslemont, original copyright in U.S. 1950 by the National Spiritual Assembly of the U.S. (NSA). The first Baha'i book I read. For my Christian family and friiends I recommend *The Challenge of Baha'u'llah*, © Gary I. Matthews 1993, George Ronald, Publisher. And, *Muhammad and the Course of Islam*, © H.M.Balyuzi 1976, also George Ronald, for our Muslim brothers and sisters.

9.1.4. *The Road Less Travelled*, © 1978 M. Scott Peck. Various editions and publication dates. The first book that opened my eyes to being dysfunctional or mentally ill and how others were adjusting. Read ca. 1980 after my first episode.

.

9.2 EPIGRAPHS — Selected as foundational themes

Dr. Wayne W. Dyer, *Inspiration Your Ultimate Calling*, © 2006, Hay House Inc. USA

Stephen R. Covey, *The Eighth Habit*, From Effectiveness to Greatness, © 2004 by Franklin Covey Co., published by Free Press, a division of Simon and Schuster, U.S.A. Revolutionary with his *Seven Habits* series

Program announcer (anecdotal), *The Naked City*, TV Series 1958 - 1963, Crime drama which took place in New York's 65th precinct.

9.3 AUTHOR'S NOTES

A1.(64 etc.) I'd been baptized and attended Catholic schools from kindergarten thru 8th grades. Received First Holy Communion, Confirmation, was an altar boy and sang in choir. Early years language (and Latin) was taught phonetically making words easy to sound, spell and read. During those years, also learning the major stories of the New and Old Testaments. After a teenage 5-year lapse I found   The Tao:

ONE

The Tao that can be told is not the eternal Tao.
        The name that can be named is not the eternal name.
The nameless is the beginning of heaven and earth.
        The named is the mother of ten thousand things.
Ever desireless, one can see the mystery.
        Ever desiring, one sees the manifestations . . . .

It's been said: "There are many Paths to truth." [39]

In concert was the I Ching, both slowly leading me to some humaneness. The Baha'i Writings and a world lit course at MCCC covering the major religions and philosophies came next. Read Rodwell's Koran (The Glorious Quran), twice. I've studied and given presentations on Zoroastrianism and other religious topics.
        I'm not a scholar of anything.

A2. (79) Invention idea. The interesting part is that when I had left the house an hour earlier, I'd no idea for an invention. The Versatile Sink (Mr. **Private**'s words), came to me fully formed while I had been driving down Route 295 to Inventions Submission Corp.

An example of finding what I needed at my fingertips.

A3. (81) Manifestation Term used by Baha'is to describe the station of Prophethood, signifying how the Major Prophet or Messenger manifests perfectly the names and attributes of God, and will one day return in spirit and being, and has again, missed by all but a few, just as In every Revelation of the past. **"Progressive revelation is a core teaching in the Baha'i Faith that suggests that religious truth is revealed by God progressively and cyclically over time through a series of divine Messengers and that the teachings are tailored to suit the needs of the time and place of their appearance."** Wikipedia.

A4. (113) College. (Graduated Ewing High School June 1968) Attended Mercer County Community College in the '80s and '90s at nights, average 4.0 for 44 credits. Then I lost interest and motivation. Maybe because I was going thru intense supervisory and managerial weekly training for 3-years in the State's Public Manager Program (with Rutgers), at HRDI, a wonderful facility and the state's best investment — improving public managers knowledge, and as a byproduct, hopefully performance. I again shook Governor Florio's hand as a vocal lobbyist for energy conservation and energy management, in our Treasury Office of Energy Savings, where I was manager of Administration.

A5. (119 etc.) OTIS HUB. The State's mega-data center, built circa late 80's.[?] At first housing only IBM mainframes, then Bull as well. (Sorry but some timings/dates lost to me in sections on OTIS, so don't take these State DP/MIS/IP/IT histories as Gospel.)

Author asides: If you've found any interesting reading herein, and would like to see more of my writing, I invite you to check out my blogs:

A Blessed Life in America Blog contains synopsized memoirs if you will, for easy reading by topic.

http://ablessedlifeinamerica.blogspot.com/

Good Ideas for New Jersey Blog, contains various thoughts and opinions mostly on New Jersey.

http://goodideasfornj.blogspot.com/

9.4 ENDNOTES AND BIBLIOGRAPHY

I apologize for many older reference books used. I've been a Baha'i over 40-years, and those are the editions I have. The first page number(s) given are from this text, the latter from the source book showing the quoted passage.

1. (7) **"Truthfulness…."** 'Abdu'l-Baha, *Baha'i World Faith* (384), Copyright National Spiritual Assembly of the Baha'is of the United States, 1943, 1956 (fourth printing 1969). Baha'i Publishing Trust, Wilmette Illinois, U.S.A. Out of print.

2. (8 & 10) **Ideal Readers** p. 215; **attribution** p. 125. Stephen King, *On Writing, A Memoir of the Craft*, Copyright 2000, Scribner, New York, NY. To date, this is my favorite book on the craft of writing; I've written a 13-page annotation I've shared at memoir writing classes. I also noted from Stephen that a little symbolism was okay.

3. (10 & 132) **"…world is but one country…."** Shoghi Effendi, The Promised Day is Come (p. 118), Copyright 1951, 1961 by the National Spiritual Assembly of the Baha'is of the U.S. Baha'i Publishing Trust, Wilmette Illinois. In this text (132), is the phrase heard more often, **"The <u>earth</u> is but one country…."** can be found in *Gleanings CXVII* (250)

4. (10) **"…50,000 words…."** Evelyn Wood, The Evelyn Wood Seven-Day Speed Reading and Learning Program, (9) Copyright © 1990 by American Learning Composition, publisher Barnes & Noble, Inc., etcetera.

5. (13) **National Alliance on Mental Illness,** *Paper on Bipolar*, 2003. Public website visited 12/7/2012. And NAMI website article *"Suicide Rates Rise Significantly Amongst Baby Boomers, Study Finds,"* by Kelana Smith-McDowell c. 5/30/2013. 2010 equaled 33,687 deaths from motor vehicle crashes and 38,364 from suicides. <u>Underlined statements used only, as cited.</u>

Note: September is Suicide Prevention Awareness Month.

Author's note: As of May 2011, 23,140 psychiatrists practiced in the U.S. according to the Bureau of Labor Statistics. Source: Website visited 12/7/12). That's one psychiatrist for every 432 bipolar individuals in the U.S., using NAMI's 10 million extreme. Current

NAMI advertising lists 1 in 4 Americans affected by mental illness (which could also mean their families?). Source: NAMI website 5/10/2013. Additional note: NIMH lists 5.7 million Americans with bipolar lately or 2.6% of U.S. population over age 18. Source: NIMH website 5/27/13: *The Numbers Count: Mental Disorders in America.*

6. p. (15 & 64) "**…nethermost fire….**" Baha'u'llah, *Gleanings from the Writings of Baha'u'llah* CXXV (266), translated by Shoghi Effendi, Copyright 1939, 1952 by the National Spiritual Assembly of the Baha'is of the U.S., Fourth printing 1969, Baha'i Publishing Trust, 110 Linden Ave, Wilmette, Illinois.

7. (18) **Allah'u'abha.** Marzieh Gail, *Baha'i Glossary* (7). Copyright © 1955 by the National Spiritual Assembly of the Baha'is of the United States of America, Fourth printing 1969, Baha'i Publishing Trust, Wilmette, Illinois. A common greeting used among Baha'is that translates into God is All-Glorious. A form of The Greatest Name of God.   Pronunciation: Allah-ho-Ab-ha.

8. (18 & 70, 299) "**Should it be God's intention, there would appear out of the forests of celestial might the lion of indomitable strength whose roaring is like unto the peals of thunder reverberating in the mountains.**" Baha'u'llah, *Tablets of Baha'u'llah Revealed after the Kitab-i-Aqdas* (197), Baha'u'llah U.S Baha'i Publishing Trust, pocket-sized edition © 1988.

9. (18 & 70) "**O Lord! Increase…**" Baha'u'llah, *The Seven Valleys and the Four Valleys* (34). Copyright 1945 and 1953, translated by Ali-Kuli Khan and Marzieh Gail, Baha'i Publishing Trust, Wilmette, IL

10. (18 & 70) "**…asleep on My couch…**" Baha'u'llah, *Epistle to the Son of the Wolf* (11), translated by Shoghi Effendi, Copyright © 1941, 1953 by the National Spiritual Assembly of the Baha'is of the United States, Baha'i Publishing Trust, Wilmette IL. Ellipses added by author.

11. (36, 83 & 90) "**O God! Refresh and gladden my spirit. Purify my heart. Illumine my powers. I lay all my affairs in Thy Hand. Thou art my Guide and my Refuge. I will no longer be sorrowful and grieved; I will be a happy and joyful being. O God! I will no longer be full of anxiety, nor will I let trouble harass me. I will not dwell on the unpleasant things of life. O God! Thou art more a friend to me than**

I am to myself. I dedicate myself to Thee, O Lord."
'Abdu'l-Baha, *Baha'i Prayers* (152). Copyright 1954, © 1982, 1985, 1991 by the National Spiritual Assembly of the Baha'is of the United States 1991 Edition, Baha'i Publishing Trust, Wilmette Illinois.

Additional note: The above is the correct version in the original text. In the narration, I changed "my" to "his," and completed the prayer that way at that time, which is not common practice for any Baha'i prayers or writings. Note: Altho attributed to 'Abdu'l-Baha, this prayer cannot be properly authenticated. It's still a favorite prayer having been memorized by innumerable Baha'is.

12. (52) **re: my cousin.** In '79 the terms autistic and mentally handicapped weren't used by me or anyone I knew. Thank goodness future labels change. I really don't appreciate T-shirts with the word, even tho crossed out. We're just teaching the kids it all over again.

13. (52) **"O my God! O Thou forgiver of sins, bestower of gifts, dispeller of afflictions! Verily, I beseech thee to forgive the sins of such as have abandoned the physical garment and have ascended to the spiritual world. O my Lord! Purify them from trespasses, dispel their sorrows, and change their darkness into light. Cause them to enter the garden of happiness, cleanse them with the most pure water, and grant them to behold Thy splendors on the loftiest mount."** 'Abdu'l-Baha, *Baha'i Prayers* (45). *op cit.*

Our Baha'i mentor Bill Foster strongly encouraged us to memorize this particular prayer and say it often for the departed. That way we could say it easily when visiting a graveyard, or caught off guard at a funeral service.

14. (54) **"…souls will recognize…."** 'Abdu'l-Baha, *Baha'i World Faith — Selected Writings of Baha'u'llah and 'Abdu'l-Baha (*p.367). Copyright 1956, The National Spiritual Assembly of the Baha'is of the U.S., Baha'i Publishing Trust, Wilmette, Illinois, U.S.A. Out of print.

15. (59) **Amru'llah** Marzieh Gail, *Bahai'i Glossary* (p. 8), op cit. This Persian word means the Cause of God or the Command of God in English. Pronunciation: am-ro-lah.

16. (81) In the text paragraph I'm paraphrasing from the *World Unity the Goal* section in *World Order of Baha'u'llah (or WOB), (203-204)* my favorite "book" written by the Guardian, especially its included treatise *The Dispensation of Baha'u'llah* (95-157). *World Order of Baha'u'llah* © Copyright 1938, 1955 by the National Spiritual Assembly of the Baha'is of the U.S., Baha'i Publishing Trust, Wilmette, Illinois.

Author's note: Many books have been written about the Guardian, *The Celestial Burning* © 2012 J.A. McLean being the most recent, a masterful tome on Shoghi Effendi's use of hermeneutics and exegesis.

17. (82 & 294) **Rational Soul. "This human rational soul is God's creation: it encompasses and excels other creatures; as it is more noble and distinguished, it encompasses all things. The power of the rational soul can discover the realities of things, comprehend the peculiarities of beings, and penetrate the mysteries of existence. All sciences, knowledge, arts, wonders, institutions, discoveries and enterprises come from the exercised intelligence of the rational soul."** 'Abdu'l-Baha, *Some Answered Questions* (p. 217), Copyright 1930, 1954, © 1964, 1981 by the National Spiritual Assembly of the Baha'is of the United States of America, Baha'i Publishing Trust, Wilmette II

18. (98) **Most challenging issue.** Shoghi Effendi, *The Advent of Divine Justice* (p.28), Copyright 1939, 1963 by the National Spiritual Assembly of the Baha'is of the United States of America, Baha'i Publishing Trust, Wilmette, Illinois. In the U.S. before the 60's and 70's, Negro, colored and black, were the most common descriptors for an African-American person, which was starting to replace them nationally. I was white like all other Caucasians. Derogatory terms then were also different, and still hurtful. In the years I refer to in the text, they were the terms in vogue at the time and the ones I used in every day speech. Political correctness didn't exist yet.

19. (100) Note: Child's Way was later updated with a new name, *Brilliant Star*, which Jan also served on. Jesse and friends even made a cover! A perk.

20. (100 & 106) **"Thy Name is my healing, O my God, and remembrance of thee is my remedy. nearness to Thee is my hope, and love for Thee is my companion. Thy mercy to me is my healing**

and my succor in both this world and the world to come. Thou, verily, art the All-Bountiful, the All-Knowing, and the All-Wise." Baha'u'llah, *Baha'i Prayers* (p. 87), op cit.

21. (114) **American-Indian.** In those early days, at least with us, Native-American was not yet the common terminology. When I was growing up in the '50s of course, thru TV shows like **Lone Ranger, Gene Autry** and many others, it was just "indians," the bad people. The Y IGP had a booklet describing principles and meetings etc., even tho information was watered down and stereotyped, in good ways. Years later I was very disappointed to see this Y program changed to **Adventure Guides,** with Indian references removed. It had been a terrific program, and taught us respect. I guess it just wasn't politically correct anymore. *Unfortunate. You'd think they'd get together and do a better job at education rather than cancel outright.*

22. (115 et al.) **OTIS.** The State of New Jersey's centralized mainframe Information Technology organization, for statewide networking and computing (not including agency departmental systems). In '98, OTIS became the Office of Information Technology (OIT), thru Whitman's EO No. 87, and later EO #42 (Corzine), and remains in place today. Altho I had worked six years at OTIS, I never worked at OIT, but worked closely with them. Executive Orders have the force of law, and regulations can result; but are usually administrative in nature. Most governor's EOs direct the State flag to be flown at half-mast for an important death, or are issued for emergencies.

Note: State employees. The Fiscal Year 2014 State Budget proposed close to 45,000 funded state employees, and another 24,000+ federal and other funded employees, for almost 70,000. Source: Official State of New Jersey website. (See my forthcoming book on my jobs, for info on state hiring practices, with a much more detailed treatment of State of New Jersey government.) I'll bet the majority of current state employees have PCs; terminals having been phased out in the prior 10 years. I do remember clearly we had 30,000 State offices/employees with PCs by '97. Source: Anecdotal. Me.

23. (124) The vision I had of the Shrine of the Bab, in Haifa, **similar to the photo on the back cover of this book,** would have been common since 2001, when the terraces and steps were actually completed and opened. I had first seen this technicolor picture in my mind in '85 (soon forgotten), when plans to build the Terraces on the semi-barren mountainside of Mt. Carmel had not yet been announced. The idea of the terraces themselves weren't shared with the Baha'i World until August 1987.

This vision, to me, means something simple to my simple mind. It must be of a far, far distant future, beyond my lifetime: modernity and nobility of kings and queens are part of mankind's ordered life on this planet; and the purposes of representative governments is to safeguard the interests of the whole human race.

I had been manic when this vision had occurred. That's all I know about it.

Janet read the first draft of this book in 2012, came to this "vision" account, and asked, "Did you really see this?"

"Until the page you're reading now, I felt I couldn't share it with anyone, lest my mental stability be questioned."

"You're right about that."

24. (140) **"Be anxiously concerned…."** Bahau'llah. *Gleanings* CVI, op cit.

25. (140) Science and religion. 'Abdu'l-Baha. *Paris Talks* (p. 146), Eleventh British Edition 1969, © Baha'i Publishing Trust, 27 Rutland Gate, London S.W.7. Approved for publication by the National Spiritual Assembly of the Baha'is of the British Isles, Fletcher & Son Ltd.

26. (146 & 178) **"Is there any remover of difficulties save God? Say: Praised be God! He is God! All are His servants, and all abide by His bidding!"** This has bolstered me many times. *Baha'i Prayers (p.28)*, op cit.

27. (174) From Tablet of Visitation of Abdu'l-Baha, *Baha'i Payers* (p. 234), op cit.

28. (195) Kathy and Red Grammar © song from *Teaching Peace* CD. Available from
http://www.redgrammer.com/index.php/store/shop

29. (205) Regarding the term Spanish and not Hispanic. In my child-hood and youth, those who spoke it or had Spanish accents were to us, Spanish. I apologize by this time of not using Hispanic or Latino, but it still slips out sometimes, like it had this time. I like American better.   World Citizen best.

30. (224) Baha'u'llah is the writer, **"And then gave utterance to one mystic word, whispered privily by her honeyed tongue. And raised the call amidst the Celestial Concourse and the immortal maids of heaven . . . ."** *Tablet of the Holy Mariner, Baha'i Prayers, (pp.221-229), op cit.*

31. (230) **Emerald Isle.** Mom and I made the trip in May 2013 during a week of heavenly clear weather. Met cousins, toured homesites and Dublin, stopped in Galway etc.

32. (246) A well-memorized prayer of the Catholic Church, my favorite, because I lied in confessions. I didn't tell mortal sins, only minor sins, absolved by saying the shorter Hail Mary's. Usually 10.

33. p.(260) *God Passed By.* A revision of the title of the authoritative Baha'i history book from the 1800's to 1944 by Shoghi Effendi, titled *God Passes By.* Copyright 1944 by the National Spiritual Assembly of the Baha'is of the United States of America, Fifth printing 1965.

34. (261) **Sadratu'l Muntaha** *Qur'an* 53:14**"Tree beyond which there is no passing."** *Another translation for example: "At the Lote Tree of the Utmost Boundary".* This passage, to me, having physical, spiritual and symbolic meanings.

35. (262) **"Good things come to those who wait."** Old English saying. Wikipedia.

36. (298) **fizz.** *Brilliant Madness* (p. 133), © 1992 by Patty Duke, A Bantam Book.

37. (302) **"For the tongue is a smoldering fire, and excess of speech a deadly poison."** Baha'u'llah, *Gleanings* (265), op cit.

38. (299) **"The world is in travail and its agitation waxeth day by day. Its face is turned towards waywardness and unbelief. Such shall be its plight that to disclose it now would not be meet and seemly. Its perversity will long continue. And when the appointed**

hour is come, there shall suddenly appear that which shall cause the limbs of mankind to quake. Then and only then will the Divine Standard be unfurled and the Nightingale of Paradise warble its melody." Baha'u'llah, World Order of Baha'u'llah (33), op cit.

39. (306) **The One**, truncated. Lao Tsu, *Tao Te Ching*, (3). This version Copyright 1972 Gia-Feng and Jane English translators, Vintage Books, a division of Random House, Inc. New York. The version I had in '69 was an earlier One; lost.

10.0 HELP

NAMI: National Alliance on Mental Illness. Helpline: 1-800-950-NAMI. **www.nami.org** Website visited 12/7/12 for Forward extracts.

Major drug companies like Merck & Co, Bristol Myers-Squibb etc., all have printed material, websites and information. Take what they say (what anyone says), with a grain of salt. In other words, they list tons of possible side effects in order to protect themselves legally in this sue-happy age, BUT (a big but), there are absolutely no descriptions or stats on how much they affect average people who take them. For example: "May cause drowsiness." Does that mean I can't drive? And besides, you'll never know how much drowsiness until you take the pills for a while. We're all slightly, sometimes massively, different in our biological and chemical reactions. My advice? Always ask a psychiatrist what the percentages are for reactions, but only avoid what you can as long as it makes sense to. I have the same attitude when it comes to pulling a tooth and surgery.

WebMD is helpful at http://www.webmd.com/mental-health/mental-health-helpline

Major hospitals like Johns Hopkins have websites too.

Check your State and local government listings as well. For example, in New Jersey there's the Division of Mental Health. Phone 1-800-382-6717. **http://www.state.nj.us/humanservices/dmhs/services/**

Enter "list of mental disorders" in Google, click Wikipedia, and find descriptions for hundreds of . . . difficulties.

These are in addition to trying to make it thru yourself using your own devices. Mine, ours, prayers and support are with you.

11.0 PERMISSIONS

1. Most Baha'i references have been reviewed and approved for accuracy by the National Review Office of the National Spiritual Assembly of the Baha'is of the United States.

2. Terraces photo, back cover. Author Arash Heshemi. Available from OTRS on Wikimedia, ticket number 2007080410006914. (Picture of Shrine and terraces) "This file is licensed under the Creative Commons Attribution: Share Alike 2.5 Generic License. "Use herein does not suggest the photo author's endorsement. Any reuse or distribution of this photo may be prohibited."

3. Trademarks. I have tried my best to identify all trademarks mentioned herein, below. If yours is missed, please write to Ablia Media Co. and it will be corrected in future editions. Here's a list of institutions, companies, names etc. that MAY be trademarked, not all are. But it would've taken me another week to pare them down. The USPTO has the worst trademarks search engine I've seen yet in 30-years of using such things.

To wit: Wawa, Sears, K-mart, Circuit City, 7/11, Dunkin Donuts, Starbucks, Polaroid, Kool, Salem, Marlboro; Chevy, Pontiac TransSport (the Boat), Camaro, Impala, BelAir, Nova, Plymouth, Toyota, Oldsmobile, VW (bug), Honda and Harley; RCA, Motor Trend magazine, Swanson, Creedence Clearwater Revival, Surrealistic Pillow, White Rabbit, ATM, Evelyn Wood, A&W, ATM, Pepsi, Coke, Perrier and RC Cola, 7UP and Mary Kay Cosmetics; Trailways, Salvation Army, Tustin Car Wash, Bank of America, VFW, B.P.O.E (elks), Princess phone, Princeton House, Helene Fuld Hospital (Capital Health), Hampton (house) Behavioral Center, Carrier Clinic, Fair Oaks Hospital, Taco Bell, Jack in the Box; The Price is Right, Disneyland, Disney World, the Times, Trentonian, NY Times, R.C. Maxwell, Sunoco and Marriott; IBM, Big Blue, MS-Outlook, Excel, Word, COBOL, RPG, SNA, 370/XA, 3084 (mainframe), CICS, SMTP, OS. DOS, MVS, IBM GUIDE and the U.N.; Waldorf Astoria, Orrington Hotel, Ravensberger, Discovery Toys; Wellbutrin, Tegretol, Haldol, Thorazine, cloropromazine, Geodon, Desyrel and GreenSpring; Avaya, Honeywell (bull), AT&T, Cisco, Computer Associates (CA), Telex, Oracle, Hitachi, Kodak; Barbie, YMCA, Camp Mason,

Adventure Guides, Amazing Grace; Dogbert, pointy-Haired Boss, Dogbert, Dilbert, Gary Larsen, Far Side; United Airlines, Continental Airlines, Alitalia Airlines, Olympia Airlines, Aegean (airlines?), Virgin Atlantic Airlines and British Airways, Fiumicino Airport, Ben Gurion Airport, Roma Termini Station, Newark Liberty Airport, JFK Airport; Sheraton Meadowlands Hotel, Jacob Javitts, Center, Better Business Bureau, WHYY (FM), Unitarian; Lakota, Rankokus Indian Reservation, Powhatan Lenape nation, Smokin' Joes; Mercer County Board of PTAs; SATs, SEB Bank (NY), Grand Hotel (Soltsjabaden), Game Boy, Water Pik; Roman Catholic, vatican, St. Peter's Basilica, Crystal City; Reader's Digest, VISA, Metropolitan Museum of Art, MOMA, Uzi, BBC; Price is Right, Naked City, ABC, the Mentalist and Castle. And AMC, my favorite Saturday place.

Both of Us?

my name is hell.

My name is Heaven.

Two persons.

Who's who?

Dual nature.

Animal and human.

Really rats in a maze.

I make choices . . .

with free will.

It -- guided by instinct.

Aware of ourselves?

Sensing, smelling, knowing —

closing in.

Time passing. Anxious.

Dead ends and detours.   Within reach . . .

Finding it.   One Voice.

One Rational Soul . . .

and food.